The Revd Dr Malcolm Brown is Director of Mission and Public Affairs for the Church of England. He was previously the Principal of the Eastern Region Ministry Course within the Cambridge Theological Federation. He has taught ethics for the Cambridge Federation's MA in Pastoral Theology (Anglia Ruskin University) and undergraduate ethics for Bangor University, Wales and the Cambridge Federation. His main research interests are the dialogue between Christian ethics and economics, the significance of 'place' in practical theology and the development of new ground rules for public theology.

His other books include: *After the Market: Economics, Moral Agreement and the Churches' Mission*; *Faith in Suburbia: Completing the Contextual Trilogy*; and with Paul Ballard, *The Church and Economic Life – A Documentary Study: 1945 to the Present*.

TENSIONS IN CHRISTIAN ETHICS

An introduction

MALCOLM BROWN

First published in Great Britain in 2010

Society for Promoting Christian Knowledge
36 Causton Street
London SW1P 4ST
www.spckpublishing.co.uk

British Library Cataloguing-in-Publication Data
A catalogue record for this book is available from the British Library

ISBN 978–0–281–05827–3

1 3 5 7 9 10 8 6 4 2

Typeset by Graphicraft Ltd, Hong Kong
Printed in Great Britain by MPG

Produced on paper from sustainable forests

For Hermione Williams,
born as this book was completed

Contents

Preface

Who studies Christian ethics today? One answer, but by no means the only one, will be students of theology and people preparing for ordained ministry, since ethics is often a compulsory element in their curriculum. This book emerges from the seven years (2000–7) I spent teaching ethics to students in the Cambridge Theological Federation – postgraduates and undergraduates from across the traditions and Churches represented there. These included Anglicans of various persuasions, Methodist and United Reformed Church ordinands, Roman Catholic lay women and some from the Orthodox Churches. Most were mature students with wide life experience under their belts already. But whether at Masters or undergraduate levels, it was interesting to see how many external students chose to take the ethics modules. Some were ordained ministers continuing their studies, others were lay people on journeys of their own where the connections between belief and action had raised questions that refused to go away. The study of ethics in such mixed groups generated levels of engagement which went well beyond the resigned acceptance of a compulsory topic.

Yet I felt there was a paradox concerning the literature available for these students. Certainly in the Federation, and in many other institutions (as I learned from discussions with teachers from elsewhere), ethics was not treated as an introductory subject for the theological neophyte. Most programmes of study started with the Bible and introduced a good deal of church history and doctrine before turning to ethics. Meanwhile, the study of pastoral practice and practical theology tended to be approached through 'long thin' modules spread over a considerable time. The result was that students had a good grounding in the study of theology, and had already begun to reflect theologically on practice, well before coming to the study of ethics at levels 2 or 3, or as a postgraduate module. (Teachers in different theological disciplines will argue about whether this is the best way to arrange the curriculum. But for better or worse, this is how it often is arranged in practice.)

Studying ethics late in the course programme meant that there were not many suitable textbooks, since most approach the subject at an introductory level roughly equivalent to level 1 of an undergraduate course. Many such textbooks are excellent. But for the student who has a decent grounding in other theological disciplines and who has been reflecting theologically on pastoral practice for some time (possibly with a good deal of experience of ethical issues in a secular context) there is not much suitable material. This, then, was the genesis of the present book. Although I began teaching ethics in Cambridge to postgraduate students, I found that a reworked version of my Masters-level module was quite suitable for use with undergraduates at levels 2 and 3. On the principle that a textbook should stretch the student by approaching the subject at a slightly higher level of detail and complexity than he or she is expected to reproduce in essays or examinations, it seemed reasonable to design a book suitable both to back up a Masters programme in Christian ethics and to be a core book for students working at the upper levels of undergraduate courses. A Masters student should be reading much more extensively than through any one textbook, but such a book may still help to forge the kind of understanding and enthusiasm for the subject which leads to further, in-depth, student-led reading and research.

But the study of Christian ethics reaches far beyond the constituency of those reading for a formal degree at whatever level. As we shall explore in later chapters, the place of religion – and Christianity in particular – within Western culture is changing rapidly, and one consequence of this is a degree of uncertainty about how to live faithfully. It is no longer possible to make the lazy assumption that Western culture is fundamentally Christian in outlook; too many tensions and contradictions challenge Christian ideas about public and private morality. Christians are being driven to think afresh about how their beliefs affect their judgements about what is just, good or right. Christian ethics can no longer be regarded as sanctified common sense. Yet, at the same time, it is far from obvious that Christian belief always points in one particular ethical direction. Despite the multiplicity of tensions between Christians and the contemporary culture around them, there is a great deal of disagreement about which tensions matter. Aspects of culture prompt members of the Churches to question their assumptions about the demands of faith – but while most would agree that the Church stands, in some way, over against the surrounding culture, there is little or no agreement about where and how a stand must be made. A good example is the deep division within the Anglican Communion (also present within many other Churches) about homosexuality – a topic we shall consider later. Underlying these specific disagreements there is something more fundamental, calling into question the whole venture of Christian ethics. It comes down to this: are Christians called to be citizens of the present world, participating in all its confused plurality, or does our citizenship of God's kingdom so transcend our earthly citizenship that we have little or nothing to learn from beyond our own tradition with its unique revelation of the nature of God, humanity and the created order? More crudely, is our faith an 'add-on' to our membership of the wider human race, or is it the most fundamental element in our identity? Do we learn what is good from the totality of our lived experience, or only by pursuing discipleship with fellow believers across the centuries and nations? Christians who are puzzled by the place of faith in the world – by the pressing question of what difference it makes to believe in God – will find themselves reflecting on questions which lie at the heart of ethics: what are sometimes called meta-ethical questions. It is my hope that this book may be of value to thoughtful Christians of all kinds, not just those studying university courses.

Before considering the structure of this book further, it may help to put my own cards on the table and explain a little about the evolution of my own thinking. In the current exciting but contested state of Christian ethics, anyone who attempts to write a book from a position of neutrality is likely to be deceiving either themselves or their readers.

I came to the study of Christian ethics as an activist. In the 1980s, I was a parish priest in a hard-pressed inner-city community dominated by unemployment and poverty cheek-by-jowl with the conspicuous consumerism of a flourishing city centre retail sector. I spent many hours working with others – a few of them Christians, but not many – on job-creation programmes, youth training schemes and worker co-operatives. I think we did some good – not least by articulating very publicly that every human being has a vision of living well which could be promoted or frustrated by economic and political visions. But when I looked to underpin my activities with a theological undergirding, I felt deeply unsatisfied. Seeking to integrate my conviction that social and political action was a true Christian vocation, I embarked on various courses of study which introduced me to two important sources – the work of William Temple and liberation theology.

Temple, dead for forty years and more, convinced me that what I was doing counted as authentic Christian discipleship, but over time I came to question his assumptions about the place of the Church within society. Not surprisingly, the church I worked within felt more fragmentary, more marginal and less confident than the Church of England in 1942. Temple (as we shall see) was arguing for Christian ethics to be at the heart of public policy-making in a way which appeared incapable of realization now. Liberation theology satisfied even less. Earnestly trying to translate ideas and processes from oppressed Latin American base communities into the context of class-bound British situations, moulded by a very different history and a different present, seemed too often to result in something lame, superficial and incapable of practical application. This is not, of course, a criticism of liberation theology as originally practised elsewhere; only of its adoption in Britain without (in my view) sufficient appreciation of contextual diversity. I felt I had to dig more deeply.

Another disquiet of those days only came into sharper focus much later during a conversation with Samuel Wells (whose work we shall encounter later). 'I realized', said Sam, 'that, having told people for years that "you don't have to come to church to be good", it was little wonder that no one came to church and that very few felt it had anything worth saying.' Building up the church had never been much of a concern for me – the institutional Church, with all its compromises and equivocations, had seemed more like the problem. I saw immense goodness and virtue among the people I worked with in community projects, trade unions and other groupings and could not easily articulate why my own faith added anything of value, let alone why they should consider it for themselves. Yet that negligence had nagged me for years – partly because I was dependent on the Church for my subsistence, but mainly because I felt profoundly, but could not articulate, that my worshipping, praying, believing self was wholly one with my political and community activism. I needed a way to understand the specific contribution of Christian faith and the Christian faithful to the 'big project' of enabling people to live well.

Some of the journey that followed will probably be evident from subsequent chapters. But is it a journey with a destination? Not exactly, because I have come to see the 'project' of Christian ethics as an ongoing conversation between incompatible, but equally authentic, lines of argument. This, I think, is one sign of a tradition in good order. What it means in practice is that strongly held views about how to do Christian ethics need to be held in tension with very different approaches – all able to trace their origins in the Christian story. One view may dominate a particular historic period, but it will, in time, require a corrective from another position if it is to answer the ethical questions the Church is called to address. As I hope to show, there are good theological reasons why this might be a good way for Christians to do ethics.

So this is a textbook which seeks balances – but not neutrality. Like the courses I taught in Cambridge, the book puts forward an underlying thesis about how ethics should be understood in today's Church. It is structured, to a great extent, around the tension between positions in Christian ethics which I have termed 'liberal' and 'communitarian' – terms which will be explained later. My own views do not fall neatly into either camp. If pressed to give a label, I tend to describe myself as a post-liberal, in the sense that I grew up in the great liberal tradition of Christian ethics as public theology (epitomized, perhaps, by Temple) and I have never completely repudiated that tradition. I still believe that theology (and Christian ethics) neglects other knowledge and other disciplines at its peril. Theology should be attentive to the world, and Christians should be citizens in their wider communities. But this tradition now seems inadequate to capture the new, more marginal, character of the Church in the West today and to risk too rapid an accommodation with a secular world which has largely abandoned its Christian roots. It is too inclined to minimize the radical challenge which Christian faith makes to contemporary social mores. It does not, in my view, do enough to build up the Church by making the Church's role in human flourishing significant.

Yet, attracted as I am to communitarian strands in Christian ethics, I am not quite ready to be a committed disciple of Hauerwas or Milbank (of whom we shall learn more). Perhaps because my journey into Christian ethics was motivated by the attempt to address social questions of justice as well as personal questions of conduct, the communitarian focus on the life of the Church often seems too introspective. And perhaps because I have worked for the Church of England for over thirty years, I am not fully persuaded by the communitarian idealization of the Church as the embodiment of all that is virtuous. So I call myself a post-liberal, although even this needs further unpacking. For some communitarian theologians like George Lindbeck, post-liberalism celebrates the demise of the liberal tradition in theology.[1] For me, the term implies moving on from one's roots without fully giving them up: openness to other traditions without adopting the convert's rage against old friends. For me, there remains much to be said for the familiar liberal virtues.

The mention of virtue gives a hint of one of my main influences. Alasdair MacIntyre's book, *After Virtue*, made an immense impact on me when I first read it. It had already created a major shift in the terms of debate not only within Christian ethics, but in disciplines as diverse as philosophy, sociology and management studies.[2] One point from MacIntyre's argument is worth noting at this point. In a well-known passage, he notes that, 'I can only answer the question "What am I to do?" if I can answer the prior question "Of what story or stories do I find myself a part?"'[3] The liberal tradition, focusing so intently on human autonomy, and so central to the predominant culture, lacks a rich account of how our roots help us understand the good, justice and so on. If the Christian inheritance is to mean anything significant to our ethical existence, it must be because the Gospel story forms us to be a certain sort of person. We belong to the story.

Reading MacIntyre brought ethics to life for me. Understanding ethical reasoning in terms of formative stories and the communities which carry them felt like a great step forward from the way I had been taught ethics, which seemed always to conceive of 'moral problems' as a fork in the road, and 'ethics' as the process of abstract reasoning by which one decided the correct choice of direction. Real-life ethics seem to me to be far more embedded in deep and complex stories of all kinds than that deracinated picture allows.

That said, some of the ways in which Christian ethicists have built upon MacIntyre's approach have felt less satisfactory. As we shall see, where MacIntyre speaks of communities and traditions mediated through narrative and story, the communitarian strand of Christian ethics treats the Christian story as superior to other traditions, and the Church itself as the only meaningful community. As a parish priest, as an academic – even as an activist – this feels like only part of the story. However completely we 'turn to Christ' in baptism, confirmation or conversion, most of us are partly formed in our reasoning and our moral understandings by the predominant culture around us and, while our faith may cause us to stand over against many prevailing assumptions, few Christians repudiate that culture entirely. Perhaps they perceive that the good is not an exclusive province of Christians and that, while going to church may help one to understand the good with far more profundity, there

---

[1] See, for example, George A. Lindbeck, *The Church in a Postliberal Age*, London: SCM Press, 2002.

[2] Alasdair MacIntyre, *After Virtue: A Study in Moral Theory*, 2nd edn, London: Duckworth, 1985.

[3] MacIntyre, *After Virtue*, p. 216.

remains much good beyond the lich-gate. Our moral sense and our conscience continue to be shaped by all the other communities we belong to apart from the Church – our working environments, our neighbours and friends, our leisure partners and so on. If Christian ethics is an aspect of practical disciple-ship, we will surely seek to explore ethics in a way which translates to the world beyond the Church and allows us to continue to engage with those we meet there. The Church has always had both a missionary vocation and a calling to holiness. In contemporary Western culture, as much as in the 'heathen lands afar' of which the old hymn speaks, mission entails a certain amount of compromise in order to make the Christian story intelligible in a strange context. Making Christian ethics – the Christian story about the good and about living well – intelligible in this way means taking seriously our membership of, and formation within, numerous, often overlapping, communities of which the Church may be pre-eminent but is only one. Yet the tension between holiness and mission is never completely resolved, and Christian ethics today is one of the most important fields in which this tension is being explored.

So this book is, in part, an exploration of the tensions between our role as citizens belonging to many communities and stories, and our identity as Christians who are committed above all to one community and one story (albeit, a story with many strands, sub-plots and divergent readings). These tensions surely capture something of the diverse demands which face prac-tical ministers in today's mainstream churches. The liberal tradition remains, in my view, an important source of wisdom which emphasizes the first aspect of our lives, while the communitarians help us to explore the second aspect in new depth. The tension remains deliberately unresolved, and I try in subsequent chapters to give a theological account of why this should be so. I note in passing that Harry Williams's spiritual classic, *Tensions*, was an early and lasting influence on my faith development, so perhaps there are deeper reasons why I find so many creative tensions in ethics.[4]

The first part of the book, therefore, is concerned, not with 'moral dilemmas' but with an exploration of how Christians might 'do ethics' in ways which honour both the liberal and the communitarian traditions. It ends with a consideration of whether it is still possible to do Christian ethics in public, arguing from Christian belief to policies and practices which could contribute to the ordering of human relationships, politics economics, and so on. My hope is that the exploration of 'meta-ethics' in Part 1 serves to show the church-member/citizen tension in Christian ethics as central to the discipline.

However, meta-ethics needs working out in practical terms, and here the temptation to stray back to the old-fashioned 'moral dilemma' approach cannot be wholly resisted, although I have tried to make Part 2 reflect as

---

[4] H. A. Williams, *Tensions: Necessary Conflicts in Life and Love*, London: Mitchell Beazley, 1976.

fully as possible the concerns and arguments introduced in Part 1. One cannot totally ignore the dilemmatic approach so long as the moral framework of Christian people continues to be formed in part by the culture around them. Christians do not always regard the ethics of the culture around them as utterly inadequate. The dilemma, however, is not the fork in the road labelled 'What shall I do?' but the deeper question: Which of the many stories which help shape my moral life is informing my reasoning and my action here?

In the course of a seminar programme, it is helpful to spend time in discussion and argument during which the bases for various, often deeply held, ethical positions can be explored. Few seminars end with a definitive presentation of the 'right' answer. While a textbook can get away with fewer loose ends, I have not used the chapters of Part 2 to point to definitive 'Christian' positions but to test differing ways of defining, and addressing, the questions. Frequently, public manifestations of Christian ethics seem only concerned to place the Church on the side of either *The Guardian* or the *Daily Mail* (respectively, the newspapers of the political left or the political right in Britain) as if popular journalism defines the ethical questions and the Church must address them on other people's terms. The richness of the Christian tradition is such that a more confident Christian ethics should also be seeking to set the questions in different terms.

If this book seems, on occasion, to be an extended conversation with Stanley Hauerwas, perhaps to the relative neglect of other voices, it is because I find Hauerwas simultaneously inspiring, infuriating, enlightening and sometimes plain wrong. Never, though, is he dull, and if I can encourage students to read more of his work, I hope it will enhance their enjoyment of the subject while causing them to question and interrogate even a guru of Stanley's stature. I wish I had found space to look in more detail at the work of Oliver O'Donovan, whose books, starting with *Resurrection and Moral Order*, would have added a further distinctive voice to the plot; but to have done so would have distorted my liberal/communitarian structure too much in one direction.[5] And if, at times, I seem to present the recent work of Rowan Williams as the light to illuminate an ethical stalemate, it is not because he is currently the Archbishop of Canterbury but because he has a rare gift for redefining the significance of the Christian tradition in contemporary contexts and, in his current post, a unique opportunity to use this gift in the public domain – rarely to his comfort, but always to the stimulation and edification of many in the Church and beyond.

Because the genesis of this book lies in a series of taught courses, I have also tried to include some of the lighter moments which are so necessary if the attention and interest of a group are to be maintained through the long

---

[5] Oliver O'Donovan, *Resurrection and Moral Order: An Outline for Evangelical Ethics*, Leicester: Inter-Varsity Press, and Grand Rapids, MI: Eerdmans, 1986, 2nd edn 1994.

weeks of the semester. In the classroom, one can introduce participative exercises or musical interludes, and share anecdotes and histories. It is less easy to translate these moments onto the page, but in the three 'Intervals' between the chapters I have made the attempt. Readers might consider taking these ideas and developing them for their own situations.

Studying Christian ethics today is a necessity if Christians are to make sense of their faith in the context of an uncertain and confusing culture. If this book is useful in generating a greater interest and literacy in Christian ethics, whether among students or others, I shall be well pleased.

Acknowledgements

Teaching is always a collaborative process. The modules on which this book is based developed year on year through the contributions of each cohort of students, as well as through the interactions between staff members from across the Cambridge Theological Federation. The invitation to design and teach a Masters module in Christian ethics, as part of the MA in pastoral theology, came from Zoë Bennett, the Federation's Director of Postgraduate Studies who was, and remains, the best sort of critical friend and colleague. Particular thanks go to Dr Susan Parsons, then of the Margaret Beaufort Institute, who worked with me to design the module from scratch and co-taught with me in the first year. Susan and I shared a desire to focus more than usual on meta-ethical questions and to resist the tendency to reduce ethical thinking to the 'solving' of dilemmas. I was very grateful that, at the outset, my own preferences and prejudices about the subject were echoed by a more experienced practitioner.

To each group of MA students between 2000 and 2007 – who included ordinands, clergy and lay people, aged from the twenties to the sixties, studying with mutual delight and occasional incomprehension – I owe a very great debt for raising questions and challenging weaknesses in the programme. The undergraduate groups on the Eastern Region Ministry Course, who worked their way through my ethics syllabuses and seminars, also shared insights and perceptions which reflected the immense range of life experiences present among today's mature ordinands. I hope some of the fruits of these sessions are present in this book.

A book, like a teaching programme, relies on a much wider hinterland of colleagues and associates. Some of the themes originated in my own doctoral studies at the University of Manchester, and here I owe a great debt to Ronald Preston, John Atherton and Elaine Graham, who nurtured my fledgling interest in ethics and its relationship to practice and to doctrine.

Since 2007, I have been greatly privileged to work with the staff team in the Church of England's Mission and Public Affairs Division – a team which combines immense expertise in public ethical issues with a profound grasp of Christian theology and a vocation to make the dialogue between public life and the Church enriching for both. They have taken me beyond the neat precision of academic theology into a world where the mendacities of the media, the default secularism at the heart of modern government and the ambiguous legacy of the Church of England's public status are daily realities to be negotiated. From this team I have learned that Christian ethics is, at heart, a missiological enterprise. It would be invidious to name individuals among one's present colleagues, but together they have given me many practical lessons in the principles enunciated in subsequent chapters.

Innumerable conversation partners, sometimes fellow members of groups pursuing defined projects, and sometimes turning casual encounters into profound exchanges, have also helped to mould my thinking. Some I work with still; others were formative in leading me to where I am. They include: Chris Baker, Nigel Biggar, Mark Bratton, Richard Burridge, Jonathan Chaplin, Wendy Dackson, Julian Eagle, Christine Fletcher, Rachel Jenkins, Neil Messer, Richard Morgan, Stephen Pattison, Alison Peacock, Chris Percy, Esther Reed, Esther Shreeve, Helen Stanton, Graeme Smith, Robert Song, Alan Suggate, Holger Szesnat and Richard Wheeler, although this is far from an exhaustive list.

Thanks are particularly due to Rebecca Mulhearn, Commissioning Editor at SPCK, who seemed to know exactly when to give another gentle push to get the author over the next hurdle before the looming deadline. And − because books don't get written without disruption to home life − to my wife Angela: apologies and thanks.

Malcolm Brown

Part 1

1

Introducing ethics: and Christian ethics

This is a book about ethics and, specifically, about Christian ethics. Even non-ethicists will probably agree with me that the study of ethics is one of the fastest-moving and most controversial fields of study within the wider theological curriculum today. This is, to some extent, a recent phenomenon. In the days when a theology degree from one of the ancient universities was regarded as sufficient preparation for ordination in the Church of England, the key subjects were the Bible, biblical languages, church history and doctrine, and when, in the late nineteenth century, the possession of a degree was felt to be insufficient by itself, it was left to the new theological colleges to cover topics like ethics and pastoralia, the two often being lumped together as adjuncts of one another. The University of Cambridge never did establish a major Chair in Christian ethics nor develop the subject in its undergraduate awards. Even into the 1980s, the study of ethics as a topic for ordination in the Church of England and the Free Churches was often almost indistinguishable from the study of the Church's pastoral ministry.

So what has changed to place ethics at the cutting edge of theological study today? While it is too simple to identify a specific date as the moment when a whole mindset changed, the year of 1979 is of considerable significance. In that year two global phenomena, often thought at the time to be mere aberrations, can now be seen as harbingers of major changes to the way we understand the world and human relationships. In Iran, militant Islam, represented by the Ayatollah Khomeini, came to power and entered the public consciousness of the West for the first time. In Britain, Margaret Thatcher's first election victory not only opened the door to an era of market economics and the marketization of increasing tranches of social relationships but also emphasized, often starkly, that the post-war social consensus was over. Soon afterwards, Ronald Reagan's election as US President confirmed the dominance of similar economic and social policies on both sides of the Atlantic. Today, despite the recession which began in 2007–8, the policies represented by Thatcher and Reagan remain dominant, driving forward the great trends of economic and social globalization. Militant Islam touches everyone's life – and not only through the increasingly onerous security measures following the attacks of 9/11. Especially in Western Europe, where the processes of secularization were well advanced, militant Islam has prompted something of a reaction against all religion and has given a new impetus to ideas of secularization, often at 'gut' level rather than as a systematic programme. Increasingly, public discourse characterizes every faith as irrational, anti-scientific and anti-democratic. A caricature of faith as mere superstition has become common currency in the liberal media. Indeed, many within Christianity, as within Islam and Judaism, seem happy to play up to that image in an increasingly aggressive confrontation with Western culture and Enlightenment notions of rationality. Religion is news again in a way that most theories of secularization have not been well-equipped to explain.

In wider social relationships, the market, with its claim to sit above mere morality, has become the principal mechanism for managing all kinds of human interactions. Even if the post-war consensus embraced a considerable diversity of interests and rival identities, its disappearance has deeply affected how people relate to each other. Nor is this just a British or European phenomenon. The coincidence of 1979 as the date which saw the rise of Khomeini in Iran and Thatcher in Britain is a convenient hook on which to hang an argument, but the changes which those two events symbolize are global in character. On the one hand, the word 'we' has been reclaimed for communal, tribal or ideological groupings. 'Is he one of us?' was a totemic question for the Thatcherites and, more generally, politics has become increasingly tribal in character so that 'we' are defined in quite distinctive groupings. In the twenty-first century, the politics of conflicting identities is, perhaps, even more acute in America as the differences between Democrat and Republican, and between factions within those parties, have become angrier and consensus less conceivable. Even as global markets bring greater uniformity of consumption patterns and media imagery, it has become increasingly difficult to give a coherent account of who 'we' are, what 'we' believe and how 'we' should live our lives – for the distinctive communities, within which ideas about what is good or right are taken for granted, are challenged through intimate media exposure to 'otherness' in all its forms.

Nowhere are these contradictions more evident than in the politics – and, behind the politics, in the moral discourses – of the United States of America. I wrote the first draft of this opening chapter against the background of the Obama–McCain presidential election of 2008. Not only were competing visions of America and 'American-ness' on offer, but the role of religion was palpable, epitomized in the Republican vice-presidential nominee Sarah Palin. Palin represented – or at least was adopted by – the Christian right which champions creationism, challenges the constitutional separation of Church and state and is furiously opposed to homosexual rights and abortion. This phalanx of American opinion celebrates tight-knit, religiously cohesive and supportive communities which still, to some extent, rest upon frontier narratives of independence and suspicion of the outsider. Obama, in contrast, ran on a platform of somewhat intellectual internationalism, recognizing America's pivotal global role and characterizing in his own person the melting-pot of groups which together make up the USA. In a highly charged election, anti-Obama propaganda portrayed him as a Muslim – an accusation which reflects the tensions between religions that characterize the post-9/11 world and simultaneously suggests that America's religious plurality has significant limits.

These various tensions have become so acute that, by the beginning of the twenty-first century, the talk was of 'culture wars'. Yet the paradox is that both groupings champion the theories of the market which, in their pure form, regard the particularities of community, culture, religion (or even, at times, nation) as irrelevant.

Where, in the middle of such heated clashes of culture, can one find the foundations for exploring what it means to live well? This is not only a question for Americans, even though the tensions within that nation epitomize the problem acutely. To be sure, American ideas and influences pervade much of the world through dominance of the global market model and media. But America's culture wars can be seen as a striking and sharply delineated version of a question which arises in almost every national context. The question is, are fundamental values essentially universal or essentially local in character? In other words, are community, religion and nation the places where we learn and practise what it is to be good, to do right and to live justly, or are these notions best discovered in looking beyond the particular so that, in a highly connected world, there can be an intelligible discussion of what these things mean between people formed in very different traditions. Most pressingly, in a world where violence can escalate into annihilation, how are we to live alongside people whose conception of what is good differs radically from our own?

Talk of what is good involves the consideration of ethics. Words which denote value or which express obligations are the basic building-blocks of ethical thought. Words like 'good', 'right', 'just', 'fair', 'ought' and 'must' only have significant meaning within a framework of ethical understanding. When such words become problematic (as they have undoubtedly become today) the ethicist is called in to repair the holes which open up in human relationships, structures and even in patterns of thought. Without some account of who is meant when people say 'we', these value-words become doubly problematical. Are 'we' the totality of the human inhabitants of the world? Or are 'we' the people who think like me?

Ethics, then, has become interesting again as a response to bewilderment about the state we are all in. The ethicist must first try to give an account of how we got here and then attempt to offer some pointers to how things could be understood better and, perhaps, even become better – working, therefore, with one eye turned towards ideals and the other towards the pragmatics of politics and the complexity of human affairs. While all ethicists are attempting to negotiate a balance between ideals and pragmatics, the debate between those who stress the one and those governed more by the other is intense. For what use are ideals if they are incapable of implementation in any recognizable form? And yet too much reliance on what is practically possible can lead to the catastrophic loss of any guiding moral compass beyond mere expediency. Once ethics is seen to address crucial questions which touch on people's lives and security, and not as a disconnected exercise in disinterested speculation, the stakes are raised and the debates become proportionately more intense and creative. I make no apology for claiming ethics as one of the most exciting disciplines in the academy today.

...and Christian ethics?

The role of Christian faith in forging a sense of shared identity and in governing aspects of public life has changed and left us in largely uncharted territory. Whereas, relatively recently, it might have been possible for a British citizen to assume that he or she was Christian by virtue of being British (an assumption that lives on in some aspects of the debate about multiculturalism) and that therefore the way the British understood concepts such as 'good', 'just' and so on, was Christian by default, that linkage no longer holds. Neither the coherent sense of a single national identity, nor the explicit grounding of that identity within a Christian framework, is tenable any longer. In their debased form, assumptions about 'Christian Britain' generated the feeling (belief is perhaps too strong a word) that Christian ethics was little more than a kind of sanctified common sense, and the surprising and often deeply challenging aspects of the Bible and the Christian tradition were subsumed in a generalized and consensual moralism.

In the United States, something different but no less disorienting seems to be happening. Vociferous efforts are being made within some sections of the Christian Churches to establish symbolic (and, in some cases, substantive) linkages between overtly Christian principles and national policies. Thus far, gestures such as the erection of a monument depicting the Ten Commandments in a state courthouse have failed, but it is clear that the constitutional separation of Church and state is not universally accepted as a basic building-block of American polity. The presidency of George W. Bush gave considerable succour to the more right-wing Christian lobbies, although it is unclear whether this represented a real influence on policy or (as the sociologist of religion Steve Bruce suggests) a new intensity to the old practice of courting the religious right's votes while, in practice, framing policy entirely pragmatically.[1] But, as in Europe, the point is that the settlement between the Christian faith and the workings of the state are in flux. The equation of Christian identity with national identity is problematic and few can ignore the shifting ground. Some new account of what it means to be Christian, and how Christian accounts of good living are to be worked out, is pressingly necessary.

Christian ethics among the other theological disciplines

The situation described above has been the occasion of some realignment between Christian ethics and other subjects in the theological curriculum.

---

[1] Steve Bruce, *Politics and Religion*, Cambridge: Polity Press, 2003.

This is not just a matter of how teachers of theology arrange their timetables but affects the wider question of what, and whom, Christian ethics is for.

One of the themes of this book is the question of public theology – whether theology has a contribution to make to public life, citizenship and the ordering of social structures, rather than being mainly about the practices of Christians. Not only do many social questions turn on an interpretation of what is good, just, right and so on, but it is precisely the interpretation of those concepts in the context of the Christian life which determines whether, and how, Christians may be called to have an influence in the public sphere.

Immediately, therefore, Christian ethics is seen to have a profound relationship to Christian doctrine – what we believe about the relationship between God, Christ and the material world shapes how we believe Christians should work within concrete relationships in practice. Christology and soteriology – the person of Christ and the meaning of salvation – are of ultimate importance in determining the Christian's relationship to the world, to the persistence of sin and to the meaning of the 'value' words which lie at the heart of ethical thought. It is, in many ways, the reconnection of ethics to systematic theology which has made the subject so lively and simultaneously so disputatious within the Churches.

That is not where ethics has always been located. Ethics has a distinctly practical side in that it addresses questions which arise from experience and in the application of Christian ideas in people's lives. Christian ethics has been helped towards a stronger consciousness of its own integrity by the rise in the last fifteen to twenty years of practical theology as a distinctive subject, thus helping to untangle the two disciplines.

Linking ethics too closely to pastoral issues has sometimes had a distinctly debasing effect on the subject. If I try to characterize the study of Christian ethics in, say, the mid-1970s in Britain, the following vignette seems to sum it up:

> There is a knock at the vicarage door. On the step is a parishioner with a look of perplexity or worry. The vicar – male, of course, and no doubt wearing a sports jacket with leather patched elbows – ushers the visitor into the study where they sit either side of the dully glowing fire in shabby armchairs.
>
> 'Padre', says the visitor, 'I have a problem ...'
>
> The vicar gets his pipe drawing to his satisfaction, listens attentively to the story and proffers a few well-chosen words of advice.
>
> 'Thank you Padre. That's helped me sort things out. Now I know what I have to do.'

A caricature, of course. But not so very far from the way ethical advice has been dispensed by the Church over the years, nor very far, I suspect, from how the Church's role as purveyor of ethics is still perceived. But ask serving clergy how they encounter ethical problems in the course of their ministry today and that kind of image rarely figures. Indeed, when I asked a large group of clergy how ethics touched on their ministries, they replied that the connection is tenuous. 'We don't get people bringing ethical dilemmas. What we get are pastoral problems.'

If the distinction is not immediately obvious, that may be evidence of the way in which ethics and pastoralia have tended to be elided in the past. The parishioner in the vignette above approached the priest with a problem prior to taking action. He or she wanted to discern what the right thing to do might be. The clergy who replied that they encounter pastoral problems rather than ethical dilemmas meant that they are called upon to respond to people after actions have been taken which turn out to have unintended or malign consequences. In such instances, it is not exactly helpful to start with a debate about what should have been done instead – although in an extended pastoral relationship that conversation could perhaps happen, bringing ethics into the picture. Ethics informs the exercise of pastoral care but is not just about responding, after the fact, to human situations, since it is also about what it means to exhibit a Christian character in one's life. Pastoral care can, in the absence of solid ethical foundations, degenerate into a desire to 'take the pain away' without ever making clear judgements about what is good, right or just. Worse, under the influence of the Churches' perceived social marginalization, the desire to build up attendance and avoid alienating potential supporters can lead to the offer of uncritical care, avoiding any challenge to social and cultural norms. An example of this might be the controversy over the Church of England's report of 1995, *Something to Celebrate*, which argued that too much emphasis on the virtues of marriage, or condemnation of couples living together without marriage, should be avoided lest it deter cohabiting couples from coming to church. The report argued its case more subtly than many of its critics supposed, but the key point remains: when should pastoral or missiological concerns trump a Christian ethic which has always regarded marriage as the proper framework for sexual relationships?[2]

When the ethicist turns towards the public sphere, the tendency to elide ethics with pastoral care begins to raise a further set of problems. To what extent should Christians support social policies which express and enforce Christian virtues and punish vices? Should Christian approaches to social policy be driven by compassion for people who face the horrendous consequences of wrong-doing – their own or other people's? Compassion, even for the wrong-doer, is itself a Christian virtue, and the chance to turn away from wrong choices and start again is fundamental to Christian notions of forgiveness. But to argue that social policy must embody compassion may be to underestimate the formative role of law and policy in shaping perceptions

---

[2] Board for Social Responsibility, *Something to Celebrate: Valuing Families in Church and Society*, London: Church House Publishing, 1995.

of what is good and just. Attempts to legislate in ways which reflect compassion for people who face tragic situations can run up against the difficulty of defining the tragic. At the time of writing, renewed attempts to legalize assisted suicide (commonly known as euthanasia) are coming forward in the British Parliament. The Churches, institutionally, are more or less unanimously against the legalization of assisted suicide on the grounds that it would undermine the supreme value of human beings and put the vulnerable at risk. In taking such a stance, the Churches not only risk media portrayal as being callous and indifferent to human suffering but must contend with many of their own members who believe that, in extreme cases, the Christian commitment to compassion can mean assisting the dying on their way.

The point, here, is that it is inadequate to drive social policy through the Christian imperative of compassion if it is divorced from a social understanding about which aspects of human experience are just part of the ups and downs of a normal life, and which are so extreme as to demand alleviation. The tendency for compassion to become generalized into a limitless desire to alleviate suffering poses a profound challenge to the Christian understanding of what it means to be human, for it is the persistence of sin and suffering in this world that, to a great extent, shapes Christian discipleship and faithfulness. In other words, the Christian virtue of compassion is virtuous only within a broader and more doctrinally comprehensive understanding of the role of humanity within God's world at this stage in salvation history.

Nothing in the above should be taken to deride compassion as a virtue. It must remain in play in all ethical thinking among Christians. My point, rather, is that the social meaning of compassion is changing and that, without a thoughtful analysis of the state of social relationships in general, once-familiar ideas end up functioning in unexpected ways. Teaching ethics in the context of ministerial training has made me anxious that this wider social analysis is too rarely part of the Churches' consciousness. The understandable desire among ministers to do good, in a world where 'doing good' is widely perceived in professionalized terms, quickly elevates pastoral care to the acme of vocation. The imperative of mission too easily becomes reduced to making the Churches' ministry 'accessible', with the result that any challenge to individualistic understanding, whether of tragedy or the 'good life', becomes muted. The dominance of pastoral care can reduce ethics to a non-subject incapable of forming a story of being human and offering guidance on what living well, seeking truth and doing justice might mean. Out of ethics flow the practices of discipleship.

Consequentialist or deontological?

It is time to put a little theoretical flesh on the bones of this approach to ethics. The tension between the doctrinal and pastoral aspects of Christian ethics is only one of the polarities which exist within the broader discipline. Even more fundamental is the tension between alternative views of how a notion of 'the good' may be arrived at. Is an action judged to be good according to whether or not it leads to good outcomes, or are some actions good simply in and of themselves? If the former, then it must be impossible to speak of actions being right or wrong without seeing them within a much wider context. If the latter, then a question arises about how we can know a priori that something is good or bad, right or wrong. These two approaches to ethics are, respectively, known as consequentialist and deontological ethics. Categories like these are helpful mainly as ways of isolating, and thereby examining, the characteristics, strengths and weaknesses of different emphases within ethics, rather than as adequate descriptions of particular schools of thought.

Consequentialist approaches to ethics not only require us to understand the immediate context within which an ethical decision has to be made, they also imply that the consequences of an action can be predicted. My action is deemed good if it brings about good consequences. Yet it is not really clear that future consequences are knowable in the kind of way that such an approach assumes. A classic example is the case of lying. Lying, in general, may be wrong, but a lie which (for example) misdirects a psychopath hell-bent on murder so that he does not meet the person he has set out to kill, may be the 'right' course of action if it leads to a 'good' outcome – the avoidance of killing. But this is to place the lie within a very constrained pattern of consequences and also makes an assumption that the hypothetical subject who is making the ethical decision is a context-less individual rather than a person who exists within a complex web of social relationships. If the ethical decision-maker is viewed within a network of present and future relationships, the rightness of the lie looks less clear-cut. Who is to say that directing the psychopath away from his intended quarry will not expose a great many more people to his murderous rage? Just as significantly, what will be the future consequence if the moral agent gains a reputation for lying whenever he or she believes that better consequences are thereby served? To be able to trust that person in any future situation, we must be sure that they were not, somewhere in their own imagination, weighing the possible outcomes of truth-telling versus lying. Without the ability to read their mind, their word becomes deeply compromised and the trust upon which myriad social relationships depend may be irredeemably weakened.

One could go on. The fact is that meeting a murderous psychopath who can be easily deflected from his course by a lie is not an everyday experience for most people, and framing ethical questions within such hypothetical situations is deeply limiting. What I have tried to show is, first, that assessing the moral consequences of an action is not straightforward, and, second, that picturing moral action as if it takes place within a simple abstracted 'scenario' is less than helpful. The particularities of real cases are usually of more significance than the general characteristics they exemplify and, in any case, the complexity of cause and effect, reaching far into an unknown future, makes it almost impossible to come to a fair assessment of the likely consequences of even the simplest action.

Even when consequential arguments are developed into quite nuanced systems, problems remain. The utilitarianism of Jeremy Bentham and John Stuart Mill sought to declare actions good according to the extent to which they maximized human happiness. Other forms of utilitarianism have sought to maximize things other than happiness, but the basic principle remains – conduct is to be regarded as good in so far as it generates more of the sought-for result rather than less. But it is notorious that utilitarianism has difficulty balancing the short- and long-term implications of actions, happiness in particular being an extraordinarily complicated juggling of immediate gratification against future benefit. Moreover, the portrayal of moral theory in abstract terms glosses over the practical difficulties of application. If, in a commonly cited example, the death of one person could secure the greater happiness of a multitude, there would appear to be no question but that the death was a good thing. Yet this does not begin to address the question of who must die to make the many happy, let alone questions of justice or the status of human life.

And yet there is still something in the consequentialist argument which is difficult to abandon completely. 'Do this, because it will lead to this or that desired outcome' remains a significant strand in the way human beings assess right action, and there is even an echo of this sort of reasoning within the Ten Commandments themselves, in that the fifth commandment requires the honouring of father and mother, 'that you may live long in the land the LORD your God is giving you'. While the cause-and-effect aspects of the commandment are not spelled out, it nevertheless appears that honouring father and mother is commended partly because it will somehow lead to desired outcomes. The power of moral example is also a significant consequential factor in that one reason to live well as an example to others is that I may benefit when others around me live according to a moral code we can share.

Turning to deontological positions, right and wrong, good and bad, are taken to be intrinsic qualities attaching to various actions. The sense is contained within the meaning of the word itself in that 'de-ontological' emphasizes that the morality of an action is bound up with the very nature of the action itself. Thus, one might say, murder is wrong in itself and cannot ever be right, regardless of the expediency or otherwise of any particular killing. This is not 'do as you would be done by' (that is, don't kill others or others might come along and kill you) but an assertion that killing another human being can never be right, even if that killing could conceivably bring about innumerable happy or beneficial outcomes.

Murder may, of course, be a rather extreme example which is unlikely to be disputed. What of other moral actions? Until comparatively recently, it was not just Christians who maintained that sexual intercourse outside

11

heterosexual marriage was always, intrinsically, wrong. Consequentialist arguments might support that stance on the grounds that such safeguards were essential to proving the paternity of offspring and, hence, the integrity of property rights. A different sort of consequentialism (often adopted by the Churches) suggests that pre-marital sex diminishes the quality of any subsequent marital relationship. These arguments were not always distinguished very clearly from the argument based on intrinsic wrongness. If pre-marital sex is deontologically wrong, then it matters not one whit if it enhances a subsequent marriage. Mixing consequentialist and deontological arguments is, in the end, unsustainable. If something is right or wrong in and of itself, the consequences are irrelevant.

But how is a deontological position to be arrived at? One possibility is that there is an overwhelming level of social agreement that something is right or wrong in a way that admits no possibility of disagreement. Murder might indeed be an example, except of course for the grey areas around judicial execution, killing in times of war, killing in self-defence and so on, all of which create scope for different understandings of the imperative. But such extensive levels of social agreement are not frequently encountered today, and even if they were, it is not easy to discern the difference between a deontological moral principle and a historically contingent social convention. In other words, a deontological principle is, by definition, true for all time and in all circumstances, and although various ages may mistake their habits for eternal truths, a view of history suggests that habits may be much more transient.

Another way of establishing deontological principles is by appeal to authority – principally, since human authority is always fragile, to a deity of some sort. An action thus becomes good or bad in itself because that is the way God has ordered the created universe and to act otherwise is to defy God's will. This position is easy for unbelievers to mock, and the characterization of religious people as those who think they have a hotline to the mind of God is common in the secular media. But one does not have to believe that God's will is known through a metaphorical heavenly telephone system to believe that God does indeed judge some human actions to be right or wrong in themselves, thus obliging believers to seek God's will and to live by it. In that believers view sacred texts as sources of true authority, moral actions may be good or bad to the extent that they reflect the eternal truths of the scriptural teachings. Leaving aside, for a moment, questions of how the meaning of Scripture is to be discerned, it remains that, with the exception of the fifth commandment, all the other nine commandments are unequivocally deontological in character. The conduct commended is good simply because it is good, and no explanation is offered which could conceivably relativize the status of the commandments or make them conditional on their outcomes.

Yet there are problems with extrapolating from clear moral teachings in ancient Scriptures to moral positions of subsequent ages. How does deontological moral reasoning cope with new knowledge? If a moral question arises which is not plainly covered by an existing moral principle, how shall it be tackled? One option is to extrapolate from already established principles, but there are limits to how far this can be taken. For example, the extent of our knowledge about being human is developing so rapidly through programmes such as the Human Genome Project that (to take one example only) the discovery that there are only tiny genetic differences between all human persons cannot but affect our beliefs about race and ethnicity (which is not to say that the genome project will eradicate racism). Any moral principle, from Scripture or another source, which emphasizes racial distinctiveness, is thus under challenge. Moreover, the recognition that a genetic difference only slightly greater separates humans from chimpanzees calls into question moralities which draw hard distinctions between humans and the animal world. In that all Scriptures are mediated through human agency, there is always the difficulty that what is taken to be divine truth may be skewed in its interpretation by contingent and culturally conditioned human perceptions.

Another problem with deontological moral reasoning involves the difficulty of securing as much moral agreement between peoples and cultures as the demands of a common humanity seem to require. As long as cultures and religions remained geographically homogeneous and had little contact with each other, social and public life could be maintained according to principles derived from authoritative sources. But no one moral universe can easily command the allegiance of a deeply plural world. One response to this is to declare one faith, one set of sources, to be true and all others to be in error, and thus to seek the domination of the world by a single ethical system. Another is to retain deontological ethics for the internal lives of communities which share a faith or an allegiance, and to dissociate such a localized ethic from any attempt to universalize its principles. Neither feels completely satisfactory.

This short review of consequentialist and deontological approaches to ethics suggests that they each entail major problems. So is such a dichotomy very helpful in the first place? It depends whether such approaches are meant to be descriptive or prescriptive. In other words, are consequentialism and deontologicalism attempts to classify the complex ways in which people do ethics, or are they 'sealed' systems which each claim to be the correct (and exclusive) way in which ethics must be done? It is best to treat the dichotomy in the way typologies should, in general, be seen: as ways of classifying complex and confusing matters so that important general points shine through the murk of particularity. Without such distinctions, ethics can descend into a babble of competing voices, each unaware that their arguments cannot be brought together with any hope of agreement since they are based on very different notions of what ethics is. As we will see, such a confusion of voices and traditions is itself a fair description of the moral predicament in which the world finds itself today – that is the perception which opens

Alasdair MacIntyre's seminal study in moral theory, *After Virtue*.[3] Provided it is understood as a simple typology and not as a normative structure for understanding all ethical positions, a distinction between consequentialist and deontological ethics helps to show that different approaches each make important claims, each display significant weaknesses and are not to be synthesized in some final solution to the problem of identifying the right, the good and the just and the obligations and imperatives which those concepts carry with them.

Inductive or deductive?

With these caveats in mind, it is worth sketching a different pair of approaches to ethical reasoning. Here I want to contrast a deductive mode of reasoning with an inductive one. If consequentialism and deontology are ways of approaching the question of the nature of the good, inductive and deductive methods are approaches to reasoning which may inform ethical debates but are not confined to them.

The distinction between deductive and inductive approaches is crucial to an appreciation of the tensions within Christian ethics. To approach deductive reasoning first, one might characterize it as starting from what is known and then deducing conclusions about what is under consideration. It works from general principles to particular applications. For example if, by definition, all swans have long necks, that bird over there with a short neck cannot be a swan. An inductive approach, on the other hand, starts with experience of the particular and attempts to establish general principles. Thus: every swan I have ever encountered has been white, so I infer that all swans are white. Clearly, the inductive argument can be falsified if the next swan to swim into view is black. When this happens, my inductive reasoning is shown to be faulty. But consider the implications if the deductive argument about swans is applied to their colour as well as their necks. It follows that, from the principle that all swans are white, we must deduce that the black aquatic bird over there is not a swan. Immediately, a dispute arises between the deductive bird-watcher and the biologist for whom the definition of a swan is not dependent upon colour. But why should biologists have the monopoly of definitional authority?

We must not push the analogy of the swans too far. Much more significant is whether, in ethical reasoning, we start with authoritative positions through which we interpret the way we perceive the world, or begin from our own experience and extrapolate from it. Both approaches raise difficulties.

The inductive approach describes how a great deal of human reasoning takes place. We learn to discern patterns in the world around us and come

---

[3] Alasdair MacIntyre, *After Virtue: A Study in Moral Theory*, 2nd edn, London: Duckworth, 1985.

to expect those patterns to be repeated. In ethics, experience leads to judgements about the nature of the good and how we ought to live. As an example, the concept of intolerable suffering is frequently deployed in the debate about assisted suicide. At once, the judgement about what is intolerable is seen to rest upon the way a person experiences things. No universal rule can tell me what level of suffering a person can find tolerable or intolerable. Thus, from a starting-point in human experience we discover a way to handle one of the components in an ethical argument. Similarly, when introducing the concept of love into a debate in Christian ethics, my experience of love may lead me to emphasize particular aspects above others – the warmth of love, perhaps, or maybe the equivocal experience of parental love. My experiences may be modified, moderated or corrected by exposure to other people's experience, but the mode of reasoning continues to be inductive, working from particular experience to general principle.

A difficulty arises when we consider how to factor God into a debate about ethics conducted on inductive principles. God is not a subject discerned in the same manner as the material world. If we are to ask in an inductive argument, starting from human experience, 'Where is God in all this?' we are likely to find that, rather like peeling an onion, analysis of the argument does not disclose a divine presence at the centre. No less significantly, an inductive approach to argument requires some consideration of how and where a person's interpretative framework is formed. My experience of the world is not simply an encounter between objective reality and an anonymous individual with no history, family or context. My ways of interpreting raw experience are not just my personal property but are forged in inherited relationships of kin and community. Questions about, for instance, the threshold of acceptable pain are, in part, learned reactions, shaped by social convention. My ways of apprehending, understanding and evaluating an external reality are products of my upbringing and social location in history, geography and politics. It matters which sources in my moral formation I choose to treat as authoritative. It is one aspect of our own age's obsession with 'the individual as moral agent' that the families, communities and political structures which shape the person have been consigned to the shadows. Inductive modes of moral reasoning need to be understood as socially contextual.

But these drawbacks do not automatically validate deductive approaches. To start with an authoritative account of how the world is, and to seek to deduce an ethic from this starting-point, raises the question of how I am to respond if my experience of the world contradicts the authoritative account of reality. Sources of authority may be accorded divine status such that dissent becomes akin to treason or apostasy. We see something of this in current disputes about the use of Scripture in debates about human sexuality where some modes of deductive reasoning from biblical texts resist alternative interpretations on the grounds that there can be only one authoritative reading and thus only one set of moral conclusions open to Christians. In the end, this sort of deductive reasoning hinges on human interpretations of authority. Deductive approaches may also encounter problems with new knowledge about the world. The earlier example about swans turns upon the willingness or otherwise of the deductive reasoner to modify his premises upon discovering a black creature which, in all other respects, resembles a swan. But the moment the premise is expanded so that the principle that all swans are white encompasses the black swan, experience has trumped authority and the deductive principle is undermined. Reverting to the hot topic of human sexuality, how does an argument, built deductively on Genesis 1.27 ('male and female he created them') to render male or female the only valid sexual identities, cope with the relatively recent discovery of the surprisingly high proportion of the population who are 'intersex' – that is, having a hormonal or chromosome make-up which defies the rigid classification of either male or female?[4] One response is simply to deny alternative readings and to assert that the world really is as 'we' have always said it was. But, followed to its logical conclusion, this can only mean the most radical kind of sectarian segregation from communities who describe the world differently and the impossibility of dialogue between ethical groupings.

So neither inductive nor deductive modes of reasoning are adequate on their own. Yet both represent ways in which people actually go about their reasoning. Once again, the best approach is to remember that such categories are essentially descriptive rather than prescriptive. Rather than setting out to privilege inductive approaches based on experience or to champion particular deductive methods grounded in authoritative sources, it helps to see each method as a corrective to the other – a prompt to remind us that each approach contains serious drawbacks and that no argument drawn exclusively from one approach or the other is immune to critique.

It is worth, at this point, returning to the specifics of ethical enquiry. Ethics is not a subject disconnected from the material world, and how we ought to live is not a question divorced from how the created order functions. Here we encounter one of the classic problems in ethics – the relationship between what is and what ought to be the case: the 'is/ought' distinction. A little reflection will suggest that an inductive reasoner is more likely to associate the fact that something is the case with the judgement that it ought to be the case. A deductive reasoner, on the other hand, may hold that the way the world ought to be has been defined authoritatively and that the way the

---

[4] See: John Hare, 'Neither Male nor Female: The Case of Intersexuality', in Duncan Dormer and Jeremy Morris (eds), *An Acceptable Sacrifice?: Homosexuality and the Church*, London: SPCK, 2007, pp. 98–111.

world seems to be may be no more than illusion or error. The stronger the bonds which tie patterns of thought to the inherited ways of the community, the tribe or the group, the more likely that 'is' will imply 'ought'. This is a classic aspect of conservatism which invests the status quo with moral virtue. But a close-knit community under the stress of persecution, or living in exile, may be much more prone to telling stories which locate goodness and right within the collective memory and contrast this acutely with the prevailing context: the gap between 'is' and 'ought' widens. And, where communal ties are weakened and all that is left are individuals, there can be as many 'goods' as persons – 'is' has been divorced completely from 'ought'. While the Christian ethicist will usually appreciate the bonds of community and be suspicious of fragmentary relativism, the problem of relating 'is' to 'ought' remains. Until all things are fulfilled in God's new kingdom, Christians are always both citizens and aliens. Human communities are important, but never the last word, and the persistence of sin thwarts the fulfilment of the kingdom: the gap between 'is' and 'ought' cannot yet be taken as closed in every respect.

Liberals and communitarians

The consequentialist/deontological distinction, and similarly the tension between inductive and deductive modes of reasoning, both help to lead us to the fundamental typology which underlies this book – the contrasting approaches which are generally labelled 'liberal' and 'communitarian' (although, in the case of Christian ethics, a close synonym for communitarian is 'confessional', since the community in question – the Church – is identified by the faith it confesses). The point of using the liberal/communitarian distinction as a framework for discussing Christian ethics is that it captures the main dividing lines within the discipline today. We shall open up the meaning of both terms in later chapters, but a brief characterization of both positions is called for here.

The inductive mode of reasoning which we looked at earlier places an obvious emphasis on experience, and privileges experience over established definitions and formulae. Similarly, a consequentialist approach to ethics gives a high priority to chains of reasoning which can, it is claimed, discern the outcomes of particular actions. Liberalism, with its high doctrine of human reason, has a natural affinity to both inductive and consequentialist approaches. This is not to say that these ways of doing ethics are capable of simplistic labelling as 'liberal', but that liberals will usually find such approaches congenial. Just so, making use of these approaches in ethical arguments may suggest a liberal outlook.

Perhaps the point becomes more obvious from the other side. A communitarian, for whom ethical ideas are primarily forged in the lives of discrete communities, according to the traditions and stories which bind those communities together, will have a natural sympathy for deontological and deductive modes of ethical reasoning, since both approaches start with firm definitions and clear boundaries. For the communitarian, experience is less to be trusted as a source of wisdom and truth than the collective wisdom of the community. It will be clear that the communitarian is likely to regard the individual as subordinate to the community whereas the liberal may put things the other way round.

That is, of course, a crude and oversimplified sketch of liberal and communitarian approaches. But it nonetheless points to a key question which will recur throughout this book: Which is the proper cultural arena for Christian ethics? The world at large, or the Church in particular? As we shall see, this is far from being a simple matter in an age when the relationship of religious faith and church life to the wider Western culture of today is both unclear and contentious.

In short, when addressing this question, a liberal mindset will tend to emphasize what Christians have in common with others, since the whole liberal project (of which more anon) is grounded in the quest to overcome the divisions that prevent human beings recognizing what they share. In Christian terms, liberals are likely to be inspired by the universal mission of God, the ways in which Jesus broke down social and cultural divisions and the ability of the Holy Spirit to make sense of strange tongues. They are also likely to draw back from notions of absolute certainty and to stress the significance of humility and doubt, since if God loves the human race, nobody's insight into truth is to be despised. Because the culture of today's Western nations is essentially liberal in character – that is, treating the autonomous individual as the basic building-block of society and looking to transcend differences rather than to entrench them – theological liberals may be inclined to minimize the tensions between culture and the perspectives of faith. For liberals, integration of their religious observances into the wider life of the various communities they inhabit may be a high priority. Ethics for liberals is usually about citizenship in the world at large, although the particular stories of the Christian faith give depth and direction to ethical enquiry.

Communitarians, however, will be much more acutely aware of how Christian ethics stands apart from the wider culture. They will resist the conflation of Christian faith and contemporary culture and will emphasize the Christian community – the Church – as the place where a distinctive ethic is worked out. The result is likely to be at odds with the wider culture in many ways and will serve to emphasize the difference and particularity of Christians. Given the more deontological approach which this position suggests, anyone who dissents from the Church's view on key issues may forfeit their membership. For communitarians, experience as such tends to be suspect since the interpretation of experience is never neutral – as we encounter the world, the pervading culture may be interpreting it to us in subtle ways which may not be consistent with Christian understandings. Thus, communitarian approaches to ethics are likely to be hard to understand from outside the community of the Church since commitment to the Church and its narratives is a precondition for 'thinking like a Christian'.

It is worth noting here that the tension between the liberals and communitarians reflects a tension at the heart of Christianity itself. Christians are called to holiness, and holiness is defined in terms of the unique Christian story and interpreted in the life of the Church. To that extent, the communitarian principle is strongly vindicated. But the Church is also called to mission – to engaging with cultures outside itself and making its message comprehensible to them. The extent to which the missionary calling of the Church entails compromising with the ethics of the surrounding culture, and how this is reconciled with the call to holiness and its implication of standing apart, is an enduring tension at the heart of the life of the Church and, hence, is central to any consideration of Christian ethics today.

A 'corrective' approach to ethics

By contrasting different approaches to ethics – inductive and deductive, consequentialist and deontological, liberal and communitarian – I have tried to open up some of the sources of controversy in Christian ethics today. But because, in none of these cases, have I put my cards on the table to declare one approach right and the other wrong, it may be thought that I have abdicated a major responsibility. If these different approaches represent genuinely divergent ways of approaching ethics, each will have its supporters and judgements must be made – neutrality is surely not an option. Ethics without commitment lacks zest.

However, it is important to remember the note of caution about how typologies and simple dichotomies should be approached. If they are seen as convenient ways of isolating and thus examining different approaches, there is no obligation to treat them as if each stood for a right approach to the exclusion of others. I have argued that there are strengths and weaknesses in the different approaches outlined above, but I now want to go further and argue that there are good reasons – and specifically theological reasons – why consequentialist and deontological, inductive and deductive, liberal and communitarian, arguments need one another.

My point is that different approaches to ethical reasoning may best be understood as correctives to one another. Thus, the respective flaws and difficulties attached to consequentialist approaches are to some extent met by the strengths of arguing deontologically, but only at the expense of a different set of problems. The question, then, is not so much about which approach is 'right' but about the intrinsic unlikelihood of ever capturing a final, universal, ethical judgement in a contingent world. And far from this being a source of despair or failure, it reflects rather well the Aristotelian point that the good life is discovered in the search for it and not in some imagined final state of perfection. For Christians this is about how disciples retain their 'eschatological hope' in a fallen and contingent world. Remembering that typologies are tools for analysing different kinds of argument rather than maps or templates for constructing ethics from scratch, it is a reasonably sound principle that, when an argument appears to rely on (say) a strongly consequentialist approach, we ought to ask how a deontological argument would shed new light on the topic – and, naturally, vice versa. Different approaches serve as critiques and correctives of each other. There are trends in ethics as in every other subject and, as new contexts and problems arise in life, so they reveal weaknesses in formerly dominant approaches to ethical thinking, and a corrective, drawing on another strand or tradition, needs to be stressed. We will pursue this theme further since one of the dominant themes of ethics – and particularly Christian ethics – today is the mutual correction between liberal and confessional (or communitarian) ethics in both the academy and the Church.

This understanding of correctives reflects an authentic theological principle. The classic Christian vocabulary about the times we inhabit speaks of the interim – the interim between the inauguration of the kingdom of God and its completion when Christ returns. A characteristic of the interim is that the gift of God to the world in Christ and the Holy Spirit is a reality which humanity can apprehend, and yet that apprehension is limited by the persistence of sin. Human fallibility means that, in matters of discernment such as ethics, absolute certainty is not ours yet, but the grace of God means that striving for understanding is not fated to fail. Where we have reduced complexity and ambiguity to neat methods and 'correct' approaches, there is almost certain to be a requirement for the corrective influence of another perspective. So, as far as I can, throughout this book, I have tried to remain alert to the corrective power of different schools of Christian ethics and their different emphases, because each has the capacity to offer a corrective to the illusion of ultimate certainty.

Further reading

As this book throws the reader in at something of an ethical deep end, one of the introductory texts on Christian ethics may be worth reading at an early stage. Among the best are: Neil Messer, *Christian Ethics*, SCM Study Guides, London: SCM Press, 2006; and, from a Roman Catholic viewpoint: Alban McCoy, *An Intelligent Person's Guide to Christian Ethics*, London and New York: Continuum, 2004.

For an excellent collection of essays introducing Christian ethics in its various dimensions, see: Robin Gill (ed.), *The Cambridge Companion to Christian Ethics*, Cambridge: Cambridge University Press, 2001.

Subject-specialist dictionaries can be a useful resource at any stage in the study of Christian ethics. These two are both excellent: David J. Atkinson and David H. Field (eds), *New Dictionary of Christian Ethics and Pastoral Theology*,

Leicester: Inter-Varsity Press, 1995; James Childress and John Macquarrie, *A New Dictionary of Christian Ethics*, London: SCM Press, 1986.

Theological dimensions to the liberal/communitarian dichotomy, which is part of the structure of the following chapters, can be explored in: David Fergusson, *Community, Liberalism and Christian Ethics*, Cambridge: Cambridge University Press, 1998.

2

Using the Bible in Christian ethics

It is a truth universally acknowledged (at least in ministerial training) that students can do excellent work in biblical studies modules but then revert to simplistic and uncritical use of the Bible in their ethical reflections. A basic grounding in biblical studies is assumed for the purposes of this chapter. The student approaching the study of Christian ethics ought, at the very least, to be able to distinguish the different genres in the biblical texts – for instance, the law and other moral instruction, history, prophecy, wisdom literature, parable and so on. It is also worth remembering that Christian doctrines are themselves grounded in the biblical texts. Many of the most interesting arguments in Christian ethics today are about the way that doctrine – for instance, the idea of the coming kingdom of God – informs how we live and what we do. And a theology of the kingdom is essentially grounded in the New Testament.

Ethical teaching in the Bible

If ethics is about what we ought to do, and how we perceive the good, there is plenty in the Bible that addresses the question directly. But even the most direct injunctions about human conduct raise hermeneutical questions. The Ten Commandments, however fundamental, require further reflection if they are to be a guide for living. 'Thou shalt not kill' – but it is clear that from earliest times exceptions have been made, as in time of war. Some translations interpret the commandment as 'Thou shalt do no murder' – whereupon the definition of murder becomes a crucial precursor to interpreting the text. The definitional questions become entangled in the relative authority of different translations. Definitions are not merely linguistic technicalities but reflect the translator's theological priorities and spiritual formation. The Commandments say, 'Honour thy father and thy mother' – but what does 'honouring' entail? To what extent must honouring entail obeying if, for example, a parent gives moral instructions which contradict other command-ments? If we are exploring, for example, the ethics of euthanasia (prompted, perhaps, by the suffering of a parent in terminal illness who asks for assistance in hastening death), it is not enough simply to refer to the Ten Commandments as instructions from God which can be applied without further reflection.

What of the prophetic literature? Can Amos 8.4–6 be taken as a direct repudiation of Sunday trading? Can the prophet's words be employed directly to condemn the retail chains which campaign for Sunday to be treated as commercially no different from any other day? Context has to be considered: we cannot jump straight from Amos to today without at least asking whether the relationship of the trader to the community is comparable. But we are also required to hear the eternal Word of God in the words of the prophets. Reading Scripture through the lens of the contemporary context must be moderated if we believe that the text itself has meaning which is not determined by context alone. If Scripture is to speak to each age, and not be reduced either to a set of quaint but irrelevant stories or to a bland affirmation of what we believe already, there must be a search for, and acknowledgement of, the text's authentic and objective meaning. Exploring the context is part of this search for eternal, transferable, meaning.

The New Testament is rich in ethical teaching. Jesus addressed ethical questions, sometimes in what seemed to be expressions of universal truth (e.g. Luke 16.18) and sometimes apparently addressed to very local situations or individuals (Luke 10.41 perhaps). But, much of the time, Jesus used parables and visual imagery – teaching methods that interact with the imagination of the listener. There are pitfalls in reading the parables as if we can tell straightforwardly what message they conveyed then, or were intended to convey. The parable of the Good Samaritan makes only incomplete sense if we know nothing of the divided history of the peoples of Jesus' time. We can, however, speak with some confidence about the theological and ethical 'atmosphere' of Jesus' teaching. Single texts are read against the background of the Gospels as a whole. Thus, it is clear that there is a particular concern in Jesus' teaching for the poor, the weak, the oppressed – the Gospel texts coming together to point cumulatively in a particular ethical direction without any single text clinching the argument once and for all.

An example of the care needed when deriving ethical positions from the Gospels might be the instance of marriage. Jesus himself did not marry and, indeed, taught that the imperatives of the kingdom were more important than the conventional responsibilities of family life (Luke 14.20, 26). St Paul seems somewhat ambivalent about marriage too (1 Corinthians 7.9). But the Church has consistently supported marriage (albeit, sometimes, as a second best to celibacy), partly as a way for human life to reflect the nature of God through the virtue of faithfulness. As God is faithful to his people so, in marriage, two people express that fidelity to each other. The sources of that ethical teaching derive, in this respect, not only from the teaching of Jesus and the apostles but from the knowledge we gain from all the Scriptures about the nature of God. Yet as the Church worked out its ethics from its understandings of Scripture and doctrine, other arguments for marriage came to stand alongside the virtue of faithfulness. The Book of Common Prayer of 1662 lists three reasons why marriage was ordained, arriving at these arguments from a consideration of scriptural sources. Marriage was instituted 'in the time of man's innocency' to signify the mystical union between Christ and his Church; it was hallowed as an institution by Christ's presence at the wedding in Cana; and marriage was commended by St Paul. Thus, the Prayer

Book goes on, marriage has three purposes: the procreation of children, a 'remedy against sin' for those 'as have not the gift of continency' and 'for the mutual society, help and comfort that the one ought to have of the other'.[1] In the course of arriving at the final form of the Prayer Book service, a great deal of argument took place before the order of those three purposes was fixed.[2] All three have scriptural warrant. But in our age, when longevity and social pressures increase the desire for escape from marriages which no longer offer 'mutual society, help and comfort' (desires from which Christians are not exempt), how shall the Church discern whether or not a marriage has met the criteria under which it was contracted? Moreover, the line of reasoning from Scripture to the Prayer Book understandings of marriage feels a little tenuous and selective in its use of texts – no mention of Luke 14.20 here. In the twenty-first century, a defence of marriage has become one of the trigger issues in defining Christian attitudes to Western social mores. Yet unambiguous biblical principles for the ordering of marriage in society are strangely elusive: how far, for example, does the Bible really envisage marriage in terms of romantic attachment outside a web of other familial networks? Which model of marriage are the Churches defending?

Turning now to the epistles, Paul's teaching is of a different quality from the Gospel accounts of Jesus' sayings. Paul's style is less allusive: less to do, perhaps, with exciting the imagination than with developing reasoned positions. In the Pastoral Epistles and in the Acts of the Apostles, we can see the earliest Church learning how to express its own nature and negotiate its relationships with surrounding cultures. Acts and the Epistles are very specifically located in time and place, yet their presence in the canon gives them universal significance. Here is the story of a group of people whose beliefs and convictions about Christ call into question everything they have been used to doing. Their ethical behaviour is shaped by their emerging doctrines. Their conviction is that God's self-giving love, offered by Christ on the cross, calls God's people to make the virtues of love and fidelity utterly central. But the early Church was also convinced of its missionary nature. Being a sect marked out by ethical purity was not enough – the imperative was to reach out to others. So a missionary Church had to work out how far it should make itself accessible and comprehensible to the surrounding cultures, without compromising its beliefs about God. This dilemma has been at the heart of the Church's ethics ever since.

There are many nuances, then, to using the Bible in Christian ethics – and it must be approached with due attention to the nature of each text in its wider context. I do not mean that we ask whether the Scripture is

---

[1] The Book of Common Prayer, Cambridge: Cambridge University Press, n.d., p. 302. Extracts from The Book of Common Prayer, the rights in which are vested in the Crown, are reproduced by permission of the Crown's Patentee, Cambridge University Press.
[2] See: Diarmaid MacCulloch, *Thomas Cranmer*, New Haven and London: Yale University Press, 1996, pp. 421f.

conformable to the assumptions and values of our present time but, rather, whether the meaning of the words is essentially the same and how the text epitomizes the nature of God so that it can be applied to situations regardless of context. In other words, is the text properly universal in application, has it been superseded by the new dispensation in Christ (as with parts of the Old Testament such as dietary laws) – or has our reading failed to capture the full significance of the text?

To illustrate the last of those points, consider Mark 12.41–44 (cf. Luke 21.1–4). This is the well-known story of the widow who puts two copper coins in the temple treasury and is commended by Jesus for having given all she had to live on. The text has frequently been used to preach an ethic of self-denial and of giving generously, especially to the Church. Now consider the same passage as part of a longer reading – Mark 12.38—13.3 (cf. Luke 20.45—21.6). The story of the widow's mite is located between a passage in which Jesus condemns the teachers of the law who claim the highest social positions but 'devour widows' houses', and another in which Jesus predicts that not one stone of the Temple will be left upon another. Suddenly, the virtuous widow appears instead as the victim of a ruthless and exploitative temple system which stands under condemnation. The ethical implications of the text become rather different. This is an example of how the meaning of Scripture can be coloured by assumptions drawn inappropriately from our own context (church collections are a good thing!) and moulded by the liturgical uses of Scripture which often dislocate passages from their contextual meaning.

Some passages contain within themselves the capacity to sustain more than one reading. The parable of the Good Samaritan is frequently quoted as an encouragement to look out for, and respond helpfully to, the wounded or otherwise disadvantaged. And so it is, for, having told the parable and identified the Samaritan's benevolence, Jesus says to his hearer, 'Go and do likewise' (Luke 10.37). But the parable itself is told in answer to a question, 'Who is my neighbour?' and, if that is the question, the significance of the answer being 'the Samaritan' is acute, for instead of the good deeds of the Samaritan being the point of the story, the outcast status of Samaritans takes centre stage and the parable turns upon the willingness to receive neighbourliness from the despised outsider. Both readings are manifestly 'right' and to emphasize either reading over the other diminishes the parable's moral significance.

The Bible operates at a number of levels simultaneously. It is the story of a people, and later an embryonic Church, discovering the ethical implications of its convictions about God. In the New Testament, living out that faith involved processes for handling ethical disagreement (Acts 15) as well as moments when new ways of living became very clear (Acts 10). And the Bible is our window into the great cosmic drama of atonement and salvation. The Christian ethicist considers moral questions in the light of the resurrection and the kingdom of God inaugurated among us, but also in the knowledge of the cross and the persistence of sin. The Bible is a 'big story' as well as many smaller stories, and together they are foundational stories for ethics.

WWJD – the imitation of Christ

Around the turn of the millennium, it became quite common to see Christians wearing wrist bands, badges and other paraphernalia bearing the initials 'WWJD' – 'What would Jesus do?' The objective was to remind oneself regularly that, in any quandary or dilemma, the faithful disciple should seek to discern the mind of Christ and act accordingly. As an approach to ethics and moral living, this has a long history as the 'Imitation of Christ' – a notion popularized by Thomas à Kempis but reaching right back to the first disciples, who treated Jesus as their mentor and model.

Nevertheless, one limitation of WWJD might be summed up as 'SWWYTSOG?' – 'Since when were you the Son of God?' Here is where Christology impacts upon ethics. Who was Jesus? The orthodox understanding is that he was fully human yet fully God also, but the implications of this for his earthly life have remained subject to argument and speculation. On the one hand, Jesus was constrained by the particularity of his time, place and individuality. I have already mentioned the difficulty of using Jesus' own life as a model for considering questions of marriage, since he apparently never married. Celibacy, then, would appear to be a prerequisite for modelling a human life on the pattern of Jesus, yet that was not St Paul's conclusion. We may conclude from the life of Jesus that absolute faithfulness against all provocation is how he might have approached relationships, although he was willing to let those who could not adapt to his requirements, like the rich young man, walk away. But questions about, say, the proper degree of equality within a marriage cannot be answered by appeal to Jesus' own practice or teaching. Significantly, it is unclear from the Gospels what Jesus believed about himself and about the future of the world. There are indications that he may have expected God's kingdom to be fulfilled very soon after his own life. Certainly, the story of the Church is, in part, about a community coming to terms with the deferral of that fulfilment and seeking an ethic for a continuing discipleship through subsequent generations, each living with persistent sin and shortfalling. WWJD is only a model for moral living in so far as it is possible to know the mind, and enter the context, of Jesus.

Fraser Watts puts this problem rather well in an essay on forgiveness.[3] While Jesus' ability to forgive is, of course, a model to strive after, we should not assume, Watts concludes, that forgiveness is hard-wired into our nature as it

---

[3] Fraser Watts, 'Christian Theology', in Fraser Watts and Liz Gulliford (eds), *Forgiveness in Context*, London and New York: T&T Clark International, 2004, pp. 55–7.

was for Jesus. Simply because I am not the Son of God, questions arise about the limitations of my ability to forgive others, and these questions are not mere reproaches to my inadequacy but cause me to ask in a profound way what forgiveness might constitute in human terms.

It remains that the imitation of Christ is an important aspect of Christian ethics. No reader of the Gospels can fail to see that Jesus' ministry involved much more than delivering the precepts of the Sermon on the Mount, challenging though the ethic of that sermon undoubtedly is. In all the Gospels, Jesus is portrayed as seeking to demonstrate the nature of God the Father – the God who is loving, faithful, knowledgeable and concerned for each person to the ultimate degree and who wishes for the creation to be restored to wholeness. Jesus taught the nature of God through parables, through precepts and by example, and repeatedly suggests that, in as much as human beings can emulate the virtues which are most characteristic of God's nature, they will be doing God's will and bringing God's reign closer on earth.

It follows, then, that what we might call the Christian virtues are those which Jesus both exemplified and taught as the defining characteristics of God's self. These virtues are learned through the study of Scripture and in particular the scriptural accounts of the ministry of Jesus. Living faithfully, loving God and neighbour and valuing each person, provides the summary answer to the question: What would Jesus do? But these demands can often seem at odds with one another, precisely because we are not in the same relationship to God as Jesus. There remains much work for us to do in deepening our insight into that relationship, and this is where the life of the whole Church, including its liturgical and prayer life, becomes central to the enterprise known as Christian ethics.

Nevertheless, it is hard to escape the fact that the Bible is read differently by Christians who each believe themselves to be reading it faithfully. Certain key concepts are, if not in contradiction, at least in tension within the texts of Scripture. Wogaman identifies six such tensions which are worthy of careful exploration:

1   Reason vs. revelation
2   Materialism vs. the life of the Spirit
3   Universalism vs. group identity
4   Law vs. grace
5   Love vs. force
6   Status vs. equality.[4]

Although there is nothing final about this particular list, the themes which Wogaman picks out are worth a little more exploration.

---

[4] J. Philip Wogaman, *Christian Ethics: A Historical Introduction*, Louisville, KY: Westminster John Knox Press, 1993, and London: SPCK, 1994, pp. 2–15.

Reason and revelation

The first of these approximates to the inductive/deductive tension which we have already explored. Extending well beyond the Ten Commandments, the self-revelation of God is a constant theme throughout the Scriptures. In the New Testament, the nature and person of the Christ-child are revealed to Mary and the shepherds by angels and to Joseph in a dream (Luke 1.30; 2.9–14; Matthew 1.20–21). Paul's conversion is arrived at, not through careful and rational weighing of evidence but through the dramatic intervention of the risen Christ on the Damascus road (Acts 9). As Wogaman points out, the prophets often justify their utterances with the formula 'Thus says the Lord' rather then seeking to persuade their hearers of the reasonableness of their position and, especially in the letters of Paul, worldly wisdom is routinely diminished as a source of understanding about God (1 Corinthians 1.20–24). Nor is this solely about miraculous interventions in human affairs by God and his angels, for Paul holds up the image of Christ crucified as providing 'a more compelling moral vision than any rational analysis could hope to do'.[5] Even the New Testament's explorations around the person of Jesus as God's ultimate self-revelation to the world draw upon categories and ideas from Hellenistic philosophy such as the 'logos'.

As we have already noted, numerous biblical stories show people, and peoples, learning about the nature of God through reflection on their own experiences. Much of the teaching of the law is pragmatic and consequentialist. The wisdom literature, and a great deal more of the biblical material, is perfectly accessible to those who do not believe in the God revealed in its pages. This is frequently borne out today by well-known public figures who treasure the Bible for its moral atmosphere while holding themselves to be atheist or agnostic about the God within its pages. To suggest, therefore, that a biblically based ethic must be grounded in revelation or reason alone misunderstands the complex and nuanced nature of the texts in front of us.

The material world and the life of the Spirit

Wogaman's second tension in biblical ethics is that between materialism and the life of the Spirit. In short, does the material world matter? In practical Christian ethics, this is one of those unresolved and perhaps irresolvable tensions which continue to fascinate, not least because of the growing significance of the environmental movement and combating climate change. In biblical terms, arguments for Christian environmentalism often start with the observation that God created the world and all that is in it, and saw that it was good (Genesis 1). The case for taking the material world seriously doesn't end with Genesis, of course: in the psalms the created order is celebrated and

---

[5] Wogaman, *Christian Ethics*, p. 4.

affirmed and the prophets emphasize the significance of material flourishing as part of God's purpose for humanity. In the New Testament, the healing work of Jesus affirms the importance in God's dispensation of physical well-being. The Johannine assertion that, in Jesus, 'the Word became flesh and lived among us' (John 1.14), underpins the doctrine of the Incarnation in the declaration that God himself is not above sharing material, human, form and hallowing the created order by living as one with it. The doctrine of the Incarnation has long been an important starting-point for a particular kind of politically active and socially conscious Christian ethics. But the materialist reading of Scripture is, as Wogaman makes clear, not the whole story.

In the biblical scale of things, it is clear that the material world is important, but not of ultimate importance. Idolatry – the mistaking of elements of the created order for the creator himself – is condemned throughout the different genres of scriptural writing. In the prophets, and in many New Testament passages such as the Magnificat (Luke 1.46–55) and the story of the rich man and Lazarus (Luke 16.19–31), God's rule is exemplified in the turning upside-down of material relationships, with the poor and dispossessed raised up over those who cherish wealth. In John's Gospel, Jesus emphasizes the spiritual nature of God who must be worshipped 'in spirit and truth' (John 4.24), and through the Pauline epistles, the contrast is made between 'the flesh' and the life of the spirit (e.g. Romans 8.7–8).

From this tension within the Scriptures, a great deal of controversy and argument follows. If the life of the spirit is emphasized to the exclusion of a concern for the material world, why should Christians care about global warming? Some openly treat climate change as irrelevant to the great questions of salvation, and for precisely this reason: that the scriptural tension has, for them, been resolved by ignoring the materialist strands in the text. The failure to grasp the tension is found no less among those for whom the transformation of the political order is the central Christian ethical imperative. Once again, we are confronted by two apparently incompatible positions which both embody wholly authentic Christian insights. They cannot easily be collapsed into a synthesized resolution. Better, perhaps, to treat them as correctives to each other and understand that, when the material aspects of Scripture are in the ascendancy in our ethical arguments, they will almost certainly require a corrective which re-emphasizes the significance of the spiritual.

Universalism and group identity

Wogaman's third scriptural tension introduces us to the disjunction in Christian ethics between liberal approaches and confessional or communitarian starting-points. Wogaman offers an interesting survey of Old Testament writings which epitomize the tension between the unity of all the created order under God and the particularity of being among God's chosen people. The tension becomes even more acute in the New Testament as the conviction grows among the earliest Christians that the revelation of God in Christ is a revelation not just to the Jews but to all peoples. Hence the missionary journeys of Paul and others and the first struggles to articulate the gospel in ways which could be apprehended in thought-patterns owing little to the Hebraic origins of the story itself.

This tension within the biblical narrative establishes the Church as called to holiness and called to mission. Promoting the hallmarks of the kingdom in peace, justice and the integrity of creation is the task of the Church in the world and wherever these marks are seen the *missio dei* is being accomplished. But for such mission to begin requires there to be some distinctive community within which those kingdom virtues are not only proclaimed but lived and exemplified – hence the significance of the Church's identity. The argument, sometimes heard, that mission always precedes ecclesiology is a red herring. As we shall see, the question of whether Christian ethics is a subject and an activity unique to the internal life of the Christian community, or whether it has a salience in the world at large, is perhaps the most significant division between approaches to Christian ethics today.

Grace and law

Here is another tension within the Bible which continues to reverberate today. Utopian Christian communities have sometimes tried, but virtually never succeeded, in living by grace with no law, and Christian ethics in general has often struggled to emphasize grace and law in ways which reflect New Testament understandings. Yet the popular conception of Christianity continues to characterize it as essentially rule-bound and legalistic – its ethic a compendium of 'thou shalt nots'. I recall being jolted, years ago, during a deanery synod debate about the remarriage of divorced people in church (then, almost as divisive an issue in the Church of England as homosexuality is today) when a speaker declared that he wanted to hear 'a lot less about compassion and a lot more about righteousness'. Up to that point, the discussion had tended to treat compassion as the 'grace filled' response and to do so had seemed to me self-evident. More than twenty-five years later, and without having changed my views about the ethics of remarriage after divorce, I can sympathize with that call for a renewed focus on righteousness – in other words, on the Bible's understanding of law. We have already considered the tendency for pastoral concerns to trump ethics – and that is part of a tendency to elevate a certain view of grace over a concern for law. To do so is to unbalance the biblical inheritance on which our ethics are based.

It is not the case that the demands of the law are unique to the Old Testament and completely bypassed in the New by virtue of grace. In many respects, Jesus intensifies the demand of the law by emphasizing its integrity and rejecting clever ways of circumventing its requirements. But at the same time, there is a major theme in the New Testament, picking up important strands of thought in the Old, in which God's free-flowing love is seen to be available to the law breaker as well as to the righteous. This culminates, of course, in the atoning gift of Christ on the cross, but it is prefigured when Jesus summarizes the law and prophets as loving God and neighbour (Matthew 22.37–40) and in the assertion that love is the fulfilling of the law (Romans 13.10). This has implications for how a Christian ethic approaches questions such as the deserving and undeserving poor.

The biblical material illustrates the tensions inherent in living in the post-Pentecost, pre-Parousia, interim. Living in the knowledge of God's grace is not, in itself, a guarantee of sinlessness, however much it may guarantee that the consequences of sin have been taken from us in Christ. We are not justified by anything other than God's superabundant grace, but attempting to live by grace alone throws us open to the fallibility of human nature and the disastrous limitation of our subjectivity. Some sort of law remains essential to hold even the Christian community together in the face of this – and, a fortiori, some sort of reliance upon law cannot be avoided in regulating the engagement of Christians in the public sphere.

As Wogaman suggests, the tension between law and grace is summed up in James 2.14–17, where the necessity of both faith and works is clearly presented as a Christian imperative. As with other ideas which work as correctives one to the other, it seems unlikely that any final synthesis of law and grace will be adequate fully to express a biblically based ethic. Law must be constantly corrected by an appeal to grace, and vice versa, if justice is to be done to the biblical inheritance.

Love or force?

What is the proper relationship between the Christian priority of love and the use of force in the name of what is good or right? Here, of course, there is a basic difference between Old and New Testaments, the former embraces an account of the emergence and development of a nation, its political institutions and their relationship to their God. While the Christian Church came, in time, to be associated with nation-building, political institutions and social codes, the New Testament is more about the emergence of a Church which not only transcended nationalities and races but which had to work out its relationship to the dominant political institutions of the time from below, Christians being a politically marginal minority.

Yet the tension is not quite so simple as Old vs. New Testaments. The Old Testament literature of the nation in exile explores how to be a faithful people under oppression and duress. There is also a considerable strand of thinking in the New Testament which calls for respect and acknowledgement for political authority and, hence, for the exercise of power (Romans 13.1 and 4, for example). The early Church recognized that some form of human authority was necessary for the good ordering of social relationships and that authorities inevitably retain the sanction of coercive force.

The Old Testament also reflects this tension. The first book of Samuel shows that the founding of the monarchy was a concession to the people by God and not itself a mirror to God's nature. Kings and rulers are not invariably venerated as agents of the divine but are frequently criticized and called upon to act humbly. It is quite clear throughout the Old Testament that, while authority and coercive power are sometimes forces for good, they are equally opportunities for abuse.

The prophetic vision, developed further in the New Testament, is one which treats peace, not war, as the condition to be envied and hoped for (Isaiah 2.4; 11.6–9). In the Sermon on the Mount, Jesus explicitly turns the law about 'an eye for an eye' on its head by commending a non-violent response to violence (Matthew 5.38ff.), and this is taken up by Paul in the epistle to the Romans (Romans 12.14ff.).

This tension between love and force intensified as soon as the Christian Church ceased to be a persecuted minority and became more closely associated with powerful institutions. This is not just a cynical accommodation by the Church to the blandishments of earthly power. As Christian faith adapted to a longer view of its place in human history, it needed some ethical structure within which to sustain the good and to regulate human affairs until the kingdom comes. The move away from fearing power need not always be a betrayal of the Church's vocation. Christian ethics had to learn to accommodate the responsibilities and challenges of power and, in a world still deeply tainted by sin, the possibility of coercive power has always to be considered even if it is often rejected. The tension will not go away, and the continuing attractiveness of pacifism to Christians, coupled with the equally evident queasiness in the Church at the violence often perpetrated by the powerful in the name of the good, testifies to the ongoing difficulty of resolving it.

Status and equality

The final tension which Wogaman identifies in the biblical material concerns the stratification of human societies and the biblical challenge to such distinctions. That there have always been those who are rich and those who are poor is not disputed by the texts. The question is whether such distinctions mirror something important about the will of God or contradict the image of God in humanity.

Over against the implication in some parts of the Old Testament that wealth is a sign of God's favour (and poverty, naturally, a sign of rejection) must be held the prophetic emphasis on the way in which wealth cuts people off from God, who blesses instead those who have little (Amos 8, for example). Over against the stories of Jesus in which wealthy people are portrayed favourably, there are the stories like that of Lazarus in which the alienating power of wealth and the blessing of the poor is again the theme. The Magnificat explicitly reverses the social order to bring down the powerful

32

from their thrones and lift up the lowly: 'he has filled the hungry with good things, and sent the rich away empty' (Luke 1.53).

Not surprisingly, this tension has fuelled a great deal of controversy as Christians have attempted to align themselves with particular political programmes. The building up of the poor, the eradication of major wealth differences and the ushering in of a new age of equality have provided the impetus for many generations of Christian social action. Yet the 'prosperity gospel', characteristic of a certain kind of Pentecostalism, which preaches that 'God wants you to be rich' and echoes without ambiguity the Old Testament theme of riches as blessing and poverty as curse, still seems grotesquely inadequate, partly because of its tendency to align itself with authoritarian politics but mainly because it too seems oblivious to the tension within the Bible itself.

It is worth emphasizing again that this particular typology of theological tensions is not by any means the only way in which the biblical grounding of ethics can be characterized. But in following Wogaman here, my purpose is to place the notion of tension at the heart of my analysis of Christian ethics. We have already looked at the tensions between consequentialist and deontological ethics and between inductive and deductive modes of reasoning, and have seen how, in both cases, emphasizing one without the corrective power of the other can mislead. But in the paragraphs above I hope I have shown that this notion of corrective tensions is inherent in the Bible itself – the key source for Christian ethics.

The deferred parousia and the theological interim

It is worth saying more about the significance of living in the interim and the consequences for Christian ethics, for here again we have a major doctrinal theme, grounded in the Bible, which gives a particular slant to ethics when explored from within Christian theology.

The Christian ethicist, however diligently she or he seeks to ground ethics within an understanding of the Bible, cannot escape the shift of perspective that is necessitated by our age's distance in time from the writers of the Scriptures. By this I mean, not that the assumptions and world-views of our own times must inevitably relativize the understanding of Scripture, although the question of relative meanings needs to be asked. I mean rather that questions about ethics in parts of the New Testament appear to have been worked out against a presumption that the world had little time left before God brought all things to completion in the second coming of Christ. There is, naturally, much discussion among biblical scholars about the extent and nature of this eschatological viewpoint. But it remains that more than two millennia of human history have necessitated a longer-term appreciation of God's timetable for the kingdom. The New Testament as a whole is not obviously oriented towards the long view of history. This has important implications when we attempt to derive a stance on (say) ecological issues from biblical sources, for while there are many biblical passages which can inform a Christian ethic on the environment, it is not self-evident that sustainability is a concern for people who look forward eagerly to a time when God would renew the fallen world order once and for all.

In many ways, the central Christian virtue in the interim is that of discernment, for it is not always self-evident whether a particular course of action, or moral judgement, is reflective of God's presence in the world or of the world's fallen nature. There is an ever-present possibility that one may sincerely, but erroneously, identify the will of God in things which ultimately frustrate godly principles or, conversely, declare a principled Christian opposition to actions which might nonetheless further kingdom values. This is one reason why ethics can be contentious ground for Christians and why the arduous search for the common mind of the Church is so important if ethics is to be done faithfully.

Clearly, the virtue of discernment in this context involves a painstaking consideration of evidence used both deductively and inductively. There is a role for using the Bible deductively to identify the way God is, the ways in which God works and how a human understanding of the good, justice and so on in particular contexts should be derived from the nature of God. Yet the biblical texts themselves include the unfolding story of how people have reasoned inductively from human experience (including their experience of Jesus) to conclusions about the nature of God. So, while the authority of the Bible requires us to use its texts deductively and to interpret our experience in its light, there are also good biblical grounds for taking our own experience of the world to be a source of insight into God's will for humanity. And, lest this sound like a hubristic attempt to elevate the individual moral reasoner above the wisdom of Scripture itself, let me emphasize that the key to reconciling – or at least moderating – the tension between inductive and deductive approaches must be the Church: the community of the faithful.

The theological concept of the interim is part of what makes the 'is/ought' question in ethics a problematic one for Christians. The created order reflects the goodness of the creator, but only imperfectly. The world has been hallowed by the Incarnation, yet sin persists. We can reason from how the world seems, and work to the conclusion that, in some respects, God wills it that way. 'Is', to that extent, implies 'ought'. But the constant influence of sin, the limitations of human understanding and, most of all, the belief that God's purposes are still being worked out in history and have yet to be fulfilled finally, suggests that Christians are sometimes called to stand over against the way the world is assumed to work by those who do not share the theological hope of the kingdom. 'Ought', then, emanates from a source different from the mere fact that something 'is' the case, since we can only imperfectly perceive God's will in creation.

The role of the Church in Christian ethics will be expanded upon later. It is not that a single, authoritative and final reading of scriptural sources can overcome the fallen nature of the human beings who read the texts – and the Church itself is a fallen and fallible human institution – but rather the opposite. A clear awareness of the different readings which Christians have made in faith is a safeguard against the tendency to assume that what seems uncontroversial and self-evident to one culture must be the only truth. It is important not to conceal the surprising and often counter-intuitive nature of texts which emanated from distinctive cultures of their own and continue to be treated as significant by people whose assumptions and knowledge are very far from ours. In short, the tendency of people in every age to take for granted the consensus around them, and to treat all other viewpoints as bizarre or deviant, is challenged by the very fact of being part of a global Church extending across two millennia.

Premature embracing of the kingdom yet to come is as problematic for ethics as is the inability to see beyond the persistence of sin to catch glimpses of the kingdom mediated through the living Spirit. Again, the Church becomes essential, for only the diverse community of the faithful can offer the constant corrective of alternative viewpoints: grace and sin, glory and finitude characterize the Christian understanding of the present human condition. The biblical story of salvation is full of these both/and issues (one thinks immediately of the Incarnation with its assertion of the nature of Christ as wholly God and wholly human). Small surprise, then, that the use of the Bible in Christian ethics also requires alertness to paradox, to alternative readings and to the pitfalls of cultural relativity.

The Bible, and doing ethics in public

Must a biblical argument always make its scriptural starting-point explicit? In other words, might it be possible to make an ethical point which is grounded very thoroughly in Scripture but which does not always parade biblical texts as marks of authentic reasoning? Nigel Biggar argues that it is.

> The Bible and Christian tradition are authorities because they are the source of certain truths. Once those truths have been grasped they can be affirmed and elaborated without constant reference back to the place where they were discovered – notwithstanding the fact that he who elaborates them should make regular pilgrimages to the place of discovery, in order to check his grasp for correction or improvement.[6]

As Biggar says, 'the truth incorporates the story on which it depends'.

This means that biblical sources must be thoroughly assimilated so that the Christian ethicist reasons naturally from biblical foundations – and this is a continual process: hence Biggar's point about constant reference back to the texts. It also implies that, while Christian ethics in the public sphere may not always 'show its working' and specify the biblical roots on which it draws, it must have the capacity to show the working if required.

---

[6] Nigel Biggar, '"God" in Public Reason', *Studies in Christian Ethics* 19.1 (2006), pp. 15–16.

In the reflections that follow, and especially in Part 2, I have not always 'shown my working' in terms of the sources in the Bible and the tradition upon which my arguments are based. I hope, however, that where the connections are not obvious, they are nonetheless discernible. In the interplay of biblical sources, theological and doctrinal insights, the contribution of disciplines other than theology, and the practical outworking of factors within and without the Churches, I trust that the influence of Scripture is not lost.

Further reading

For four excellent introductory essays, see the following chapters in: Robin Gill, *The Cambridge Companion to Christian Ethics*, Cambridge: Cambridge University Press, 2001: Gareth Jones, 'The Authority of Scripture and Christian Ethics', pp. 16–28; John Rogerson, 'The Old Testament and Christian Ethics', pp. 29–41; Timothy P. Jackson, 'The Gospels and Christian Ethics', pp. 42–62; Stephen C. Barton, 'The Epistles and Christian Ethics', pp. 63–73.

For one of the most imaginative and thorough recent studies of the ethics of the New Testament, see: Richard A. Burridge, *Imitating Jesus: An Inclusive Approach to New Testament Ethics*, Grand Rapids, MI, and Cambridge: Eerdmans, 2007. Burridge looks at the New Testament through the prism of narrative biography to explore how the ethics of Jesus were presented by the evangelists and St Paul, and the implications for today.

For an accessible study of how the ethics of the Bible look different from different social perspectives, see: Christopher Rowland and Mark Corner, *Liberating Exegesis: The Challenge of Liberation Theology to Biblical Studies*, London: SPCK, 1990.

3

Roots of Christian ethical thinking

The history of Christian ethics is a major subject in its own right and it is not possible to do it full justice in a book which focuses more on contemporary issues in the discipline. Nevertheless, the distinction between historical and contemporary is somewhat arbitrary, since where we are now is the outcome of where we have been. Exploration of the history of Christian ethics not only establishes the roots of the subject but helps to explain the contemporary situation better as the great figures of the past are seen to have been struggling with particularities and circumstances.

For the purpose of this chapter I will look briefly at three major figures: Augustine, Aquinas and Luther, illustrating their thinking through texts which are also used by Robin Gill in his *A Textbook of Christian Ethics*.[1] By referring to the same texts in Gill, the student can make use of his more detailed commentary and see how Gill locates them within a wider historical picture of Christian ethics in a way which cannot be attempted here.

My objective is not to cover these three sources in depth but to locate the emergence of questions in Christian ethics within a historical perspective, to establish the link between Christian ethics and Christian doctrine which was considered in Chapter 1, and to consider how certain emphases in ethics can be seen as responses to specific historical issues. Other representative figures could have been chosen for this purpose, but Augustine, Aquinas and Luther have a particular salience in terms of the arguments which will follow in later chapters of this book.

It would be hard to ignore the significance of Augustine in any work on doctrine or ethics. As Wogaman and Strong put it, 'The thought of Augustine of Hippo (c.354–430) was to dominate Christian theology for a thousand years, and it continues to exert great direct and indirect influence on Christian thinking.'[2] Augustine was, perhaps, the first thinker to give Christianity real intellectual stature. Thomas Aquinas (1225–74) not only dominated the thinking of the later Middle Ages but continues to be highly influential in Roman Catholic theology. Aquinas's synthesis of Augustine's thought with that of Aristotle established the place of reason (as understood in antiquity) in the Christian approach to God. In his emphasis on natural law, Aquinas

---

[1] Robin Gill, *A Textbook of Christian Ethics*, Edinburgh: T&T Clark, 1st edn 1987, 3rd edn 2006. NB: the third edition contains much new material.

[2] J. Philip Wogaman and Douglas M. Strong (eds), *Readings in Christian Ethics: A Historical Sourcebook*, Louisville, KY: Westminster John Knox Press, 1996, p. 51.

epitomizes an enduring strand of ethical thought which is significant in many contemporary arguments. Luther (1483–1546), in contrast, stresses the limits of human reason in apprehending the nature of God and the good. His Pauline emphasis on faith alone, not works, as the means of salvation establishes again the distinctiveness of Christian life and ethics. Standing as he does at the doorway to the Reformation and on the cusp of modernity, Luther's influence reverberates today in the tensions between reason and revelation, and between the universality and peculiarity of Christian ethics. These tensions, as we will see, remain not only unresolved but by turns creative and frustrating, in ethics today.

It is several hundred years since the most recent of the three, Luther, was writing, and there is always a temptation to regard the past, in L. P. Hartley's words, as 'another country'. It is important that these three historical figures do not become conflated in the imagination and that the different ages in which they lived are clearly differentiated. It is salutary to recall that Augustine was more distant in time from Aquinas than Luther is from our century. As Alasdair MacIntyre observes in *After Virtue*, it is vital to keep in mind that the great thinkers of the past were addressing particular contexts and circumstances: 'We all too often still treat the moral philosophers of the past as contributors to a single debate with a relatively unvarying subject-matter, treating Plato and Hume and Mill as contemporaries both of ourselves and each other.'[3] It is equally tempting – and equally misleading – to read back contemporary disputes into the work of theologians from other times and to make judgements on the basis of what their ideas stand for now rather than in the context of what they wrote or said. Thus, while Aquinas and Luther certainly emphasize different approaches to Christian ethics, the subsequent polarization of those approaches, and the division within the Churches which has attached to such differences, does not fully characterize their thinking. While there are aspects of Aquinas's thinking which are important to some contemporary aspects of the liberal tradition in Christian ethics, and Luther does much to underpin some of the more communitarian or confessional approaches, that is not to say that Aquinas *is* a liberal (the term would have been meaningless to Thomas) or Luther a communitarian in the sense in which the word is used today.

Augustine of Hippo

We know that St Augustine grew up with a Christian mother and a 'pagan' father. He himself experienced an intellectual journey which placed him, variously, under the influence of the neo-Platonists and the Manichaeans[4] –

---

[3] Alasdair MacIntyre, *After Virtue: A Study in Moral Theory*, 2nd edn, London: Duckworth, 1985, p. 11.
[4] In brief, neo-Platonism is the third-century rediscovery of Plato's work in a specifically religious context with a focus on the divine unity. Manichaeism is a philosophy characterized by a strong sense of the conflict of good vs. evil.

the first influence remained strong within his thinking while he explicitly rejected the second. Augustine followed a monastic vocation, largely in Africa, before ordination and consecration as Bishop of Hippo.

Most importantly, however, Augustine's life coincided with enormously formative episodes in Christianity's relationship with Roman political power. The Council of Milan, some forty years before Augustine's birth, had effected a shift in status for Christians from being a fringe Judaic sect – sometimes tolerated, sometimes persecuted – to a new, more comfortable relationship with Roman imperial power in which new challenges emerged as the faith sought to make the move from outsider to insider. But within Augustine's lifetime, Rome had fallen to the Goths and the Church found itself part of the inevitable process of scapegoating that accompanied political disaster. The accusation was made that Constantine's conversion to Christianity had fatally weakened the Roman empire, making it vulnerable – politically and morally – to barbarian invasion. Part of Augustine's intention in writing his *City of God* was to rebut this charge. Far from the fall of Rome being a sign that the emperor's adoption of Christianity had angered the gods, he argued that Christianity's God had intervened to punish the pagan empire. Intrinsic to his argument is his opposition to central tenets of Rome's pagan inheritance and his development of countervailing Christian themes which he presents as triumphantly superior, intellectually and rhetorically (Augustine had been a professor of rhetoric in Rome). Among the key arguments which he deploys in this task is the defence of free will, since it is important that he can demolish the pagan notion of the fates and thus establish a stronger sense of human responsibility and, hence, the possibility of morality. In this, there are some very contemporary resonances with the twenty-first century as Christian beliefs about the nature of God and the nature of human agency are difficult to articulate in a way which a secular consciousness can comprehend.

In the text below, taken from Augustine's *City of God*, Book V, we can see how Augustine attempts to establish the reality of free will without compromising the Christian conception of a God who is all knowing and powerful. The text is interspersed with my comments to draw attention to the developing argument.

St Augustine, *City of God*[5]
Book V, chapters 9–11

If, on the other hand, we define 'necessity' in the sense implied when we say that it is necessary a thing should be thus, or should happen thus, I see no

---

[5] Augustine, *City of God*, Penguin Classics, trans. Henry Bettenson, ed. David Knowles, Harmondsworth: Penguin, 1972. Quoted in Robin Gill, *A Textbook of Christian Ethics*, 1st edn, Edinburgh: T&T Clark, 1985, pp. 72–3.

reason to fear that this would rob us of free will. We do not subject the life and the foreknowledge of God to necessity, if we say that it is 'necessary' for God to be eternal and to have complete foreknowledge; nor is his power diminished by saying that he cannot die or make a mistake. The reason why he cannot is that, if he could, his power would certainly be less; and he is rightly called 'all-powerful', although he has not the power to die, or to be mistaken. 'All-powerful' means that he does what he wills, and does not suffer what he does not will; otherwise he would be by no means all-powerful. It is just because he is all-powerful that there are some things he cannot do.

See how Augustine grounds his argument in the nature of God himself. Although we know something of God's nature from Scripture, it is important that we do not derive our image of God entirely from analogy with our own nature, otherwise we will forget that God is not bound by finitude as we are. Our finitude means that our understandings of power and necessity cannot capture God's all-powerful nature. Before we can understand free will, we must first see the difference between our power as we understand it and power as it would be to an all-powerful God. Here, Augustine gives us a model for deductive theology which argues from the nature of God to human experience. He goes on to establish the implications of this for free will and, hence, for ethics.

> The same applies when we say that it is 'necessary' that when we will, we will by free choice. That statement is undisputable; and it does not mean that we are subjecting our free will to a necessity which abolishes freedom. Our wills are ours and it is our wills that affect all that we do by willing, and which would not have happened if we had not willed. But when anyone has something done to him against his will, here, again, the effective power is will, not his own will, but another's. But the power of achievement comes from God. For if there was only the will without the power of realization, that will would have been thwarted by a more powerful will. Even so, that will would have been a will, and the will not of another, but of him who willed, although it was incapable of realization. Hence, whatever happens to man against his will is to be attributed not to the wills of men, or angels, or any created spirits, but to the will of him who gives the power of realization.

Even as his argument turns to human experience, Augustine places God absolutely at the centre of all that is. Appealing to the common experience of finding that one's will may be thwarted or may prevail, he allows each person's will to be their own and thus prevents a person from being merely God's puppet. But this does not push God out of the picture since, given the diverse things people intend, human will cannot be the whole explanation of why things happen in the world. Human freedom and God's power are placed hand in hand.

> It does not follow, then, that there is nothing in our will because God foreknew what was going to be in our will; for if he foreknew this, it was not nothing that he foreknew. Further, if, in foreknowing what would be in our will, he foreknew something, and not nonentity, it follows immediately that there is

something in our will, even if God foreknows it. Hence we are in no way compelled either to preserve God's prescience by abolishing our free will, or to safeguard our free will by denying (blasphemously) the divine foreknowledge. We embrace both truths, and acknowledge them in faith and sincerity, the one for a right belief, the other for a right life. And yet a man's life cannot be right without a right belief about God. Therefore, let us never dream of denying his foreknowledge in the interests of our freedom; for it is with his help that we are, or shall be, free.

So, having started with the nature of God and then considered human experience of how the world works, Augustine pulls this together as a recipe for a 'right life', that is, an ethical life in which beliefs shape conduct. And, in the following extract, he goes on to show how attempts to influence the behaviour of others are consistent with believing in a God who knows all and is all-powerful, since the key to understanding ethical behaviour is to grasp the significance of human freedom.

By the same token, it is not true that reprimands, exhortations, praise and blame are useless, because God has knowledge of them before; they are of the greatest efficacy in so far as he has foreknown that they would be effective. And prayers are effectual in obtaining all that God foreknew that he would grant in answer to them; and it is with justice that rewards are appointed for good actions and punishments for sins. The fact that God foreknew that a man would sin does not make a man sin; on the contrary, it cannot be doubted that it is the man himself who sins just because he whose prescience cannot be mistaken has foreseen that the man himself would sin. A man does not sin unless he wills to sin; and if he had willed not to sin, then God would have foreseen that refusal.

There is a very contemporary ring to these arguments which, perhaps, serves to emphasize the continuing tension in Christian thinking between free will and God's foreknowledge. The persistence of the tension suggests, also, that Augustine did not resolve the argument to the extent that subsequent generations of Christians felt that it had been conclusively answered. My purpose in choosing this text is, however, to illustrate precisely the persistence of certain key issues in ethics, and this example is, in that respect, important. For without free will the possibility of ethics seems remote. Since Christian faith, as portrayed in the New Testament, requires a human response to the call of God in Christ, free will would seem to be fundamental to the Christian dispensation. The relevance of the question to ethics is that an acceptance of free will establishes the principles of agency and responsibility. A connection then becomes inescapable between my actions, the moral reasoning that informs them, and the concepts of goodness, justice and so on. Ethics becomes meaningful when something significant turns upon my decisions. It is my belief that my actions bear such significance which creates the space for ethics – if I believe I have no free will and allow that belief to shape my actions, ethics becomes moribund.

41

On 31 October 2006, the Archbishop of Canterbury, Dr Rowan Williams, was interviewed on the BBC's influential *Today* radio programme by the renowned broadcaster John Humphries. Among themes on which they touched was the problem of the persistence of evil in a world which Christians believe is governed by a good, omniscient and all-powerful God, and the question of whether human freedom of action is incompatible with such beliefs or not. Humphries was incredulous that the Archbishop conceded that there were some things about the nature of God and God's purposes which he didn't know. The question itself, about the apparent incompatibility of God's knowledge and power and humanity's freedom, was one of Augustine's central themes in *The City of God* long before.

It is not irrelevant that Augustine was writing *City of God* in a period of profound political instability. Empires usually promote the notions of stability, progress and virtue. Power confers the ability to define, to a great extent, the nature of what is good, what is just and what is right behaviour, since consistency in such concepts is one factor which distinguishes an empire from a mere coalition of interests. It then becomes conceptually straightforward to equate what is the case with what ought to be the case. But when empires wobble or are defeated, the resultant uncertainty cuts deep. The very foundations of truth appear to be in question and not only is there a powerful impetus to find simple and superficial explanations (like blaming the Christians – or, if one might dare a contemporary parallel, blaming Islam) but also the conditions for advancing new world-views may become viable. It is possible to see Augustine as occupying precisely that space, even as his arguments are directed to addressing specific issues of his time.

A few more observations about Augustine's thinking are relevant here. First, we can see the evidence of his strongly deontological approach in the 'givenness' of both God's nature and human free will. We can also discern the convert's rejection of former views in Augustine's desire to make free will and a prescient God compatible rather than to stress the rigid either/or which his former Manichaean self might have preferred. Gill also makes the interesting observation that a defence of free will might be a more pressing issue to the well-born Augustine than it would be to someone born into the lower orders of Roman life for whom freedom of any kind would be largely beyond their experience. Without wanting to go too far down the line of arguing that economic and political status determine ethical stances, it is nonetheless possible to note that what seems significant and contentious in one context is not universally so when the conditions of human existence differ so radically, both geographically and in time.

Thomas Aquinas

Aquinas (1225–74) is, perhaps, the foremost thinker of the late mediaeval period, which became much enlivened by the rediscovery (through contact with Muslims) of Aristotle's thinking. It is interesting that this intellectual ferment took place in a period of relative political stability, thus acting as a corrective to the notion that new intellectual movements emerge from crisis and the collapse of established modes of thought. Aquinas lived through an age when the Christian faith, mediated through the Catholic Church, provided the deep structures of social, political and personal relationships – this was Christendom, the inherited memory of which was to haunt the post-Enlightenment Church to the present day.

Aquinas, born into the aristocracy of Lombardy, became a Dominican monk, studying in Naples, Paris and Cologne. He became professor of theology in Paris, returning later to Italy where he continued to teach. His two great works are the *Summa contra Gentiles* and the *Summa Theologica*, the latter written as a book of instruction for novices. Its style is didactic; raising a question, offering objections (and objections to the first objections) and summing up in a reply and conclusion. And it is here, in this textbook for novices, that Aquinas develops his majestic synthesis of the Christian teachings of Augustine and the early Church Fathers with the philosophy of Aristotle.

From this, it becomes clear that part of Aquinas's argument must be that the insights of Christian faith are not incompatible with knowledge and wisdom derived from human reason. If Aristotle can be adapted for Christian purposes, then teachings which are not predicated upon monotheism, let alone upon the unique revelation of God in Christ, can contribute to a Christian understanding of the world and to a Christian ethical outlook. Once it is conceded that theology and philosophy are not mutually exclusive disciplines, the way is opened for a theology which is accessible through the exercise of reason and therefore for knowledge of God and God's purposes to be open to the processes of human discovery and not just through God's self-revelation in ways which transcend human reason. This is what we know as natural theology, based upon what Aquinas called the natural law.

For Aquinas, natural law took its place alongside eternal law, human law and divine law. Eternal law is the mind of God which only God can fully know, but humanity can participate in eternal law to the extent of their ability to perceive the natural law through which the created order reflects God's will. Because humanity is a flawed creation, it is necessary to have human laws to make good the imperfection of our apprehension of the natural law. In case Aquinas is here interpreted through modern eyes as arguing that human salvation is capable of being realized through human endeavours, it is important to remember that he also posits the divine law as representing God's intervention to enable humanity to perceive its true end in salvation.

But it is for his thinking on natural law that Aquinas is especially important to this book, for the tension between advocates of natural theology and the primacy of revelation continues in Christian ethics today. And behind that tension lies the crucial question of whether Christian ethics leads, in principle, to positions which non-Christians may share or whether the uniqueness of the revelation of God in Christ and the primacy of God's grace over human works means that Christian ethical positions are independent of human reason and are grasped solely through divine grace. This has immediate missiological consequences for Christians and for the Churches, for on this question rests, to a great extent, the possibility of the Church engaging in ethical debate in the public arena. It is worth recalling that this problem would not have presented itself to Aquinas in the way it appears to us since, for Thomas, living and working in the heyday of Christendom, there was no such distinction between the Church and the public realm. But if natural law is a delusion, and the only source of moral insight is God's self-revelation to those who accept Christ, then the task of Christian ethics looks very different and its interface with the concerns of wider civil society is much more attenuated.

If the idea of natural law is to be sustained, then it must possess some universal properties such that it both is a trustworthy source of moral insight and can be apprehended by people from diverse cultures and perspectives. In the passage below, Aquinas addresses precisely this point. Immediately, the context in which Aquinas is writing becomes significant. In a relatively stable political climate, where Christian faith stands at the heart of the structures and thought-processes of most people, the concept of universality is likely to be much less strained than in more self-consciously plural and diverse societies, or societies where Christians are a small minority. Of course, Aquinas was not unconscious of social diversity. But the kind of incorrigible plurality of which our present age is so keenly aware would have been beyond his ken. Thus the usefulness for today of Aquinas's arguments about natural law turns, to some extent, on the question whether we view the plurality of our own context as an essentially new breakdown of even vestigial consensuses, or whether we see it more as a deepening of old differences without being in any way a qualitative shift in, or ultimate fracturing of, the way commonality and difference is understood.

Thomas Aquinas, *Summa Theologica* 1a2ae, 96, 4–6[6]

Can natural law be changed?

OBJECTIONS:

1 It seems that natural law can be changed. For on the text of Ecclesiasticus, 'He gave instructions and the law of life' (17.9). The Gloss comments, 'He willed the document of the Law to be written in order to correct natural law. Now what is corrected is changed. Therefore natural law can be changed'.

2 Moreover, the killing of the innocent is against natural law, and so is adultery and theft. Yet you find God changing these rules, as when he

---

[6] Thomas Aquinas, *Summa Theologica*, vol. XXVIII, London: Blackfriars with Eyre & Spottiswoode, and New York: McGraw Hill, 1966. Quoted in Gill, *A Textbook of Christian Ethics*, pp. 83–4.

commanded Abraham to put his son to death, the people of Israel to spoil the Egyptians, and Hosea to take a wife of harlotry. Natural law, then, can be altered.

3 Furthermore, Isidore says that 'common ownership of property and the same liberty for all are of natural law'. Human law seems to change all this, and therefore natural law can be changed.

ON THE OTHER HAND it is said in the *Decretum*, 'Natural law dates from the rise of rational creation, and does not vary according to period, but remains unchangeable'.

Here, Aquinas is exploring the tension between the world as commonly experienced and the demands of faith in God. Does faith require us to overturn our perceptions about how things are? On the one hand, some scriptural passages, along with certain respected thinkers, imply a gap between the way things seem to be according to natural law and either the demands of God or the way human law intervenes to promote justice. On the other, authoritative sources (for Aquinas) suggest that natural law operates rather like the laws of physics in that it reflects human interactions with the world and is therefore independent of context. This is another example of the is/ought distinction.

REPLY:

A change can be understood to mean either addition or subtraction. As for the first, there is nothing against natural law being changed, for many things over and above natural law have been added, by divine law as well as by human laws, which are beneficial to social life.

As for change by subtraction, meaning that something that once was of natural law later ceases to be so, here there is room for a distinction. The first principles of natural law are altogether unalterable. But its secondary precepts, which we have described as being like particular conclusions close to first principles, though not alterable in the majority of cases where they are right as they stand, can nevertheless be changed on some particular and rare occasions, as we have mentioned in the preceding article, because of some special cause preventing their unqualified observance.

Although this might seem like a linguistic quibble, Aquinas makes a fair point: adding to something in order to elucidate or clarify the original point is a different matter from declaring that what once applied no longer does so. It is in the working out of natural laws that the need for change may occur. To put the point in anachronistic jargon, the interface between the human and the divine is always going to need a certain amount of adjustment (and note how conservative Aquinas is in this, stressing how the need for change is rare rather than frequent) because of the incompleteness of human understanding. Translating this point to contemporary church life, it may suggest that conservatives in the argument about homosexuality are right to stress that the Church's ethic must not be changed lightly or under pressure to conform to passing trends, but that the liberals are right to believe that the possibility of the Church's perception of natural law changing remains open.

HENCE:

1 The written Law is said to have been for the correction of natural law because it supplied what was wanting there, or because parts of natural law were decayed in the hearts of those who reckoned that some things were good which by nature are evil. This called for correction.

2 All men without exception, guilty and innocent alike, have to suffer the sentence of natural death from divine power because of original sin, according to the words, 'The Lord kills and brings to life' (1 Sam. 2.6). Consequently without injustice God's command can inflict death on anybody whether he be guilty or innocent. Adultery is intercourse with a woman to whom you are not married in accordance with divinely given law; nevertheless to go unto any woman by divine command is neither adultery nor fornication. The same applies to theft, the taking of what belongs to another, for what is taken by God's command, who is the owner of the universe, is not against the owner's will, and this is of the essence of theft. Nor is it only in human affairs that whatever God commands is just, but also in the world of nature, for as stated in the *Prima Pars*, whatever God does there in effect is natural.

Aquinas here appeals to the nature of God in a similar way to Augustine. God's commands may appear to contradict natural law, but the apparent contradiction is a result of our assumption that God is, as it were, like us only bigger. But the difference between God, who is over all things, and finite humanity is not just one of scale but one of kind. See how, in the passage which follows, this allows Aquinas to sit light to human structures (private property and slavery), not dismissing them as ungodly, but relativizing them as human additions to natural law and thus subject, in principle, to being changed.

3 You speak of something being according to natural right in two ways. The first is because nature is set that way; thus the command that no harm should be done to another. The second is because nature does not bid the contrary; thus we might say that it is of natural law for man to be naked, for nature does not give him clothes; these he has to make by art. In this way common ownership and universal liberty are said to be of natural law, because private property and slavery exist by human contrivance for the convenience of social life, and not by natural law. This does not change the law of nature except by addition.

Central to Aquinas's thinking, here and throughout the *Summa Theologica*, is his teleology – his focus on good ends. Through the exercise of practical wisdom, it is possible for humanity to understand what constitutes moral and ethical living, and here Aquinas recognizes the influence of sin and error – including erroneous customs and habits which may be culturally embedded – in distorting our perception of the principles whereby morality is discerned. Here, of course, the essentially consensual nature of Aquinas's world may contrast sharply with our own. It is one thing to hold, in a context of general agreement and uniformity, that diversity of moral perception is entirely accounted for by sin and error, but where there is greater and more confident diversity such a view condemns a considerable proportion of the world's population to being radically more sinful than those who have perceived God's law. This may not be a theological problem for many, but it does shape the relationship between the Church and the world in ways which many Christians find uncomfortable. And (thinking back to Augustine and free will) there may indeed be theological difficulties lurking here since sin and error are consequences of free human agency and many will draw back from a position which regards all non-Christians as having made a free decision to live their lives in opposition to the truth.

Aquinas's concern for natural law touches significantly on today's questions about the public role of Christian ethics. Some kind of natural law position does seem necessary to underpin a commitment to the Churches' involvement in public dialogue on ethics. (The stress here is on the word 'dialogue'. As we will see, there are other modes of engagement which rely on rhetoric and assertion and which are not dependent on any significant shared ground or even a commitment to a common notion of reason. But that is not dialogue.) However, it remains that, while Aquinas may have been able to assume that authentic Christian principles were so embedded in the political and social structures of his day that highlighting the distinctiveness of Christian ethics was not a germane issue, subsequent generations were not always willing or able to pass over the question. At least to some extent, the intellectual ferment generated by Aquinas's synthesis of Christianity and Aristotle, and his consequent focus on human reason, laid the ground for the relativizing of Catholic teaching as diverse cultures could no longer be excluded by definition from any knowledge of God. While the Crusades had broadened Christendom's awareness of other peoples and cultures, the rise of international trade in the later Middle Ages deepened the process, paving the way for a mercantile society in which the need to establish questions of value which could be shared between cultures and traditions required a further loosening of the tie between specifically Christian revelation and an ethic based on reason. It is possible to discern, in the rise of mercantilism, both the natural development of a Thomist ethic founded on reason, and the intensification of the process of ethical relativism which made possible the revolutions of thinking which constituted the Reformation. It is also possible to discern in this process the trend towards an increasingly global, and less tribal, human consciousness which remains a challenge to a Christian faith originating in a much more tribal communitarian context, and also the significance of economic interests as major factors in the shaping of ethical structures – another process which remains significant today.

Martin Luther

In contrast to Aquinas's position at the heart of the age of Christendom, Martin Luther (1483–1546) occupied a period much more conscious of radical social dislocation and unease. While Luther is often portrayed as one of the chief instigators of the seismic historical shift which we have come to call the Reformation, the relationship between major social changes and individuals is subtle and complex. Luther was able to take his stand against the corruption of the Catholic Church of his day, partly because of the wider context of thought and events. He was both a parent and a child of the new ways of thinking.

In Luther, as in Augustine, it is possible to trace the zeal of the convert in his stance towards established patterns of thought. An Augustinian monk, and an ascetic, Luther's stance against the practices of the Church of his day came to a head in 1517 when he promulgated his *Ninety Five Theses* as a public statement of faith and as an invitation to debate. The 'presenting problem' may have been the open sale of indulgences, but Luther's action constituted a serious challenge to the authority of the Pope. While Luther's theology at this time was not entirely original, owing something to Wycliffe and Hus, the timing of his action was critical, coming as it did at a moment when papal power and authority were already weakening and wider social developments, especially in economic life, were generating an atmosphere of turbulent change. Knowing himself to be vulnerable and recognizing the seriousness of his rebellion against established religious structures, Luther committed his theology to writing in an immensely productive period between 1517 and his excommunication in 1520, followed swiftly by the Diet of Worms, which caused his books to be banned and his opinions to be outlawed.

It is difficult to assess Luther's theology without considering the turbulent times in which he lived. The notion of Christendom, which Aquinas had been able to take as his fundamental frame of reference, was visibly crumbling. In its place, the concept of the nation-state was growing in salience and the early manifestations of capitalism were beginning to emerge as a dominant economic structure. The stresses of change were, as ever, being felt most acutely by the poorest. In 1525 came a peasants' rebellion which Luther vehemently opposed. At first sight, it seems odd that Luther, who in theological terms might be seen as a radical prepared to challenge the most powerful of orthodoxies and the most entrenched of establishments, should not have sided with the peasants. Indeed, this apparent paradox still causes a degree of discomfort to modern Lutheran scholars such as Cynthia Moe-Lobeda who feel that the relevance of Luther's theology for today requires that his opposition to the peasants be explained in some acceptable way.[7]

---

[7] Cynthia Moe-Lobeda, *Healing a Broken World: Globalization and God*, Minneapolis: Fortress Press, 2002. See especially pp. 95–9.

Moe–Lobeda, to her credit, concludes after much consideration that imposing notions of ideological consistency from today upon a figure from such a different social, political and theological context is a lost cause. Yet a couple of general points might still be made here. First, Moe–Lobeda is surely right that we cannot interpret historical figures and their thinking against some kind of template drawn up from contemporary concerns and categories. Nevertheless, there does seem to be some correlation between times of profound economic and social change, with all the social insecurities which ensue, and shifts in the ways in which religion is understood to shape human understandings. In ethical terms, periods of significant upheaval and change seem to generate simultaneously a new interest in the religious foundations of ethical reasoning and fresh emphases on the distinctiveness of religious perceptions over and against the prevailing moral climate. Without wanting to make too much of this rather broad generalization, a recurring theme in subsequent chapters will be the way in which Christian ethics gains its vitality from addressing questions to which the general consensus of the time seems to have no adequate answers. It seems likely, then, that the more far-reaching the uncertainties of the age, the more challenging to the status quo will be the Christian ethical response. Luther is a very sharply focused example of this.

Note how, in the passage which follows, Luther is emphasizing the uniqueness of the Christian revelation over against any concept of the good derived from 'common sense' or accessible to anyone regardless of faith. It is not what is done – works in themselves – that constitutes good living but the faith that motivates good works. And yet Luther is able to draw an example from a universal human context as he compares faith in God to the confidence of a married couple in one another. So the concept of faith as the grounds for moral action is not, of itself, incapable of being apprehended by 'a heathen, a Jew, a Turk, a sinner' – but it is through the unique revelation of God in Christ that humanity is able to enter that relationship of trust with God. From this, it follows that the good, for Luther, is whatever faithful Christians do – it is not a set of practices which Christians can teach the rest of the world (unless the rest become Christian) or exercise in the public sphere independently of commitment to Christ. Ethics, then, is not a set of precepts but the consequence of certain commitments. Luther's world was at the threshold of an early process of globalization (as we would now call it). Heathens, Jews and Turks (Muslims) were starting to impinge upon the consciousness of Christendom, and new trade-driven contacts were creating relationships across religious divides, which inevitably suggested some common human understandings which transcended the particularities of religion. In the face of what we can now recognize as the emergence of Enlightenment liberalism in its earliest stages, Luther reasserts difference and Christian distinctiveness in ways which run counter to the dominant trends. In the face of the emergence of the nation–state, he posits a different kind of community grounded upon faith. In these respects at least, Luther can be seen to offer an example of Christian ethics in counter-cultural mode which will offer interesting parallels with Christian counter-culturalism today.

Martin Luther, *Treatise on good works*[8]

Now everyone can notice and feel for himself when he does what is good and what is not good. If he finds his heart confident that it pleases God, then the work is good, even if it were so small a thing as picking up a straw. If the confidence is not there, or if he has any doubt about it, then the work is not good, even if the work were to raise all the dead and if the man were to give his body to be burned. This is the teaching of St Paul in Romans 14 (.23), 'Whatsoever is not done of faith or in faith is sin.' It is from faith as the chief work and from no other work that we are called believers in Christ. A heathen, a Jew, a Turk, a sinner may also do all other works; but to trust firmly that he pleases God is possible only for a Christian who is enlightened and strengthened by grace.

Unlike Augustine and Aquinas, Luther appeals here to feelings – to the Christian's sense that actions undertaken in faith are different from those where faith is absent. His arguments do not proceed according to the laws of logic alone but draw on the specific Christian insight that faith is God's unique gift to Christians which distinguishes Christian ethics from common wisdom – as the next paragraph shows.

That these words seem strange, and that some people call me a heretic because of them, is due to the fact that they have followed blind reason and heathen ways of thinking. They have set faith not above but beside other virtues. They have made faith into a kind of work of its own, separated from all works of the other virtues, although faith alone makes all other works good, acceptable, and worthy because it trusts God and never doubts that everything a man does in faith is well done in God's sight. In fact, they have not let faith remain a work but have made it a *habitus*, as they call it, although the whole of Scripture gives the name good, divine work to no work except to faith alone. Therefore, it is no wonder that they have become blind and leaders of the blind. And this faith soon brings along with it love, peace, joy, and hope. For God gives his spirit immediately to him who trusts him, as St Paul says to the Galatians, 'You have received the spirit not from your good works but because you have believed the work of God' (Gal. 3.2).

In this faith all works become equal, and one work is like the other; all distinctions between works fall away, whether they be great, small, short, long, many, or few. For the works are acceptable not for their own sake but because of faith, which is always the same and lives and works in each and every work without distinction, however numerous and varied these works always are, just

---

[8] From: W. A. Lambert and James Atkinson, *Luther's Works*, vol. 44, Philadelphia: Fortress Press, 1966. Quoted in Gill, *A Textbook of Christian Ethics*, pp. 92–4.

as all the members of the body live, work, and take their name from the head, and without the head no member can live, work, or have a name.

As Luther expands on his theology of faith, one can sense behind it the targets which have aroused his ire. Because he is appealing to felt experience rather than shared logic, the reader is likely either to identify with his struggle or to be confounded by it. Moreover, the sense that Luther is arguing against the practices of a historically specific Church will inevitably invite the reader's sympathy to the extent that the same practices are perceived to be problematic. This is one of the potential pitfalls of assuming too readily that an ethic developed in response to particular questions can always be translated into our contemporary context without further interpretation.

> It further follows from this that a Christian man living in this faith has no need of a teacher of good works, but he does whatever the occasion calls for, and all is well done. As Samuel said to Saul, 'You shall become another man when the spirit enters you; do whatever your hand finds to do, for God is with you' (I Sam. 10.6–7).

> We may see this in an everyday example. When a husband and wife really love one another, have pleasure in each other, and thoroughly believe in their love, who teaches them how they are to behave one to another, what they are to do or not to do, say or not to say, what they are to think? Confidence alone teaches them all this, and even more than is necessary. For such a man there is no distinction in works. He does the great and the important as gladly as the small and the unimportant, and vice versa. Moreover, he does them all in a glad, peaceful, and confident heart, and is an absolutely willing companion to the woman. But where there is any doubt, he searches within himself for the best thing to do; then a distinction of works arises by which he imagines he may win favour. And yet he goes about it with a heavy heart and great disinclination. He is like a prisoner, more than half in despair, and often makes a fool of himself.

My purpose in offering these three short texts from the history of the Church is not, of course, to give a comprehensive analysis of the ethics of Augustine, Aquinas and Luther or even to suggest that these three figures somehow set the agenda for all the thoughts on Christian ethics which follow. Rather, I hope that three points have emerged.

First, each of the three texts exemplifies how the direction of Christian ethics is often set by the specific questions which the wider social and political context thrusts to the foreground. Augustine, Aquinas and Luther were all writing in periods of ferment – political, in the cases of Augustine and Luther, and intellectual in the case of Aquinas. Indeed, the continuing significance of these three figures is not just that they epitomized their respective ages but that they each helped to mould the eras that were to follow them. Their work emerges from their context, addressing questions for which the prevailing patterns of thought had no reply, and changes that context by the nature of the responses they conceived. From the viewpoint of our own age, it is important to avoid, not only the tendency to imagine all historical figures as intellectual contemporaries engaged in an ongoing conversation with each other, but the fallacy of imagining that their renown was somehow instant, that these were the celebrity theologians of their own day or even the only theologians around at the time. Our own perspective on their work is mediated through the prism of ensuing centuries. The key point is that movements in Christian ethics need to be understood through a grasp of the pressing problems to which they were once regarded as answers. Augustine, Aquinas or Luther are all reference points for modes of thinking today, but their usefulness as sources depends, as with the use of the Bible, upon the understanding of not only what they said but why they were moved to say it. This is no less true of much more recent developments in Christian ethics where, without an appreciation of the context into which key ethicists are speaking, their work can appear as little more than an intellectual game or an exercise in academic point-scoring. One side of the current vibrancy of Christian ethics is its contentiousness. But separated from the determination to address the problems and tensions of contemporary living, contentiousness can be self-indulgent. Ethics matters precisely because it is a discipline motivated by a desire for the peoples of the world to flourish.

Augustine, Aquinas and Luther each brought about a significant shift in the way the task of ethics was framed, and they did so by exposing the inadequacies of the received wisdom of their times. There are important parallels here with what Alasdair MacIntyre has called an epistemological crisis. MacIntyre characterizes an epistemological crisis as the consciousness that 'a schema of interpretation which he [the agent] has trusted so far has broken down irremediably in certain highly specific ways'.[9] The resolution of such a crisis is found in

> the construction of a new narrative which enables the agent to understand *both* how he or she could intelligibly have held his or her original beliefs *and* how he or she could have been so drastically misled by them. The narrative in terms of which he or she at first understood and ordered experiences is itself made into the subject of an enlarged narrative.[10]

MacIntyre speaks of a tradition in crisis coming to a point where 'by its own standards of progress it ceases to make progress', throwing up 'new problems for the solution of which there seem to be no resources within the established fabric of belief'.[11] An epistemological crisis is thus a moment in the history of traditions where they must either develop, die or defeat one another. If one sees Christian theology as a number of traditions in tension with one

---

[9] Alasdair MacIntyre, 'Epistemological Crises, Dramatic Narrative and the Philosophy of Science', in Stanley Hauerwas and L. Gregory Jones (eds), *Why Narrative? Readings in Narrative Theology*, Eugene, OR: Wipf & Stock, 1997, p. 143.

[10] Hauerwas and Jones, *Why Narrative?*, p. 140.

[11] Alasdair MacIntyre, *Whose Justice? Which Rationality?*, London: Duckworth, 1988, pp. 361–2.

another, as well as in competition with other religions and ideologies, one can see how Augustine, Aquinas and Luther each in their different ways expose an epistemological crisis in the prevailing understandings of Christian ethics and generate a new narrative which (by virtue of its grounding in Scripture) offers an explanation of why the old narrative was inadequate to the context which new political or social developments demand and which enable the Church better to address the problematics of the age.

Second, our three historical theologians demonstrate the continuing difficulty of reading the trajectory of change. Luther's opposition to the peasants' rebellion is the most obvious example of this – a move which probably felt wholly consistent at the time but which has left our present generation struggling to reconcile Luther's radicalism with this failure to back what has emerged as a trend towards inclusiveness and democracy. The fallacy of judging historical situations according to our own categories has been noted, but the fact remains that the Christian ethicist faced with social change has to discern the will of God within flawed and fallible social movements. Simply because great historical figures made 'the right call', it is tempting to regard their position as self-evidently right, but this is again to mistake the view from today as the viewpoint of the times. But in all ages, the decision to reaffirm the established narrative of Christian ethics, or to pursue a radically different approach which may be damned as heresy or prove to be the foundation of a great Christian revival (or some point in between), is one which faces the ethicist and the theologian. 'Conservatives' and 'liberals' in today's ethical disputes within the Churches are involved in precisely this dilemma, and neither side has the privilege of knowing which of their honestly held and authentically reasoned theological perspectives will endure.

Third, Augustine, Aquinas and Luther each demonstrate an approach to authentic theological reasoning in a missiological context. By this I mean that each is attempting to convince fellow Christians of the truth and validity of their arguments while relating their arguments to a world beyond the Church. In other words, their concern is not simply internal church politics but the Church's calling to address the world's questions and to bring the world to Christ. Augustine, then, argues not from Scripture so much as from the nature of God as all-knowing and all-powerful – if you accept these characteristics as essential to God, he says in effect, certain consequences follow in terms of your understanding of humanity. The argument is both authentically rooted in Christian understandings of God and simultaneously accessible to those beyond the community of faith who can accept the basic premises. Aquinas, in a different age and at a very different stage in the Church's history, seeks to synthesize Christian thought with that of Aristotle. His arguments draw upon Scripture and established Christian thinking but aim to show that Aristotelian thinking does not diminish, but rather complements, Christian theology and exposes new depths within it. Those beyond the Church who are nonetheless steeped in Hellenistic thought patterns can come to Christ without having, as it were, to unlearn everything they thought they knew. God's love for the world is sufficiently capacious to employ the thought patterns of antiquity as pointers to the truth of God-in-Christ. Yet for Luther, such a conjunction of narratives is mistaken: God's truth can be apprehended only through faith preceding works. Not surprisingly, Luther makes more foundational use of Scripture in his arguments than either Augustine or Aquinas. The Bible as a source of truth is only authoritative to those who have already committed themselves to the God revealed in Scripture. Luther could expect most of the population of his time to accept Scripture as authoritative, but arguments from Scripture are only persuasive to those who accept that premise already. Yet Luther's case is directed very explicitly to a Church that has, in his view, allowed compromise with other narratives to corrupt its character. As such, his theology, and the ethics which flow from it, epitomize a Church in a different relationship to the world beyond its boundaries from that conceived by either Augustine or Aquinas. Where we might, with the benefits of hindsight, see Augustine as the apologist for a Church rising in confidence and power against a declining pagan establishment, and Aquinas as representing the adaptability of a supremely confident Church in the face of radical social developments, Luther might (again, with the benefit of our knowledge of subsequent trends) be interpreted as the slightly defensive spokesman for a Christian ethic which is preparing for minority status. Distinctiveness, over against prevailing mores, becomes the hallmark of authenticity. The Bible, authoritative only to those who have accepted its revealed wisdom already, becomes the fundamental building-block of ethical reasoning. It is a vexed question which context best equates to the situation of the Church today. In the West, the Church retains considerable powers and privileges despite significant social marginalization. Christianity still offers an acceptable – even an essential – discourse for public figures. Yet Christian ethics can no longer take for granted its role as an agreed narrative which moulds public policy. Plurality has usurped Christendom, yet the legacy of Christendom remains and the Church cannot undo its centuries of power to return unsullied to the pure status of an emerging, misunderstood but righteous, sect. History does not, in fact, repeat itself – but without a grasp of historical trends, the tension between holiness and mission in the contemporary Church will not be easily negotiated.

Further reading

Robin Gill, *A Textbook of Christian Ethics*, in any of its editions but especially the latest (2006), is an extremely useful guide to ethics in the historical context.

J. Philip Wogaman and Douglas M. Strong, *Readings in Christian Ethics: A Historical Sourcebook*, Louisville, KY: Westminster John Knox Press, 1996: this book covers a much wider range of ethicists from the first to the twentieth centuries, though inevitably in less depth than Gill.

J. Philip Wogaman, *Christian Ethics: A Historical Introduction*, Louisville, KY: Westminster John Knox Press, 1993, and London: SPCK, 1994: a discursive study of the history of Christian ethics and a fine companion to Wogaman and Strong's *Readings in Christian Ethics*.

For short introductory essays on Augustine and Aquinas, see: Gillian Evans, *The Mediaeval Theologians*, Oxford: Blackwell, 2001, especially the essays by: John Rist, 'Augustine of Hippo', pp. 3–23; Fergus Kerr, 'Aquinas', pp. 201–20. For a thorough consideration of Luther's significance for ethics, see: William Lazareth, *Citizens in Society: Luther, the Bible and Social Ethics*, Minneapolis: Fortress Press, 2001.

4

Modernity, plurality and their consequences

An alternative title for this chapter might be 'The state we're all in'. The brief consideration of some of the historical roots of Christian ethics in the previous chapter opened up the idea that Christian ethics may be not about timeless principles for addressing abstract problems so much as a matter of reflecting on the resources which faith brings to the deep questions raised by the political and social nature of the times. In other words, ethics is shaped by change – the emergence of new questions for which established ways of thinking seem to offer inadequate answers. If this is so, then the accelerating pace of change through the twentieth century and beyond would be expected to throw up new challenges for ethics, rival interpretations of what a proper response might be, and little time or space for the conversation between context and ethics to deepen and bear fruit. Not surprisingly, any attempt to evaluate the state of ethics in contemporary society is going to be difficult, partly because of the pace of change but also because it is harder to assess trends and issues from a contemporary perspective than it is to analyse the context of Luther, Aquinas or Augustine with the benefit of hindsight.

Part of the problem of describing the condition of ethics today is that words which describe the contemporary context are contested in their meaning and value. The word 'modern', for example, is frequently used in the sense of 'recent', 'up to date' and the opposite of things outmoded or no longer relevant. The implication, then, is that 'modern' is a term of approbation. And yet the term 'postmodern' has gained considerable currency with its strong implication that 'modern' is rather old hat. Ideas connected with 'modernity' need a good deal of analysis, as there are serious definitional problems about what it means to be modern.

One must hope that the teaching of history in schools has progressed since the late 1960s when my contemporaries and I were taught that 'modern times' began in 1485 with the accession of the Tudors to the throne of England, as if life in 1486 possessed a totally different character from life in 1484. (The tendency to speak of modernity as essentially a temporal phenomenon runs into similar problems of historical definition.) But if, broadly speaking, a period of several hundred years can be regarded as 'modern' it is clear that the word is not fully synonymous with the times we now inhabit. What we are talking about here is a mode of understanding human society and structures, and the idea that from time to time in history there are periods when the way these things are conceived undergoes a rapid and lasting shift. The question now is the extent to which we may be living through just such a shift ourselves, and whether a mode of thought that has served for a long time is simply evolving or is in the process of being replaced.

We saw in the last chapter how Luther's thought developed in the context of emerging capitalism and the rise of the nation-state. For Luther, it was natural to speak of 'the heathen, the Jew, the Turk' – defined as outsiders from Christendom by their religion, rather than their nationality or racial characteristics – and his quarrel was with the Pope, not with the king, the emperor or the German people. This feels more characteristic of the Middle Ages than the modernity of the nation-state. Yet Luther's willingness to challenge papal authority marks him out, as with other great figures of the Reformation, as essentially a character of modernity since the importance of conscience, and thus the significance of the individual moral agent, is one key feature of the modern period. Once the individual agent becomes the basic building-block of ethics, differences take on a new salience and ethics has to face intractable questions about the extent to which morals are particular to specific communities and traditions, whether they are essentially universal and common to all persons or whether there is no morality at all except that which the individual takes to him or herself.

To illustrate the transition into modernity in simple terms, we might consider why it is an era so closely associated with the economics of capitalism and the market. To do so, let us follow that great apostle of the free market, Friedrich Hayek, in his analysis of the times.[1] Hayek is using a very broad brush, but it is still possible to find his analysis useful without necessarily sharing the value judgements in favour of market economics for which he is arguing.

The tribal society and the 'great' society

Hayek contrasts the 'tribal' societies which preceded modern times with the vision of the Great Society towards which he believes modernity is progressing. In a tribal society, morality is 'traditional' in that the ways of the tribe constrain behaviour not only by sanctions imposed against transgressors but by setting the limits of imaginable conduct. Where there is no contact with other ways of behaving or reasoning, differences are not only transgressive but may simply be beyond imagining as there are no concepts which allow difference to be recognized as human. Thus outsiders from the tribe, whose moral precepts may be strikingly different, may not only be incomprehensible but are in danger of being categorized as less than fully human and unworthy of survival. And lest this tribal construct is imagined to be essentially primitive and irrelevant to the developed world, it takes only a little reflection on the twentieth-century history of Nazism or apartheid to realize

---

[1] F. A. Hayek, *Law, Legislation and Liberty*, vol. 2: *The Mirage of Social Justice*, London and Henley: Routledge & Kegan Paul, 1976.

that similar forms of tribalism are rather frighteningly close to home. If tribal societies are understood as pre-modern in character, it is yet another reminder that concepts of modernity (including pre- and post-modernity) are not strictly temporal phenomena but reflect distinct philosophical ways of understanding the world such that modern, pre-modern and post-modern manifestations interpenetrate each other.

In the tribal society, everything continues to be peaceful and to justify itself by the internal logic of the tribe – until there is an encounter with difference from without. What is right is right because it is right. Justice is understood identically by all and is therefore uncontroversial. Obligations are inherited or simply imposed by the mass will. The good is whatever is good for the tribe, and the good of the individual can only be conceived within an understanding of tribal flourishing. The outsider must be quickly assimilated or equally quickly repulsed. But this ethical unanimity is seriously challenged when the outsider is encountered not as a threat but as one who brings enough promise to be regarded, in all his enduring difference, as a fellow human being.

It is no surprise that this moment has, historically, coincided with major developments in economic activity and, in particular, with the growth of world trade. The visitor from another continent, religion or culture remains the outsider who is less-than-fully-human when he comes only in the guise of explorer or refugee. But the potential of trade ensures that the fellow humanity of the outsider cannot be ignored. Some degree of social intercourse is essential if the mutual benefits of trade between tribes are recognized. World trade emphasizes the essentially local character of religion by bringing the Christian into contact with the Hindu, the Confucian or the Muslim on terms in which each has need of the other. Where conquest, occupation and domination are not viable options, some form of mutual recognition is essential. At the very least, such trading encounters reveal the existence, and sometimes the internal coherence, of other beliefs and moral codes. The world is seen to be explicable through a number of narratives, not just the one with which I am familiar, even if I firmly believe my tradition to surpass all others. I become aware that other peoples derive their understandings of what is good, right, just and so on from roots quite different from mine; sometimes with strikingly different consequences for morality, sometimes with surprising overlaps. But what is more, trade between cultures requires some common foundation of value which can be shared between tribes or traditions. Thus emerges the great modernist project of seeking a shared morality on the principle of universal reason.

For Hayek, it is self-evident that a world which makes possible this kind of exchange across the boundaries of culture, religion and tribe, must be superior to a disparate collection of self-contained tribes warring at their boundaries. The vision he offers is that of a 'Great Society' in which the connections between people and cultures are not dependent upon the diverse accounts of the good which various groupings assert. The difference is between what he calls an 'ends-connected' society and a 'means-connected' one. For the tribe, Hayek argues, it is perfectly possible to secure agreement about what human life is for. Ends, for the accomplishment of which society is ordered, can be known and agreed. Indeed, agreement about ends is one mark of belonging to the tribe. Ends are usually expressed in precisely the language of ethics: the nature of the good, an understanding of justice and so on. But this kind of agreement is impossible, claims Hayek, when tribes who live by different ethical codes, grounded on different traditions and rooted in different myths and stories, encounter one another. Unless one tribe conquers the other, some means must be found for accommodating a diversity of ends without jeopardizing the fruits of exchange between tribes. But whereas agreement about ends may prove impossible, Hayek argues that it is perfectly feasible to forge effective connections on the basis of a shared understanding of means. Thus, ethics abandons any attempt to agree on the goals of good living and substitutes instead a series of second-order agreements about how people of differing beliefs and values are to conduct their business with one another. As Hayek puts it, agreement about means is possible 'precisely because it is not known which particular ends they will serve'.[2] Hayek holds up the market as a key example of means-connectedness. In a market economy, the value of goods is set, not by a social consensus as to what things are worth, but by the interplay of millions of independent transactions. This is the 'hidden hand' which Adam Smith noted. Participants in a market cannot know in advance how goods will be valued. At the simplest level, if people will not buy my products at the price I set, I must lower the price until they do. Each 'player' enters the market with his or her own ideas about purpose and morality. I may sell eggs in the expectation that their price will reflect the value which people place upon eggs in their diet, the availability of other foodstuffs and so on. But, should an unpopular political party be staging a march past my stall, I may find that the public is willing to pay an inflated price for my eggs since they are the only suitable missiles to hand. It is not my business, nor is it in my interests, to dictate what the proper end of an egg shall be. Omelette chefs and protesters alike are in the market for eggs, connected only by a commitment to the market mechanisms of supply and demand as arbiters of price (these are, presumably, pro-capitalist protesters!). In other words, the market can accommodate any number of disparate ends, and requires only that participants agree to the mechanisms of the market as the means by which their wants can be met. Hayek, indeed, makes even bigger claims. The ability to disagree about ends while ensuring that social and trading relationships can continue is precisely how freedom is to be understood. 'It is the absence of prescribed common ends which makes a society of free men all that it has come to mean to us.'[3]

---

[2] Hayek, *Law, Legislation and Liberty*, vol. 2, p. 3.
[3] Hayek, *Law, Legislation and Liberty*, vol. 2, p. 111.

The market is the supreme instance of the means-connected society. It is difficult to think of any other social institution which meets the case anything like as well, except for the principles of representative democracy. I use my vote according to conscience and, while many others may vote for the same party as me, we may do so for wildly different reasons. We may agree with the manifesto, seek to keep the other lot out, accept a party's social policies but not its economic ones, or vice versa, and so on. The outcome of the election is the product of millions of votes cast by people who have no idea how far they agree with each other. So Hayek's means-connected Great Society is, of its essence, a democratic market economy. We will consider the moral claims (and disclaimers) of the market in Chapter 10 and see how some of its apologists bind markets and democracy together as a single theme.

Hayek is addressing a real problem. How is morality to be worked out in a plural context which embraces adherents of numerous religious, cultural and moral codes? At this point, a word needs to be said about the use of the terms 'plural' and 'plurality'.

By plurality I mean the absence of any shared story or narrative sufficient to establish mutual identity in a given society. This is commonly characterized as the loss of overarching narratives which provide the fundamental account of morals to a community. It is the tension between the 'liberal' acceptance of plurality and the persistence of rich strands of narrative in the lives of many communities (particularly in religious traditions) which gives communitarianism much of its sense of potential, as we will see in subsequent chapters.

In *After Virtue*, MacIntyre (whose work will assume a larger role in my arguments as we proceed) identifies the emergence of plurality as a direct consequence of Enlightenment liberalism. The project of discerning morals through universal reason having failed, he says, we are left with no means of adjudicating between the good as perceived by different agents. 'In the domain of facts there are procedures for eliminating disagreement; in that of morals the ultimacy of disagreement is dignified by the title "pluralism".'[4]

Charles Taylor has a helpful insight into the ramifications of these different approaches, stressing the importance of distinguishing an ontological statement from an advocacy position.[5] In other words, describing the condition we are in, and developing an argument about how things should be, are different projects, connected but often confused. In any discussion of plurality, modernity or post-modernity, it is worth trying to apply Taylor's distinction by scrutinizing the motives of any author using such terms. Is the author in question seeking to describe and analyse an actual situation so that it can be

---

[4] Alasdair MacIntyre, *After Virtue: A Study in Moral Theory*, 2nd edn, London: Duckworth, 1985, p. 32.
[5] Charles Taylor, *Philosophical Arguments*, Cambridge, MA, and London: Harvard University Press, 1995, pp. 181–2.

better understood, in which case one should expect complexity and ambiguity to be part of the picture, or is the author seeking to draw a contrast in order to illustrate an alternative? If the latter, one should expect a certain starkness, or even exaggeration of key characteristics, in order to emphasize either approbation or condemnation. An ontological account of plurality would be alert to residual common bonds as well as nuanced understandings of difference (it is possible for people and groups to be more, or less, different from each other). An advocacy approach, however, tends to stress the breakdown of common bonds and the sheer extent of difference in order to make a point.

Plurality, then, is a deeper issue than just the coexistence in society of people of diverse origins, cultures and habits. Diversity *per se* is relatively unproblematic. In the opening chapter of *After Virtue*, MacIntyre describes a situation in which difference is not only a matter of diversity but also a situation in which people have become detached from shared stories which give meaning and content to moral utterances. The tragedy of the liberal Enlightenment, he says, is that the pursuit of universal grounds for morals, transcending tradition and thereby uprooting moral language from the narratives within which it made sense, has left liberal societies without grounds for adjudicating between different moral discourses and, hence, has brought about the 'interminable' character of moral disagreement. As we will see, a lot depends on whether that suggestion is really true.

Liberalism and the Enlightenment project

The term 'liberal' arises frequently in discussions of modernity and plurality and deserve a little further explication. 'Liberal' has come to have a range of meanings, differing according to the context in which the word is used and frequently at odds with each other.

It is important to distinguish the uses of the term 'liberal' in theology, economics and politics. A liberal in theology tends to stress the essentially rational and ethical character of religion, seeks universal ideas, especially a universal conception of human reason, rather than focusing on the particularities of faiths, and holds out hope for the perfectibility of the human race. In economics, liberalism refers to the prioritizing of individual choice over against state intervention and is often a kind of shorthand for a supporter of unrestrained free markets. However, in politics, especially in the United States, this meaning is stood on its head, with 'liberal' coming to be used to denote scepticism about free market assumptions coupled with tolerance of social diversity. In the British context, additional subtleties apply to the political use of the word, not least because of the enduring presence of a Liberal Democrat Party which no longer stands for laissez-faire liberalism in economics (a principle which has instead become identified more with the policies of the Conservatives). Although it is possible to construct a genealogy of the word which shows how these meanings come to be related, there are clearly some considerable tensions between the three contexts. A political liberal and an economic liberal are likely to be at odds. Economic liberalism has sometimes gone by other titles (neo-conservatism or the New Right) and the political programmes embodying such policies have been socially authoritarian and derisive of political liberalism. On the other hand, economic liberalism has sometimes (and perhaps more coherently) been coupled with social libertarianism, as in the work of Robert Nozick.[6] Theological liberalism has often run alongside political liberalism, but the emergence of theological apologists for market economics (such as Novak or Griffiths)[7] forces a reconsideration of the nature of liberal theology and its relation to social and political programmes. This confusion is part of the institutional crisis of liberal-minded church structures.

For MacIntyre, a particular philosophical conception of liberalism is at the heart of his argument. He understands it as the pursuit of criteria for judging rationality and truth – especially in morals – independently of tradition or context. This is the 'Enlightenment project' of deducing morals from universal reason. MacIntyre's case is that this project has inevitably foundered, leaving us with nothing more than emotivism and a world in which politics is 'civil war conducted by other means'.[8] MacIntyre's excursion into the history of ideas in his successive books is dedicated to exposing the lineage connecting classical liberalism with its various (and apparently contradictory) contemporary manifestations, thereby drawing attention to our present plight and pointing a way beyond it.

Amid the confusion of definitions and name-calling, the interesting question is whether there is any useful sense in which liberalism remains an ongoing project which contributes to a theological approach to ethics. MacIntyre's point is that the classical liberalism of the Enlightenment has failed in its quest for a universal, traditionless, morality – not least because, far from separating ethical enquiry from communities, narratives and traditions, liberalism is itself only one such tradition. As Stout puts it: 'Liberalism . . . is a tradition, but one whose necessarily frustrated project is to cease being what it is.'[9]

It is possible to identify some common characteristics of liberalism, found in various degrees and combinations within the discourses of theology, politics and economics.[10] Among them are: a preference for individual

---

[6] Robert Nozick, *Anarchy, State and Utopia*, Oxford: Blackwell, 1974.

[7] Michael Novak, *The Spirit of Democratic Capitalism*, Lanham, MD: Madison Books, 1982; London: Institute of Economic Affairs Health and Welfare Unit, 1991. Brian Griffiths, *Morality and the Market Place: Christian Alternatives to Capitalism and Socialism*, London: Hodder & Stoughton, 1982.

[8] MacIntyre, *After Virtue*, p. 253.

[9] Jeffery Stout, 'Homeward Bound: MacIntyre on Liberal Society and the History of Ethics', *Journal of Religion* 69.2 (1989), p. 228.

[10] See the extended discussion of this in S. Mulhall and A. Swift, *Liberals and Communitarians*, Oxford: Blackwell, 1992. Mulhall's and Swift's treatment of the liberal/communitarian debate acknowledges the plethora of definitions of 'liberal'.

liberty over traditional authority; for justice as fairness (as is seen notably in Rawls's *A Theory of Justice*);[11] for tolerance over coercion; for complexity over closed accounts of reality; and for agreement about procedural rules rather than agreement about ends. Most of all, liberalism is characterized by the search for a narrative of universal reason which does not understand itself to be directly derived from, or dependent upon, arguments particular to any single tradition. This does not mean that all forms of liberalism are wedded to this notion of universality in a way which truly transcends particular narratives or traditions – if it did, the idea of Christian liberalism would be a nonsense. But the tendency within liberalism towards this goal of some kind of universal reason introduces a certain equivocation to the liberal's commitment to tradition. Theological liberals will usually treat claims about the ultimate and universal truth of Christianity with a degree of qualification – frequently (and perhaps with some justification) drawing on the theological insight that the human grasp of God's truth is always inadequate and partial.

Communitarianism

While we are in the business of definitions, it is worth looking briefly at the main antitheses to liberalism which, together, tend to be bound together under the term 'communitarianism'.

Communitarianism, which like liberalism takes both political and philosophical forms, describes a set of ideas which claim a long lineage but whose current manifestation derives its impetus from being framed principally in terms of a reaction against liberalism.

In its political form, communitarianism's best known contemporary exponent is Amitai Etzioni. Etzioni enjoyed a certain vogue in the mid-1990s when Tony Blair (then in opposition but formulating plans for his time in government) appeared to be drawing strongly on his work. (Interestingly, at the time of writing, David Cameron's Conservative Party stands similarly on the brink of government, and a political philosophy similar to Etzioni's – the 'Red Toryism' of the philosopher and theologian Philip Blond – is being hailed as a major influence on opposition thinking.)[12] Etzioni's definitions of the communitarian project are frustratingly vague and propagandist, but clearly his target is fragmentary individualism, equated with the dominance of liberalism, and his political goal is the restoration, through politics and law, of a new settlement between rights and responsibilities expressed in the lives of communities. Communitarians, he says, are: 'people committed to creating a new moral, social and public order based on rational communities, without allowing puritanism or oppression'.[13] (How puritanism is to be denied without resorting to oppression is not quite clear.)

---

[11] John Rawls, *A Theory of Justice*, Oxford and New York: Oxford University Press, 1972.
[12] Philip Blond, 'Rise of the Red Tories', *Prospect* (February 2009).
[13] Amitai Etzioni, *The Spirit of Community*, London: Fontana, 1993, p. 2.

Etzioni goes on to outline, though in highly polemical mode, a political programme for communitarians. Despite attempts to enlist philosophers like MacIntyre to the political project, philosophical critics of liberalism tend not to identify themselves with the political communitarian movement.[14] Their concern is rather that liberalism fails to take into account the importance of community for personal identity, moral and political thinking and so on. The desire to re-emphasize the centrality of 'community' does not necessarily entail the endorsement of a particular political platform.

In so far as communitarianism understands itself to be in opposition to liberal notions of individualism and a universal rationality, its focus must be on the understandings and agreements which bind communities together: the traditions, narratives and practices which distinguish communities from each other. In theology, this usually means the Church and the factors which determine the Church's identity and relationship to those outside it. The theologian's concern is particularly for the defining narratives of faith which mark the nature and boundaries of the Christian community. It is also clear that in contemporary theology the emphasis on confessional identity is understood as a central feature of the reaction against liberalism. Confessional theologies indeed exhibit many of the characteristics of communitarianism, and so the liberal/communitarian dichotomy in moral philosophy and socio-economic thinking is paralleled by a liberal/confessional divide in theology. The line of continuity between political and philosophical communitarianism and theological confessionalism is found in the way they both posit 'community' as superior to 'liberal individualism' or metanarratives of universal reason. Communitarians reject the idea that abstract philosophical reasoning enables us to grasp coherent understandings of the good, and this is also a central characteristic of confessional theologies (especially those of Milbank and Hauerwas, whose work we shall explore further). This serves to explain my equation of confessional theologies with communitarian positions.

MacIntyre, and the nature of the problem

Having considered the meaning of some of the key terms to which we will return frequently as this book progresses, let us go back to the problem of 'the state we are in' and turn to MacIntyre once more to get to grips with his analysis.

After Virtue begins with what MacIntyre calls 'A disquieting suggestion'. He asks us to imagine a catastrophe in the natural sciences in which the public turns upon scientists, destroys laboratories and books and, under the influence of a Know-Nothing political movement, science is banished from schools and places of learning. Then comes a reaction against this movement

---

[14] See: Alasdair MacIntyre, 'I'm Not a Communitarian, But . . .', *The Responsive Community* 1.3 (1991). This was a journal closely associated with the work of Amitai Etzioni.

and an attempt to revive science from the fragments that remain. While people believe they are practising physics, chemistry or biology again, they do not know, and have no way of knowing, that they are working only with disjointed fragments of what were once whole systems of learning. Terms which once made sense within a body of knowledge are now used with no awareness that the framework which gave them meaning has disappeared. For MacIntyre, this is a parable of what has happened to the language of morality. His claim is that the modernist project of seeking a common basis for moral discourse which could transcend the differences of culture, religion or tribe (and thereby provide a moral basis for exchange, markets and global politics) has extracted moral language from its location within the particular traditions which make morality meaningful. In other words, means-connectedness is not enough, indeed it is impossible to separate morality from ends, as Hayek tacitly acknowledges when he declares the amorality of the market. Instead, we have only the 'simulacra of morality'.[15]

Some 260 pages later, MacIntyre closes his book in a similarly dramatic vein. Comparing our situation with the condition of the Roman empire in its decline towards the Dark Ages, he concludes that

> the barbarians are not waiting beyond the frontiers; they have already been governing us for quite some time. And it is our lack of consciousness of this that constitutes part of our predicament.[16]

So the only hope lies in

> the construction of new forms of community within which the moral life [can] be sustained so that both morality and civility might survive the coming ages of barbarism and darkness.[17]

After Virtue is devoted to establishing the weakness and inevitable failure of the liberal Enlightenment and the essential 'embeddedness' of moral discourse within traditions. By connecting the nature of a tradition to the idea of community, MacIntyre is able to point a way beyond 'the new dark ages which are already upon us' through 'local forms of community within which civility and the intellectual and moral life can be sustained'.[18] It is Aristotle's particular concept of the virtues, in which the exercise of virtue is itself part of 'the good life', which allows MacIntyre to make his later move towards the mediaeval Christian Aristotelianism of Aquinas, thus opening the way for his engagement with Christian theology in *After Virtue* and its sequel *Whose Justice, Which Rationality?*[19]

A crucial component throughout MacIntyre's argument is that the liberal Enlightenment project contained the seeds of its own destruction. His case

[15] MacIntyre, *After Virtue*, p. 2.
[16] MacIntyre, *After Virtue*, p. 262.
[17] MacIntyre, *After Virtue*, p. 262.
[18] MacIntyre, *After Virtue*, p. 262.
[19] Alasdair MacIntyre, *Whose Justice? Which Rationality?*, London: Duckworth, 1988.

is that the emergence of scientific rationalism detached the notion of moral enquiry from the concept of ends (the human *telos*), not only abandoning Aristotelian modes of moral enquiry but, by detaching moral language from traditions and communities, paving the way for the incommensurability of contemporary moral debate. 'Liberalism', he says, 'is a set of agreements to disagree', which, 'as a form of social life is partly constituted by its continual internal debates between rival incommensurable points of view'.[20] And this is unsurprising, given that the central component of Enlightenment thinking was the rational, autonomous individual. Divorced from a shared concept of human ends, moral utterance became detached from factual content – the division between 'is' and 'ought' breaks down. In this setting, moral debate quickly acquires an interminable character, since no appeal to facts can ever settle disagreement over values.

MacIntyre also notes how, with the loss of the Aristotelian teleological framework, other foundational concepts crept in to take its place – whether 'happiness' in the case of utilitarianism, or 'rights'. His point is that these concepts 'purport to provide us with an objective and impersonal criterion [for morality] but they do not'.[21] MacIntyre is here illustrating the point with which he opens *After Virtue*: that we have only the decontextualized fragments of a moral vocabulary. As a result 'the mock rationality of [political] debate conceals the arbitrariness of the will and power at work in its resolution'.[22]

MacIntyre's comments about the interminable nature of moral arguments are instantly recognizable to anyone who follows American, or British, politics. Two examples which MacIntyre cites are the argument about abortion and the controversy over nuclear deterrence. There seems no possibility of reaching agreement between the Pro-Lifers and the Pro-Choice lobby in the first instance and between the deterrence theorists and the unilateralists in the second. MacIntyre's analysis of our moral condition helps us see why the hope of agreement is in vain and the arguments literally interminable. In the abortion debate, arguments which proceed from an assumption of the sacredness of all human life are grounded at some point in a religious tradition which makes the concept of the sacred intelligible. Wrenched out of this religious framework, it is not clear what meaning the word 'sacred' might carry. Similarly, the pro-choice lobby uses the vocabulary of rights to argue for a woman's right to choose what happens to her own body. Yet, talk of rights has its own history and framework, and this may not be congruent with many religious traditions in which human rights do too little justice to the relationship between humanity and its creator. Similarly, the advocate of nuclear deterrence draws upon a particular tradition of understanding human fallibility. This assumes that, where a new power is available to humanity, that

---

[20] Alasdair MacIntyre, 'A Partial Response to my Critics', in J. Horton and S. Mendus (eds), *After MacIntyre*, Cambridge: Polity Press, 1994, p. 292.

[21] MacIntyre, *After Virtue*, p. 70.

[22] MacIntyre, *After Virtue*, p. 71.

power will be used if, by its use, a human advantage can be realized. Meanwhile the unilateralist draws on a more optimistic account of human nature which does not discount either the positive influence of example, the power of a consequentialist argument based on horrendous levels of destruction, or sometimes the deontological principle that some actions are intrinsically wrong. No resolution of the argument can be conceived unless one party simply gives way and ceases to press their case. Both, in their way, can claim a theological rationale within the Christian tradition; the first by reference to the persistence of sin and the second appealing to the abundant grace of God. And yet both these theological insights are somewhat rudimentary. Unaware that all they have to work with are the fragments of older, richer, traditions of ethical discourse, the arguments continue unabated and are literally interminable. What purports to be moral debate degenerates into mere assertion and counter-assertion. With morality and ethics cut loose from the historical cultural and religious contexts which give meaning and consistency to the language of morals, all we are left with is what MacIntyre calls civil war by other means. We are left with no mechanism or criterion to distinguish your version of the good from mine, or my understanding of the demands of justice from yours. The language of morality is reduced to the assertion of preferences ungrounded in any wider narrative or sense of common agreement.

Countervailing voices

At this point, it is worth recalling how such a state of affairs came about and, lest the impression should be given that MacIntyre's is the only voice worth listening to in this branch of ethics, to consider where his case may be less than fully convincing. Jeffrey Stout puts his finger on the matter when he comments that civil war by other means is at least less appalling than civil war as prosecuted by arms. It was, argues Stout, precisely to escape from the pre-modern notion that difference could only be dealt with by conquest and war that an ethic to transcend the particularities of rival traditions became an imperative. Where agreement about the sources of goodness and justice might be impossible between rival communities and traditions, the most promising common factor transcending all religions, cultures and communities appeared to be human reason. If ethics could be derived from pure reason, the possibility of a schema of morality, independent of specific traditions, holds out the possibility of an end to crusades and other bloody wars waged for the purpose of defeating a rival tradition and establishing the dominance of one's own.

Stout concedes, with MacIntyre, that the Enlightenment project of establishing ethics upon reason alone has not, as a matter of fact, overcome tribalism and civil war of the old, murderous, sort. Reason itself is not so universal and independent of culture as might have been assumed. But that failure should not blind us to liberalism's virtues to the extent that we fall back into old ways, armed now with more dangerous weapons than in pre-Enlightenment times. For Stout, and for others, MacIntyre is in danger of being so alert to the failures of modernity and the Enlightenment project that he risks a return to old evils. The risk, Stout argues, is that we end up belonging to strong, virtuous, communities with no mechanism for negotiating encounters with other communities, equally certain of their virtue, except a rapid recourse to warfare. As we will see, the trend in theological ethics to reaffirming the unique revelation of God in Christ and the special role of the Church in mediating that dispensation, has at times offered weak or negligible accounts of how Christian communities are to live peaceably alongside or in the midst of those who do not share their ethical narratives.

This chapter, so far, has tried to weave together the concepts of modernity, plurality, liberalism and the Enlightenment Project, along with the market as a very significant manifestation of all they stand for. It has also attempted to address the problems of modernism, liberalism and so on, through some reassertion of the centrality of community and tradition, in a story about how ethics has become the contentious subject that it now is. It will not be lost on the reader that one can quite easily discern a prominent religious thread in the very warp and weft of the story.

Naturally, MacIntyre's call for 'another – doubtless very different – St Benedict' in the closing line of *After Virtue* has excited Christian commentators. At last, it seemed, theology was being brought in from the cold, rescued from being a tentative appendix attached to a public discussion of ethics from which overtly religious language had been rigidly excluded. Religions never quite reconciled themselves to the Enlightenment project of transcending tradition since religions are patently specific to time, place and communities. While a particular faith may regard its precepts to be universal, and may be committed to converting the whole world to its precepts, it remains incontrovertible that other, rival and incompatible, religions exist and have their own account of ultimate truth and their own universal aspirations. As religion in the West has felt increasingly marginalized within the surrounding culture, it has sought to emphasize the distinctiveness of faith over against the prevailing culture. (Even where religious adherence is mainstream, as in the USA, and where it plays a powerful role in politics, the tone of the narrative is invariably one of marginalization, potential persecution and under-dog status.) Naturally, then, the backlash against liberalism and the Enlightenment project has been strongly supported by religious voices.

Redeeming liberalism?

However, there have also been strong religious reasons for backing the Enlightenment and for sustaining liberal principles. First is the historical lineage of liberalism itself, emerging as it did from Christian thinkers who understood their quest for a universal framework of ethics to be entirely consistent with their commitment to God's purposes for the world.[23] Second, and reflecting Stout's objections to MacIntyre, many religious voices are acutely aware of the atrocities committed in past ages (and the present age) in the name of their faith. The shadow side of religion is a present reality to many who, in faith and in commitment to the common good of all in God's creation, seek the flourishing of humanity rather than just the temporal interests of their own faith community. This is not a position unique to Christianity, although it is one which many Christians would share. Their problem is that the liberal programme of transcending the particularities of tradition leaves scant support or encouragement for the very specific trad- itions of faith which sustain that kind of concern for the common good. Is it possible to have one's ethical cake and eat it, as it were? In other words, can one conceive of a way of practising religion which is simultaneously concerned to uphold its own tradition and narratives and to ensure the flourishing of humanity beyond its own adherents without insisting on co- opting or converting them first?

Ian Markham sums up the MacIntyre/Stout controversy in a way which helps us answer this question. Markham seeks to understand liberalism, not so much as the project which purports to transcend tradition but as a tradition in its own right, alongside others – one which both engages in dialogue and seeks to bring out the dialogic elements present within other traditions. 'Stout', he says, 'wants to resist religious solutions [to conflict between traditions] because he does not trust religion. He wants to affirm liberalism because he wants to affirm tolerance. Much of his argument would crumble if it could be shown that a religious culture can also be a tolerant culture.'[24]

Markham's six arguments for tolerance

Can such a proposition indeed be demonstrated? Markham offers six theses which he claims support the idea that liberal principles can be reconciled with orthodox Christian doctrines.[25]

First, he argues that the commandment to love one another must involve the toleration of difference. The objection may immediately be raised that the divine commandment to love does not embrace tolerance for sin, only for the sinner as a child of God. But this implies that love is conditional on agreement about what constitutes sin. As long as the other person is truly perceived as other and not as a glass in which I see only a reflection of myself,

---

[23] See, for example, Jeremy Waldron, *God, Locke, and Equality: Christian Foundations of John Locke's Political Thought*, Cambridge, New York etc.: Cambridge University Press, 2002.

[24] Ian Markham, *Plurality and Christian Ethics*, Cambridge: Cambridge University Press, 1994, p. 134.

[25] Markham, *Plurality and Christian Ethics*, p. 183. Here, I have taken Markham's six theses and developed my own arguments around them.

then the sense that he or she is indeed 'other' and therefore to some degree not fully explicable in my own terms, points strongly towards tolerance being a virtue.

Second, Markham takes a principle from Aquinas to argue that it is always a sin to act against one's conscience. This principle applies as much to others as to oneself, so difference and diversity must be tolerated when they reflect the imperatives of conscience. To this one might object that conscience has to be formed somehow and that a malformed conscience (say, the conscience of a person brought up to believe that eliminating adherents of another faith is a godly virtue) cannot be tolerated. Perhaps the best that Markham can say is that conscience is such a serious consideration in understanding morality that there must be a strong presumption of tolerance until the character of the conscience in question is understood.

Third, Markham turns to the principle of free will which we have already examined in the work of Augustine. Because God alone saves, free will must entail the freedom to rebel against God, hence, the Christian must tolerate those who reject God since they cannot be saved by human intervention alone. But there seems to be a sleight of hand here, equating the fact that some people reject God with the assumption that the Christian has no obligation to seek to persuade them otherwise. Is it intolerant to seek to change the mind of someone you believe to be in error? Once again, if toleration means the acceptance that difference is more than skin deep, all is well and good, but Markham seems to be implying a version of tolerance which looks somewhat more like resignation to the impossibility of differences being reconciled.

Nevertheless, Markham's next three arguments may be more robust. His fourth argument is that human sinfulness has not left religion unaffected, so the orthodox Christian believer will humbly admit to the possibility of being in error. It becomes essential to tolerate difference since, although I may strenuously seek truth myself, others may be right and I may be wrong. In so far as liberal ideas of tolerance prevent premature foreclosure on arguments where absolute certainty is not to be had, then accepting the possibility of error in a world mired in persistent sin may be a real Christian virtue.

Markham's fifth point is another version of the fourth: there can be no absolute certainty until the eschaton. Until God brings all things to completion in himself, it behoves us to tolerate others lest, in the final analysis, it is they, rather than us, who turn out to have been right all along. It remains that tolerance of this sort can only go so far. If we believe that God has indeed been revealed to us in Christ and in the Scriptures, our lack of certainty is not the same thing as being completely at sea. There may, therefore, be significant limits to an authentic Christian capacity for tolerance, even as Christians remember that utter certainty must wait until the end of all things.

Finally, Markham makes the surprising claim that 'God desires freedom and dialogue, hence the deliberately ambiguous nature of the world'. In other words, if God had intended us to know with certainty that we were right and others wrong, God would have made the world so that the truth was self-evident. Instead, we have a world which is open to myriad different interpretations, in which pointers to truth give ambiguous messages and the same phenomenon can be read in wildly different ways by different witnesses. This is true even among those seeking to follow Christ faithfully. It seems, so Markham argues, that since this is how the world appears to us, we may surmise that this is how God intended it to be – an argument parallel with Augustine's claim that free will is a deliberate act of creation by God to God's greater glory.

Clearly Markham's six arguments for liberal understandings of tolerance are not conclusive by themselves. They do, however, point the way towards the possibility that the alternative to a failed version of liberalism may not entail the total rejection of all that liberalism has stood for. Liberal virtues may be thoroughly grounded in Christian theology rather than in some narrative that stands beyond traditions. But is it possible to separate liberal virtues from the hubristic liberalism that saw itself as the culmination of history and the transcendence of the particularities of tradition? This is one question which we will consider further when we examine more closely the potential for Christian ethics to take a role in the public sphere.

Meanwhile, the developing argument about modernity and ethics must consider the practical out-working of the liberal strand in Christian ethics through the course of the twentieth century, its strengths and its weaknesses when lived out by the Church rather than confined to the theoreticians. And then it must turn in greater depth to the alternatives to liberalism and the communitarian emphases in contemporary Christian ethics. These themes are tackled in the next chapters.

At this stage, however, we have established the centrality of plurality as a governing consideration for Christian ethics today. How are Christians to live well among peoples who do not share the foundational stories of Christian faith? Three possible responses have emerged. The first is to muddle on with a more or less covert liberalism, treating the failings of the liberal settlement as passing glitches rather than fundamental flaws. But this offers no satisfactory response to the devastating account of our condition put forward by MacIntyre, and, indeed, the inability of inherited liberal structures to give an adequate account of plurality and difference is born out by the intractable nature of the problems which a plural society poses to its own governance (as, for example, in the difficulty governments have in articulating a satisfactory narrative of Islam in a Western context).

A second response is to follow Markham in seeking out the intrinsically dialogic elements in different traditions so that encounters 'across the borders' can take place without jettisoning the narratives that constitute those traditions. Thus the danger of 'holy wars', waged out of ignorance and fear of the other, might be minimized. There is a great deal of work to do before this project becomes fully convincing and, if there are major traditions and narratives which turn out to have no authentic dialogic component, the venture may be incapable of fulfilment anyway.

The third approach is to reassert a single tradition and its narratives as intrinsically superior to others, and to seek its dominance. This may sound like a dangerous strategy, as indeed it may be, but as we will see shortly, it is a serious and thoughtful approach adopted by a number of influential voices in Christian ethics.

But first, we turn from the theoretical to a consideration of Christian ethics in practice – and as practised by the Churches.

Further reading

There are a number of books which take the themes of this chapter further. Each author listed here is putting forward a particular thesis about the current condition of society and of ethics, and each provides much food for thought which may touch on the matters dealt with in my later chapters:

Jeffrey Stout, *Ethics After Babel: The Languages of Morals and Their Discontents*, Cambridge: James Clarke, 1988.

Nicholas Boyle, *Who Are We Now?: Christian Humanism and the Global Economy from Hegel to Heaney*, Notre Dame, IN: University of Notre Dame Press, 1998.

Richard H. Roberts, *Religion, Theology and the Human Sciences*, Cambridge: Cambridge University Press, 2002.

For more on MacIntyre, see: Mark C. Murphy, *Alasdair MacIntyre*, Cambridge: Cambridge University Press, 2003.

First interval: 'cutting the cake'

The political philosopher and theologian Raymond Plant has commented that the dilemmas of distributional justice can be likened to four people sitting around a table trying to decide how to divide a cake. One of them bought the ingredients. Another baked the cake. A third missed breakfast and the fourth has just passed an exam. What are the rival claims of those four people to shares of the cake? And, just as importantly, how will they decide between them a fair way to cut the cake?[1]

Searching for ways to enliven a class in ethics, it seemed to me that Plant's brief illustration could be developed as a participative exercise with real people dividing (and eventually eating) a real cake – not only as a way of involving students in the questions which, as ethicists, they ought to be considering, but also as a way of gathering data about how people actually go about deciding ethical questions of this sort. By working out the exercise with different groups of people, it became, in fact, a kind of exercise in game theory; an idea that has become increasingly popular as a way of modelling how choices are made by imagining them in the context of a game where participants seek to maximize benefits for themselves (whether altruistically or otherwise). Some ten years after first trying the exercise of dividing the cake, I have now played it with over a hundred different groups with wildly diverse outcomes and much interesting learning. As a way of showing that ethical concepts like justice and fairness are not straightforward, and that perspective can alter ethical perceptions, the game is an excellent way of establishing the central problematics in a memorable and relatively light-hearted way. One does not have to play the game 'for real' to discern some of the ways in which it illustrates the ethical issues, and the variety of outcomes which participants have developed through the years are revealing of some of the ways people actually think about ethics today. However, this is definitely an exercise which (in the immortal phrase from Children's TV) you can try for yourself at home – with a suitable cake you prepared earlier.

It is important to be clear from the outset that the game has limitations. I will explore these later, but the point is that the game works as an illustration of some of the points made in the preceding chapters and is not intended to be a method of solving major issues of distributional justice in some final manner.

If you want to try the game for yourself you need nothing more than four participants, a cake and a knife, but a few tips culled from experience may

---

[1] Raymond Plant, *Social Justice, Labour and the New Right*, Fabian Pamphlet 556, London: Fabian Society, 1993, pp. 7f.

be helpful. Choose a cake which is of a fairly solid consistency – it will need to be divided accurately, possibly into quite small pieces. A uniform consistency and few adornments help keep the range of solutions to the problem under control – when participants start dividing the cherry on the top, as well as the cake itself, the game may be getting out of hand. A circular cake tends to work better than a rectangular one. It helps if the participants are not all from a very uniform background – too much uniformity of view limits the potential for learning. Finally, don't take the notes offered here as the definitive way to play the game – the participants' handling of the issues is what leads to learning, not the objective of getting a 'right' answer.

The four participants – who respectively bought the ingredients, baked the cake, missed breakfast and passed the exam – represent significant social roles. These are, of course, capital, labour, need and merit, but this can be revealed after the game if participants don't catch on immediately. To begin, they are seated one on each side of a square table with the cake in the middle and a knife to hand. The brief is that, knowing their roles, they should together come to an agreement about the fairest way to cut the cake and proceed to cutting it – but not (yet) to eating it, as the cut cake will be evidence for their decision. It helps if participants are briefed to note not only how the cake is to be cut but also how the decision was arrived at. These simple instructions having been given, the process of discussion and decision-making can begin.

I said that a degree of diversity between the participants, at least in their moral outlook, helps make the game work – it can also prolong the process. At some point, preferably when the cake has been cut, the game ends and the participants begin to explain their decisions and arguments. Every group is unique – but there are often patterns of discussion and outcome that emerge, and it is in identifying and developing these that the connection can be drawn between the game and the wider issues of ethics.

Of the many groups with whom I have attempted the game, the most extreme cases were a group of Finnish diaconal students and a group of military chaplains from the Royal Air Force. I quickly gave up using the game in my sessions with the Finns because every group simply divided the cake in four equal pieces, usually with only the most perfunctory discussion, and found it incredible that anyone could contemplate any other outcome. In their culture, they said, equality was considered to be of crucial importance and equality was always interpreted as equality of outcome. More on that in a moment. The RAF chaplains, however, were still arguing after nearly an hour. On one table, voices were raised and a struggle was taking place for control of the knife. Another group of chaplains contemplated a pile of crumbs as successive individuals had attempted to impose their version of fairness on the others. Without drawing any superficial conclusions about the combative tendencies of military chaplains, clearly something very different was going on here compared to the Finnish context.

74

I found over time that group responses fell into three categories. The Finns were not the only ones who settled immediately and uncontroversially on a cake cut into equal quarters. The RAF chaplains were a particularly extreme case, but other groups, too, failed to come to an agreement even after protracted wrangling. A third and very common solution involved a complicated division of the cake such that, having been allocated a share of their own, each member then proceeded to divide their share between themselves and their colleagues.

In the analyses that follow, I will attribute to the players a range of motives behind the respective outcomes to the game. These are distilled from debriefing various groups, but I am not insisting that every player over the years has held the motives attributed here.

The obvious retort to the Finns' outcome is that the person who missed breakfast remains, relatively speaking, as disadvantaged as when the game began. Nothing has been done to address the inequality which brings about that player's need. By dividing the cake into four equal parts the players are showing that redressing need is of less significance than demonstrating a particular understanding of equality. Finland is well known as a country in which social cohesion is regarded as an overriding political objective and, although degrees of material inequality exist, the country does exhibit a practice, as well as a social narrative, of equality that is quite observable. It may be that a strong and comprehensive welfare state, coupled with an absence of American or British levels of material inequality, make it harder for players to extrapolate from the trivial problem of a missed meal to the situation of the socially needy. Indeed, a public expression of equality is not a negligible ethical stance to take. What is more interesting is the lack of discussion leading up to this outcome – most players who come up with this solution are hard put to see that any alternative might have been contemplated. The 'right' answer is obvious and not a subject for debate. What is considered ethical is simply 'known' and not fought over. No other solution is discussed because no other solution than one which expresses a basic equality has ever been seriously considered. This is what Hayek was referring to when he spoke of a 'tribal' society (others would call it a pre-modern context) – one where the demands of morality are uncontroversial because there has been no exposure to alternative ethical narratives. This is not a derogatory judgement. Everybody, some of the time, operates in an essentially tribal ethical environment – frequently in the family, although often in workplaces or in churches – where there is such a basic level of moral agreement that issues which are, in other circumstances, contentious, appear straightforward and are solved simply and obviously.

But the solution involving four equal pieces of cake is rare if the backgrounds and styles of the four participants are significantly different. Another group might quickly realize that they are unlikely to agree a simple way forward, but they still place a premium on arriving at a solution acceptable to all. A common response from groups like this is to divide the cake according to a simple formula – maybe in four equal pieces, though sometimes only the buyer of ingredients and baker of the cake get to share in the cake at this stage, presumably reflecting the idea that their economic roles as capital and labour take priority over other claims to cake. But they then agree that each person will divide their own share in ways which reflect their personal understanding of fairness. Thus, from four (or two, or however many) original pieces, subdivisions are made which may overwhelm the hungry player with the gift of more than he or she can eat or, conversely, may reward the exam-passer with an embarrassment of cake at the expense of the hungry one. It is just as possible that the outcome may reflect the right of the 'owners' of the cake to keep their whole share to themselves, although a redistributive practice is more common.

The point here is that, in the absence of an agreement about what would constitute a fair outcome, the moral question is left to each individual to answer. Expressed like that, the extent of the retreat from a shared understanding of fairness becomes more explicit. The group may congratulate itself for having reached a solution to which all four can assent, but in reality their agreement runs only as far as an agreement about means. They have not achieved any agreement about ends since none of them could predict from the decision itself how much cake any one of them would end up with. For all they can tell when the cake is cut, the hungry member may remain hungry or be utterly sated. There is a degree of unpredictability about the outcome which makes it questionable whether it can be termed 'moral' at all. The group has managed to reproduce rather well the philosophy of the market economy – a modernist construct in which agreement about ends is taken to be impossible and the best that can be hoped for is a conditional agreement about means. Thus, the market ideology claims, it is unknowable whether I will end up rich or poor because my wealth or poverty is the outcome of many individual decisions which I cannot control. In a market economy, the players assent to the distribution of goods through the workings of an amoral invisible hand – that is the limit of their moral agreement. Hayek praised this system as one fitted to a global, or 'Great', society: what Jeremy Bentham termed a society of strangers. Modernity can be understood as the era in which social bonds were based on only limited levels of moral agreement – primarily about means such as the market – rather than any attempt to come to agreement about moral outcomes or ends. But the existence of a third group of cake-cutters, exemplified by the RAF chaplains, suggests that the veneer of social agreement in modernity is thin and vulnerable.

Superficially, it is easy to dismiss the chaplains' game as being more about the macho culture which they are assumed to inhabit, in which compromise and backing down are deplorable weaknesses. It is doubtful if any of the players actually believed this. But below the surface, the response of these players, which was not unique although quite extreme, is revealing about the state of ethical discourse today. Indeed, they exemplify what happens when even limited agreements about means cease to hold. If no agreement about means or ends is possible, all that is left is the exercise of coercive power. Hence, perhaps, the struggle over who held the knife. Hence the raised voices, jocular put-downs and general 'alpha male' behaviour. If the Finns stood for a pre-modern culture in which the good is simply known because its nature has not been contested, and the multiple-dividers represent a modernist, market-led, individualist culture seeking to hold onto some sense of community, can we tentatively identify the chaplains' group as exemplars of post-modernity? There is, naturally, much more to post-modernity than the naked struggle for power (just as there is more to modernity than the market, and to pre-modernity than the tribal consensus), but the implications are suggestive. Post-modernity has been described as elevating rhetoric above reasoned argument, presentation above substance and the individual above the group – and all these characteristics were observable among the groups who cut (or, rather, mangled) the cake in this way. If the identification with post-modernity is even partially accurate, it seems to imply that either the winner takes all or everybody loses. The heap of crumbs that was the cake allows no one to benefit from its nutritional value or oral delights. And if one player claims the whole cake on the basis of his or her power over the others, there remain three hungry people who have played the game for no gain at all.

One of the joys of this game is that each group plays it their own way and new insights appear with every round. For example, no reason is given why the hungry player missed breakfast although groups often supply their own 'back story'. If that player missed the meal because they were up partying all night and woke with a hangover, it is quite likely that the group will not make the alleviation of their need a particularly high priority. Whereas if the one who missed the meal had been delayed getting a reluctant child ready for school, they can usually rely on receiving a goodly slice of cake. Thus, often unconsciously, the group will have established a distinction between the deserving and the undeserving poor. Ethically, they are giving substance to a position which argues that it is not need alone that obliges others to respond but how that need arose. Responses become inseparable from the story which the person in question tells about themselves. This illustrates, simply but rather well, the division between a human rights approach to ethics, in which every individual is entitled to a certain level of treatment simply by virtue of their humanity, and a more communitarian, narrative-based, ethic in which one's social history, wider relationships and biographical story all work together to determine one's place within the group and, therefore, the outcomes one may enjoy.

Then again, it is not uncommon for the person who passed the exam to forgo any claim to cake at all. 'My success is its own reward', they may say. This may be challenged by the group on two grounds. First, it may be argued that the cake is an incentive – if the group fails to recognize and encourage the passing of exams, why should any of its members feel motivated to take exams in future? But a stronger challenge often arises if the group chooses to portray themselves as a family gathering of some sort. In a family, celebration and participation are important in themselves, and sometimes this leads to the reflection that these things are, ideally, just as important in wider social relationships. There is a fascinating parallel here with the philosophy behind the British welfare state at its inception in the 1940s and through most of the subsequent period until the late 1970s. The initial understanding of social welfare was that all were perceived to have a stake – it was not merely a safety net for the most vulnerable but an institution of social cohesion which bound all together. Thus, for example, family allowances were paid to all mothers regardless of wealth. Only in the 1980s was the whole structure turned around to 'target' the most needy, thereby signalling, not mutuality, but that reliance on welfare entailed a separation from wider social relationships. Groups playing the cake game sometimes allude to a eucharistic principle here – participation in the common meal is of far more significance than addressing hunger. So if the passer of exams chooses not to share in the cake, they are announcing that they do not belong to the group: even a token mouthful is better than outright refusal. It is worth bearing in mind that, although no religious imagery was overt in the British welfare state as created, the friendship between Archbishop William Temple and William Beveridge, the architect of the welfare state, may have contributed a Christian insight in the way the project was conceived to bind together the national 'family' rather than simply to offer a safety net. Indeed, it was Temple who first coined the term 'welfare state', contrasting the way in which the state might gain legitimacy through ensuring the welfare of its citizens with the totalitarian concept of the state legitimated through power and military strength.

It is noteworthy that, after innumerable rounds of the game, the potential for conflict between the purchaser of the ingredients and the baker of the cake has never surfaced in my experience. Whatever the outcomes for the hungry or virtuous members of the group, the two who represent capital and labour have never yet shown any desire to make claims on each other. When I devised the game in the mid-1990s, the era of overt and public conflict between capital and labour in the life of the nation was largely over. It would have been interesting to have played the game during the miners' strike some years previously. But framed within an implicitly familial setting, the mutual dependence of capital and labour appears uncontroversial. There is, perhaps, one moment at which this consensus is damaged – a moment which few groups are aware of until it is drawn to their attention. In about three-quarters of the groups with whom I have played the game, it is the purchaser of the ingredients who is the first to pick up the knife, assuming a strongly controlling role as if by right, even though, as the game progresses, the knife may well be passed on to another player. Is it reading too much into a simple game to suggest that there remains, deep down in the most consensually minded players, an assumption that capital (or perhaps the *paterfamilias*) has an ultimate right to power which may be benevolently shared but which is nonetheless instinctively recognized?

I have called this a simple game, which it is, and it is not difficult to think of variants which might develop it further, although complication often diminishes the learning potential. As an exercise in game theory, playing the game once is only a beginning. Ideally, the same group should play the game repeatedly and observe how their conclusions change over time. For instance, a benevolent attitude to the hungry member might well become more punitive if it appeared that they took their cake for granted and continued to miss meals. Few groups have the stamina or interest to undergo repeated rounds, but one round is often sufficient to enable future rounds to be imagined and changes in attitude to be predicted.

Then again, in so far as this is a model of economic relationships, the cake does not offer a fully comprehensive analogy. A better metaphor for economic life might be the ginger-beer plant where a judgement has to be made about retaining (i.e. investing) some of the production so that more can be produced later. But a group can hardly sit down to divide a bottle full of fermenting liquid. I draw attention to these questions to show that too much should not be claimed for the game as an analogy of economic decision-making. Rather, its value is to show, first, that understandings of justice and fairness are rarely simple or unanimous. This is important in Christian ethics where talk of justice often leaves unexamined the problematic questions of 'justice for whom?' Second, the game exposes the importance of perspective in ethics. Where you sit, and where your interests lie, affect your perception of what constitutes a just outcome to a distributional problem. Third, the game has the potential to examine the tensions and congruencies between what is regarded as moral in terms of close personal relationships and what is moral in wider political contexts. Because the game uses an implicitly familial setting to consider a clearly political problem, the strength with which the body politic is understood as an extended family can be helpfully exposed. Fourth, the game offers few opportunities for Christian perceptions directly to short circuit the often complex process of exploring difference and seeking agreements. The difficulty of defining distributional justice remains as problematic for the faithful as for the secularist, and thus the question of how Christian perceptions can engage with social and political problems is seen to be worth examining rather than taking for granted.

Perhaps the fifth reason for playing the game is as important as any. It allows the study of ethics to be more fun than an unbroken series of lectures or seminars and enables students to discover the existence of a problem rather than simply having a problem presented to them. That is, perhaps, an outcome worth having for both the student and the teacher of ethics.

5

The Christian social tradition

Although this book is not intended as a historical survey of Christian ethics, it is nonetheless important, for at least two reasons, to review the ways in which the Churches have approached ethical issues in the recent past. First, the legacy of the way Christian ethics was done by the Churches through most of the twentieth century is part of the inheritance against which the adequacy of more recent developments in ethics may be evaluated. Second, movements in academic disciplines do not happen all at once – much in Christian ethics is still informed (whether knowingly or not) by the ways the subject was approached in the past, and many Christians still owe something of their formation to the tradition of ethical engagement which has been practised by the Churches.

Consideration of the practice of Christian ethics in recent history enables us to look further at the proposition which I advanced in Chapter 3 – that is, that the emphases in Christian ethics are shaped, in part, by the questions which the condition of the world poses in any one period. In other words, changing social contexts test the adequacy of any approach to ethical reasoning and, from time to time, a question arises for which the established way of working seems inadequate. This is of more than historical significance, for it implies that there is a contingency about moral positions and arguments which, despite frequently being presented as eternal truths, can seem less adequate over time.

Social Christianity and 'the social gospel'

Let us, then, attempt to trace the development of thinking and practice from the late nineteenth century to the present day, in terms of the Churches' engagement with ethical issues to do with the shape of society. In America, this tradition of doing ethics in the public sphere has usually gone under the title 'The social gospel'. As such, it has frequently been a target of criticism and derision from more pietistic branches of the US Churches – ostensibly for appearing to promote salvation through (good) works and for transgressing the convention that religion and politics do not mix. The paradox, of course, is that the evangelical movement in America – always the sternest critic of the social gospel – has, since at least the 1980s, been thoroughly committed to an engagement with politics and a presumption that Christianity requires certain active political stances. Yet the condemnation of the social gospel continues. Only one conclusion is possible. The contention is not so much about salvation by works or the boundary between politics and religion but the tension between the politics of the right and politics which, by American standards, are capable of portrayal as mildly left. The social gospel has always been concerned with the flourishing of humanity in this life as well as the next, and has usually sought to take in a broad picture of the good for all God's people and not just a narrow segment of humankind.

Interestingly, 'the social gospel' has always been American terminology. Where the term arises during debates in the British Churches it is almost always used as a term of disapproval. The critics seem to miss the fact that the name denotes something with a very different history from any trend in ethics in the British Churches. It suggests that the ammunition discharged by critics of the British Churches' social ethics is frequently manufactured across the Atlantic. There is, in fact, no single parallel term for the tradition of social ethics in Britain – Christian socialism (although that label now applies only to a small, more party-political, grouping), ecumenical social ethics, or, less neatly, the social tradition in Christian ethics.

In 2001, the American theologian Max Stackhouse published an essay in which he identified five phases in the development of the social gospel in the United States, from the late nineteenth century to the present. I shall follow this interesting typology in the first part of this chapter and then go on to take a similar historical look at the British scene. Here, I draw on John Atherton's book *Social Christianity*.[1]

Let us consider the American experience first, and see how Stackhouse links developments in the social gospel to major political and economic shifts of consciousness.

Stackhouse chronicles the way the social gospel movement emerged first as a reaction to the carnage and trauma of the American Civil War – the first major war to be fought with industrial-scale military technology, railways and machine guns. What is more, it was a civil war fought between people who essentially shared a language, worshipped the same God and who shared a great deal of recent history. Yet it was a war fought over a fundamental question about human identity and models of governance. This revelation of the brutality of human beings to those who otherwise had so much in common left scars in the American psyche which, while some say they have never fully healed, must have been open and agonizing for a very long time. A war does not 'end' on the day an armistice is signed. How might the Churches heal such profound rifts? What strands within the Christian narrative could be highlighted in order to bind a fractured country together again?

That this was not a uniquely American malaise became all too clear when Europe collapsed into world war in 1914. Here, the mechanization of war entrenched (literally) a new and terrible insight into the destructive capacity

---

[1] See: Max Stackhouse, 'The Fifth Social Gospel and the Global Mission of the Church', in Christopher H. Evans (ed.), *The Social Gospel Today*, Louisville, KY: Westminster John Knox Press, 2001; John Atherton, *Social Christianity: A Reader*, London: SPCK, 1994.

of humanity and the failure of politics to prevent carnage. Any presumption that the Christian peoples of either the New World or the Old were enmeshed in a trajectory of human progress, in which the kingdom of God was inexorably approaching through human achievement, became rapidly unsustainable. Faith had not prevented the slaughter. The Churches' message had, on occasion, been enlisted on both sides in the conflicts and their authority emerged significantly diminished.

In response, many in the Churches reached for the simple doctrine of human unity under God. Old divisions, exacerbated by defeat and victory, could be healed by a renewed commitment to discipleship as fellow children of the one Creator. Crudely abbreviated to BOM-FOG (reputedly the marginal note which reminded President Theodore Roosevelt to deploy this particular rhetorical strand), the emphasis lay heavily upon the Brotherhood of Man under the Fatherhood of God. Especially in America, this conceptual device served another purpose: the forging of a nation out of successive waves of immigrants, sometimes Christian in origin, but with widely differing traditions, languages and social structures. The invocation of the Christian principle of humanity's common status as God's children not only served a rhetorical purpose but also implied the direction of social policy. Equality – at least as a good, if not as a material reality – took a stronger place in the political lexicon. Some form of social security, however meagre, became an embodiment of the shared identity of all citizens and not just the deserving poor. The point is not that these political objectives were realized but that they became goods recognized in public and political discourse. And in this, the Churches were able to reinforce the attendant political programmes.

The writings of the theologians who embodied and drove forward the social gospel movement in this first stage of its development are not especially easy to get hold of today, although extracts can be found in readers and anthologies such as Atherton's. The great names include Washington Gladden (1836–1918), Shailer Mathews (1863–1941) and Walter Rauschenbusch (1861–1918). Rauschenbusch's *Christianity and the Social Crisis* (1907) and *Christianizing the Social Order* (1912) were especially significant texts, some of whose themes reappear in the works of Reinhold Niebuhr, J. Philip Wogaman and other more recent theologians. Together, they represent what Stackhouse calls the first phase of the social gospel movement.

Christian realism

But the flaw in the BOM-FOG social theology was that, by optimistically emphasizing the idea that human unity could lead to human progress, it neglected the Christian doctrine of the sin which separates humanity from God – the estrangement between the heavenly Father and the rebellious children. The politics of the period when this theology flourished proved insufficiently robust to survive the disappointments following the First World

82

War, the collapse of the American (indeed, global) economy and the ensuing social crisis. The Great Depression demanded the corrective power of a theology of sin to rebalance a theology too wedded to the potential of human goodness. What emerged between the two world wars remained deeply influential until relatively recently. Often known as Christian realism, this second phase of the social gospel is most sharply demonstrated in the work of Reinhold Niebuhr (1892–1971) in publications such as his *Moral Man and Immoral Society*.[2]

Christian realism argues from a position close to a theology of the interim and seeks good structures for living well and justly. These need to be sustainable when human sin is factored in alongside the possibility of goodness. There is a pragmatism about this approach which fits well with the belief that it is the Churches' role to contribute to the political process – even to advise and support the powers, authorities and governments of the day. Just as practical politics requires not only a moral compass but a hard head for the law of unintended consequences – not only a commitment to good ends but a willingness to determine the means also – so Christian realism is about seeking concrete social programmes and policies which can be endorsed by the Church and can be understood as promoting Christian ends in a fallen world without violating Christian principles through the means adopted.

The great challenge to Christian realism came with the rise of totalitarianisms in Europe and the Soviet Union during the 1930s. It is arguable whether or not a pragmatic understanding of Christian ethics was in fact well equipped to sustain resistance to totalitarianism. On the one hand, its relative social pessimism, congruent with a sharp consciousness of the persistence of sin, allowed Christians to realize that they had to get their hands dirty in order to defeat ideologies which sought the extermination of other ways of interpreting the world. Christian ethics was not reduced to the role of a bystander piously hoping that people might be nice to one another again. On the other hand, it is at least arguable that the pragmatism of Christian realism dulled the ideological gulf that lay between a Christian understanding of humanity and those of the totalitarians. Something more passionate, more visionary and, perhaps most of all, less ready to accept the necessity of compromise, might have sustained a stronger and more prophetic faith which not only sought human flourishing in this world but had something more to say about the world to come as well. The threat of totalitarianism was an immense challenge to a liberally minded understanding of plurality. When the ability of the Church to exist at all (at least in ways which could embody Christian virtues) was under immediate threat, a Christian ethic which shied away from practical politics, and which had no adequate doctrine of humanity's capacity

2 Reinhold Niebuhr, *Moral Man and Immoral Society: A Study in Ethics and Politics*, New York: Charles Scribner's Sons, 1932.

for evil, would have seemed like mere abdication. What was at stake was precisely the question of eschatology. Is the Christian vocation about living faithfully, even unto death and committing the fate of future generations entirely to God's hands, or does it entail a responsibility for ensuring that evil shall not triumph in this world? Niebuhr, like many others in the twentieth century, was convinced of the second position.

Niebuhr's influence persisted long after the Second World War and into the years of prosperity that followed. William Temple was a friend of Niebuhr's, and in Britain, as well as in the USA, this became the dominant mode for doing Christian ethics. Nor was Christian realism without influence in Western Europe, although the bitter experience of Churches which had had to live under Nazism provided the background to Karl Barth's powerful emphasis on deductive orthodoxy, of which we shall hear more. My point here, however, is that Christian realism had its roots in the political, social and economic upheavals of the first half of the twentieth century and proved sufficiently robust, and sufficiently in tune with changing times, to remain a dominant voice in Christian ethics through most of the second.

While Christian realism was never a style adopted by a majority of Churches in the United States, it nonetheless achieved prominence by being the method of Christians who would, in today's political parlance, be described as part of the liberal elite. Nor is this label entirely inappropriate since, with its implicit assumption that the task of Christian ethics is to inform policy and influence the 'movers and shakers', this was indeed an approach to ethics which spoke to and for an upper social stratum. As Stackhouse notes when he turns to the third mode of the social gospel, the next challenge would come from below.

The post-war period coincided with unprecedented growth and prosperity – certainly in the United States but also, once the ravages of war had been made good, across Europe. Material prosperity, following the experience of the Depression and the privations and uncertainties of wartime, rekindled the hope that human society was capable of improvement. In terms of Christian ethics, a continued realism about humanity's propensity for sin was combined with a more optimistic sense that, with totalitarianisms defeated or contained, strides could still be made towards the kingdom values of justice and peace. In the American context, this awareness threw new light on the unfinished business associated with the melting-pot origins of the nation. The civil rights movement began largely in the Churches of the black communities, the scandal of effective racial segregation at worship providing both a presenting issue and, at a practical level, the meeting places and cultural focus which enabled the black communities to organize. To a considerable degree, the movement for civil rights in the USA sustained itself on a gospel tradition which was not afraid to engage with the public sphere through political action and yet which did so in a highly visionary, prophetic, manner very unlike the polite pragmatics of Christian realism.

Theologies of liberation

The sheer vibrancy of the civil rights movement and the Christian ethic that sustained it gave encouragement to other equality movements. Driven in part by a Christian conviction of the fundamental equality of all people before God, and yet also influenced by the growing scepticism of received authority and old ways of thinking, attention turned, paradoxically, to difference. Plurality became a key term in social analysis, and the competing claims of diverse social groupings tested the mechanisms and structures through which a patchwork nation was held together. Years of plenty had loosened the ties of obligation which had upheld elites and power-brokers for so long. The new focus on black people, women and other groups which had reason to feel excluded or marginalized, called for a Christian ethic which was not dispensed from on high by authority figures but which emerged from the faithfulness of those experiencing discrimination.

And so Stackhouse identifies a fourth phase of the social gospel, this time drawing heavily on the liberation theologians of Latin America, but in time developing into a whole set of genres reflecting the particular experiences of different groups, each speaking in their own voice about the implications of Christian faith for real lives. Although, for reasons of brevity, it may be impossible to avoid lumping together black theology, feminist theology or the Dalit theology of the Indian caste of untouchables, this risks overlooking the subtle work done within each genre. Worse, it risks perpetuating a top-down perspective which treats all marginalized groups as essentially alike and, by definition, non-mainstream. But there is also some justification for taking these theological movements together, seeing them in Stackhouse's terms as representative of a new phase in the social gospel, for together they mark a point at which today's intractable concerns within Christian ethics rise to prominence. The philosophical and ethical problems associated with plurality arose primarily because consciously plural cultures could no longer be adequately represented in any single narrative and attempts to do so were seen as ways of entrenching sectional interests and power. Since the beginning of the fourth phase of the social gospel, Christian ethics could no longer be characterized as one activity working with a single mode of reasoning.

Finally, Stackhouse turns to the future and attempts to predict what the next turn in the development of the social gospel might be. With some prescience, since he was writing just before the cataclysmic events of 9/11, he sees the next big question being posed by other faiths and specifically Islam. Globalization, at first primarily an economic phenomenon, is having much the same effect as mercantilism, global trade and the rise of capitalism in earlier centuries. Cultures, communities and traditions which had, hitherto, been able to conduct themselves in more or less splendid isolation from each other, are no longer able to make sense of their context without some account of why other, very different, cultures should exist and how they might find ways to live on one planet together. In other words, Stackhouse says, we need a 'theology of the religions'; an account from within the Christian tradition of a world in which we are not the only people present or the only people who matter. The question of the encounter between traditions and of dialogue across differences comes once again to centre stage.

Like all typologies, Stackhouse's five phases of the social gospel are not to be taken as mutually exclusive categories rigidly delineated by time. Although there is a clear historical sequence here, the earlier phases persist through the later ones. But Stackhouse enables us to see that the social gospel through the decades has been a movement seeking to respond ethically to the new questions which changing culture, politics and society continually pose. Each era has something to contribute to the next, but each mode of doing Christian ethics is eventually found wanting by failing to address convincingly some new challenge or context. Theologically, the weaknesses of one phase, often found to lie in the over-emphasis of one doctrinal motif over other equally important ones, are corrected by bringing back to the foreground the neglected aspects of the Christian tradition – only, of course, to set up a newly imbalanced position which requires later correction from elsewhere in the tradition.

The story in Britain: industrialization and urbanization

In the British context, it was not war but radical social change that first elicited a strong Christian social response. The processes of industrialization and urbanization had overturned a long-established and semi-feudal social order. The growth of cities with their teeming working class, employed in factories rather than in homes or tight-knit small communities, posed a massive challenge to a Church which had always been geographically defined and part of the social fabric. Long before the industrial revolution, the Church had been understood as part of the solution to the social pressures of urban growth; for example, church building in cities was often intended as a civilizing and moral influence on the otherwise unruly and threatening proletariat. As industrialization progressed, it was initially thought that the social problems of slum housing, and the 'moral degeneracy' accompanying poverty and overcrowding, were but passing phases to be solved in some mysterious fashion by progress and the market. When, instead, they proved to be intractable, the Church began to respond with more thoughtful measures than just the provision of places of worship.

The practical social responses came both from the evangelical and what would now be called the liberal wings. Indeed, any account of twenty-first-century British evangelicalism has to reckon with the enduring legacy of the evangelical social reformers of the nineteenth century – a tradition that has never gone away and persists quietly but effectively in many of the hardest-pressed communities of the land. Charles Kingsley is, perhaps, the best-remembered figure from this evangelical movement. Theologically, the movement is significant for the insight that saving souls without thought for the bodily needs of the person was not only evangelistically ineffective but theologically lopsided. The wider public concern may have been for the threat posed by the immoral and degenerate masses, but the Church was concerned with the salvation of Christ's children. If, as a result of social interventions by the Church, both problems could be addressed, well and good.

An interesting light can be shed on the emerging Christian social conscience of the nineteenth century by the story of the missionaries to the navvies who built the railways of Britain. The gangs of itinerant navvies were the epitome of the social threat posed to once-stable communities by the upheavals of industrialization and were a by-word for lawlessness and dissolution. They drank heavily, fought wildly, consorted with 'women not their wives', and few towns or villages were spared a visitation. Somehow, along the way, they constructed a mass communication system like nothing seen before, mainly by human muscle power and on a timescale that eclipses most subsequent public works. But the navvies were frightening, unconnected to structures of social obligation, and appeared to threaten the whole ordering of Christian society. As with the heathen tribes of Africa or Asia, so the heathen navvies (a good number were Irish Catholics, but in Protestant England that was as bad as being heathen) became the object of missionary ventures grounded upon the principle that a converted soul would become refined, peace-loving and deferential.[3]

This is not to underestimate the courage of the navvy missioners. Many, such as Elizabeth Garnett, were middle-class women for whom the navvy shanty towns must have been as foreign as an African encampment and the language of the navvies as incomprehensible as Swahili. Many started with a strategy of providing improving tracts and opportunities for worship (contending with the contractors' desire to work around the clock seven days a week). But those who had eyes to see recognized that personal morality was not the only barrier to converting navvies to civilized values.

Drunkenness, for instance, was endemic, and not solely because of moral weakness. When men were paid partly in tokens, redeemable only at the company shop, and when that shop sold cheap booze and not much else, heavy alcohol consumption became a way of life. The missionaries were not going to stamp out alcohol altogether, despite the power of their temperance preaching. But they did, eventually, get the law changed to prevent a man being paid in 'tommy shop tokens', thus freeing the navvies to follow their consciences in their spending and freeing them from economic slavery to the company shop. The so-called 'Truck Acts' are still in force today and generations of British workers have been spared this one aspect of economic exploitation thanks to the evangelical zeal of the navvy missions.

---

[3] See: Terry Coleman, *The Railway Navvies*, Harmondsworth: Penguin Books, 1968.

Then there were the unmarried couples – a source of shame and a shock to Victorian England. Yet the missionaries who looked beyond the individual navvy, and observed the system within which he worked, began to see the logic that drove serial cohabitation of this kind. Railways are not built from start to finish by one gang of men. First came the rockmen, the blasters and shovellers who created the cuttings and embankments. Then came the masons who built the viaducts, cattle-creeps and retaining walls. The track layers followed – and so on until the job was done. A rockman might bring his wife to the shanty town until his contract ran out. Then he had no option but to 'go on the tramp' around the country until he was taken on at another set of works. Then he would send for his wife, but in the meantime she stayed behind on the site, probably making ends meet by taking in lodgers from among the men now working there. But without a husband on the contract, she had no right of tenure, for the lease on the shanty would be in her husband's name. The week would come when the company's rent collector would ask whose (male) name to enter in the book this time, and before long she was that man's woman. Contact with her husband would have been intermittent if it happened at all: she might not hear from him for months if ever. And life had to go on for the alternative was starvation.

All this, the more thoughtful navvy missioners could understand. They took ameliorative steps by publishing news-sheets which included, among the pious sentiments and moral uplift, news of navvies passed on by those they had met on the tramp. What they never quite admitted publicly, although it must have been apparent to many, was that a new economic order was eroding the institution of marriage as quickly as it was eroding the insularity of rural England. The seed was sown for a more radical Christian socialism which openly opposed the economic order and the exploitation which appeared inseparable from it. And because some of this theological reaction was prompted by the perceived threat to a social order which had seemed not only timeless but God-given, there was more than a hint of romantic conservatism in the socialistic ideas.

Christian socialism and the return to Christendom

F. D. Maurice (1805–72) is the figure most associated with Victorian Christian socialism, his reputation as a theological liberal being cemented by his removal from a professorial chair at King's College London in 1853 for doctrinal unorthodoxy, having rejected the notion of everlasting punishment. The Christian socialists' response to industrialization was to condemn capitalism and plead for the restoration of a system of craft guilds after a mediaeval model. In this respect, Maurice and his allies were Christian versions of romantic reformers like John Ruskin, William Morris and the arts and crafts movement, although their social engagement was driven by a strong theological commitment to doctrine and an understanding of human relationships grounded in a theology of the Trinity. While there was to be no return to a pre-capitalist, pre-industrial social order, Maurice did lay the foundations of a style of ministry which became characteristic of the Church of England in the mid-twentieth century by establishing groups which met outside the liturgical rhythms of the Church to discuss issues of concern and support one another. This approach to working among the people of a parish, interweaving social action with liturgical observance in a rich and active discipleship, would later enable the Church rapidly to establish a sense of community and shared purpose in the anonymous suburbs that sprang up around most big cities in the 1920s and 1930s.[4] By then, the explicit Christian socialism and the theological challenge to capitalism and industrialization had largely vanished from the parochial outworking of the model, while they remained central to one important theological school of the inter-war period – the Christendom movement.

Christendom

A flavour of the Christendom idea can be gained from the writings of G. K. Chesterton, although the movement was far from confined to Roman Catholics. In Chesterton's capacious and often humorous writing, one constant undercurrent is the inadequacy and disappointment of modernity, industrialization and commerce, and the superiority in all things of the Middle Ages, craftsmanship and tight-knit communities in which the Church acts as the social glue. Ethics are discovered in the principles of chivalry and honour. The closer society can come to a mediaeval model, with human relations ordered hierarchically under God and secured by a universal Church, the better. Chesterton's famous hymn, 'O God of earth and altar', captures something of the Christendom vision:

> Our earthly rulers falter, our people drift and die
> The walls of gold entomb us, the swords of scorn divide.
> Take not Thy thunder from us, but take away our pride.
>
> . . .
>
> From sale and profanation of honour and the sword,
> From sleep and from damnation, deliver us, Good Lord.
>
> . . .
>
> Bind in a living tether the prince and priest and thrall,
> Bind all our lives together; smite us and save us all.

The message is clear: civility and honour have been destroyed by cynical politics and the love of money embodied in commerce. Instead, salvation is to be found in submitting to the rule, and the wrath, of God, and in a new order which binds together the 'prince and priest and thrall'. Political power

---

[4] See: Malcolm Brown, *Faith in Suburbia: Completing the Contextual Trilogy*, Contact Monograph 15, Edinburgh: Contact Pastoral Trust, 2005.

and spiritual power, united with the whole people in a proper bond of care and obligation, restores the right ordering of society under God.

The Christendom movement continued to be of significance up to, through and beyond the Second World War, with V. A. Demant its most articulate spokesperson. In sharp contrast to Christian realism in the United States and to the 'middle axiom' approach of Temple and Oldham which we will explore shortly, Christendom had little time for forms of knowledge that were not interpreted through the prism of theology. Any notion that the natural sciences, economics or sociology might be autonomous disciplines whose methods expanded human understanding were subordinated to the ideological insistence on Christian theology as the 'queen of sciences', the summation of all that was worth knowing and the interpretative framework through which other branches of knowledge must be understood. Modernity had toppled theology from its pre-eminent position in universities and in public allegiance, but the failings of modernity (and, as the twentieth century wore on, examples of human fallibility, the misapplication of science and the promotion of violence backed by technology were not hard to find) required a humble turn back to a pre-modern world-view and the accompanying social order. As we shall see in the next chapter, these motifs return in post-modern form in the work of John Milbank.

In the 1920s and 1930s, as the Churches reassessed their social role in the face of immense political and economic turbulence, Christendom theology vied with a very different set of emphases, influenced by Reinhold Niebuhr but 'Anglicized', as it were, in the work of Joseph Oldham and William Temple. It was Temple's work, building on Oldham's, which came to fruition between the wars in a series of well-publicized conferences and achieved immense coverage through Temple's small Penguin book, *Christianity and Social Order*, of 1942. As a result, it was the Oldham/Temple approach which came to characterize the social ethics of the Church of England for almost four subsequent decades.[5]

William Temple and middle axioms[6]

William Temple was successively Bishop of Manchester, Archbishop of York and, for two short years, Archbishop of Canterbury before his early death in 1944. In the world of post-war academic theology, Temple's approach to social ethics is most strongly associated with the work of Ronald Preston, whose long career brought him into contact with Temple and other great figures of

---

[5] J. H. Oldham (ed.), *The Churches Survey Their Task: The Report of the Oxford Ecumenical Conference on Church, Community and State*, London: George Allen & Unwin, and Chicago: Willett, Clark & Co., 1937. William Temple, *Christianity and Social Order*, Harmondsworth: Penguin, 1942.

[6] Parts of this and subsequent sections of this chapter appeared in an earlier form in my 'Preface' to Mark Bratton (ed.), *God, Ethics and the Human Genome*, London: Church House Publishing, 2009.

the 1930s such as Reinhold Niebuhr. Preston's later work with the Church
of England's Board for Social Responsibility, and with the World Council of
Churches, made a bridge between theology as practised in the university and
theology as the servant of the Church in the world. Preston was concerned
that the Church's engagement with political and social issues should not only
be theologically literate but should give due weight to empirical evidence
and the knowledge found in disciplines other than theology – and he emphasized this for reasons that were themselves theological: a conviction that an
incarnate God makes himself known to us, not only through direct revelation
in Scripture and the traditions of the Church but also through our daily
encounter with his created order.

Here is Preston's last published account of the approach to Christian social
ethics which he had championed all his working life:

> I have thought for a long time that the best method has three stages. (1) Identify
> the problem. This involves a negative judgement on the *status quo*. Christians
> have a radical faith. They are taught not to be satisfied with things as they are
> and in particular to be sensitive to all who are marginalized, so they are not
> likely to lack issues to take up. (2) Get at the 'facts' by searching for the
> relevant evidence from those involved in the problem, whether as expert
> witnesses or as experiencing it personally. (3) Try to arrive at a broad con-
> sensus on what should be done – first of all at a middle level. This indicates
> a general direction at which policy should aim. Since there are always
> disagreements on public policies, among Christians, no less than the general
> public, this puts the onus on the objector if a Church Report can produce
> agreement on a general direction of policy. If it chooses, a Church Report can
> go on to recommend detailed policies, though the more detailed they are the
> more likely they are to be affected by the inevitable uncertainties in obtaining
> facts; these can often be evaluated and interpreted differently. Still more are
> the uncertainties in forecasting the effects of any detailed policies that are
> advocated.[7]

This is the classic account of what is often known as the 'middle axiom'
approach to Christian social ethics, exemplified by Temple between the wars
and by the Board for Social Responsibility of the Church of England between
the 1960s and the 1980s.

Middle axioms are emphatically not about 'splitting the difference' between
opposing points of view. Rather they seek a middle way between excessively general or vague pronouncements which cannot be translated into
meaningful policy, and excessive specificity which not only appears to align
God's will with detailed and fallible human programmes but tends to leave
no room for legitimate disagreement between Christians about the means by
which good ends can be achieved. A good example of middle axioms can

---

[7] From: Ronald Preston, 'A Comment on Method', in Malcolm Brown and Peter Sedgwick (eds),
Putting Theology to Work, London and Manchester: CCBI and William Temple Foundation, 1998,
pp. 36–7.

be found in the Appendix to Temple's *Christianity and Social Order*, such as his principle that 'Every child should find itself a member of a family housed with decency and dignity ... unspoilt by underfeeding or overcrowding ...'. This goes beyond the generalization that God wants children to flourish but stops short of saying (for example) that taxes should rise to pay for social housing. While this is essentially the approach championed by Preston, he tended to avoid the term 'middle axiom', regarding the word 'middle' as misleading. I use the term here because it is a familiar expression for encapsulating Preston's methods.

Middle axioms emerged from a period in which the Church of England sought to maintain its role of guiding the conscience of the nation in an age of insecurity, rapid change and theological turmoil. The First World War had brought an end to the certainties – some would say complacency – of the Edwardian era, had demonstrated the grotesque inhumanity of technological warfare, and was followed by a depression which put at risk any sense of a social contract between the classes, sowing the seeds for political turmoil across Europe and the totalitarianisms which would lead to a further world war and decades of cold war. What was the vocation of an Established Church in such a world, and how might that calling be articulated publicly? On the one hand, there was the Christendom movement, seeking to turn away from modernity, industrialization and urbanization and looking for inspiration in an idealized mediaevalism in which all human activity was ordered under God and the benign rule of God's Church. On the other hand were voices like Temple's calling for a reappraisal of the role of theology, no longer as the discipline to which all other learning was subordinate, but as one significant discipline among many – one which must listen with respect to the knowledge and wisdom of those whose specialisms lay elsewhere, and through whose work, it was believed, God's purposes could be discerned. At the Conference on Christian Politics, Economics and Citizenship (1924), the Oxford Conference on Church, Community and State of 1937 and, most famously, perhaps, at the Malvern Conference of 1941, it was Temple's skill as chair and in influencing the ensuing reports which, if it did not fully synthesize, nonetheless managed to elide the differences between, these two approaches. But the most significant thing about this series of conferences was that, under the influence of Temple, theologians and church people listened with respect to the thoughts of people eminent in subjects and specialisms other than theology. What we would now call a 'knowledge explosion' had made any return to mediaeval social structures impossible. No one discipline could now claim a monopoly of knowledge, and theology had to learn how to locate itself alongside empirical sciences and other modes of theorizing.

The conferences mirrored the extraordinary ways in which friendship created networks between prominent figures in different spheres of life. As an example, Temple sought the advice of John Maynard Keynes to ensure that the passages in *Christianity and Social Order* which touched on economics made sense to an economist. He was close to the political theorist R. H. Tawney, whose book *Christianity and the Rise of Capitalism* first established the interweaving of Christian faith and economic development and who also advised Temple in his public pronouncements. And there was a close relationship between Temple and William Beveridge, the architect of the post-war welfare state. There is something in this network of influential friends which adds credence to the claim that the model of ethical engagement pioneered by Oldham and popularized by Temple was, at bottom, distinctly elitist.

The Malvern Conference is worth dwelling on further for a moment. In 1941 the British could feel no sense of a secure future. The Battle of Britain had postponed Hitler's invasion ambitions, but the threat had not disappeared and the great military turning point of El Alamein had not yet taken place. Nevertheless, it was not only possible but apparently natural for a group of eminent Christian men and women to gather to address the agenda of post-war reconstruction. Malvern was convened to articulate the kind of world for which the nation was fighting and (without seriously questioning the fact of the Church of England's centrality to the nation) to paint a picture of a Church for a more just, peaceful and technologically forward-looking society.

The precise findings of Malvern do not concern us here. Like many attempts to shape the future they look, with hindsight, either bland or bizarrely over-optimistic. What is important is to recall the social environment from which commitment to the middle-axiom approach sprang. This was a world in peril but one which held real faith in an uncertain future. It was a world which knew too well the capacity for evil inherent in the strange blend of modernism and mediaevalism that was Nazi fascism (although it had yet to learn the full horrors either of that creed or of totalitarian communism). In the lifetimes of most participants, powered flight had gone from being a mere fantasy to becoming what we would now call a weapon of mass destruction; a development that symbolized the advances and ambiguities of industrial modernity. In short, there were engaging parallels with our own times, but some very significant differences. A widely held dream of post-war reconstruction was one of classlessness and social (and material) equality. The autonomy and distinctiveness of the nation-state was not questioned. Those dreams have faded and now have little political currency. And England in 1941 could take for granted its 'Christian' nature and the central role of the Church of England as the Church of all the people, an estate of the realm and a major part of the fabric of civilization. While the vestiges of this view persist today, few if any would regard the place of the Church as beyond question.

The Church of England's tradition of social ethics

In the ensuing era of consensual politics, middle axioms became the hallmark of the work of the Church of England's Board for Social Responsibility

(BSR), from which flowed a stream of reports on social issues of all kinds. The American theologian Henry Clark, writing of the 1980s, was able to follow Paul Abrecht in describing the BSR as one of 'the two most effective ecclesiastical social action groups operating in the world today' (the other being the Roman Catholic bishops of the USA).[8] But already the BSR stood for a tradition under question, both in the Church and in the academy. The turning-point had come at the end of the 1970s when the post-war social consensus spluttered to a halt and the election of Margaret Thatcher's first government ushered in an age of monetarism, overt individualism and a reassertion of management's right to manage which seemed to many to involve a good deal of retribution for decades of trade-union power. Consensus was over and, along with it, the assertion, however tentative, of human equality as a political goal. Many saw, in the place of consensus, something approaching war between the classes – a view which gained greater currency as the government's determination to close down the coal industry saw violence break out between miners and an increasingly militarized police force.

In British politics, the consensuses forged by wartime had proved impossibly fragile after decades of peace. In theology, the middle-axiom methodology – the handmaiden, in its way, of social consensus – proved similarly unsatisfying. The charges against the BSR's characteristic approach were, in retrospect, somewhat akin to the arguments deployed by the Thatcherites against many British institutions. The method was elitist: it was, essentially, the conversation of the educated middle classes, portraying an easy, yet bogus, consensus because the voices of conflicting interests and distinctive dissent were automatically excluded. It was, moreover, a theological betrayal, reducing the distinctive voice of the Christian tradition to a baleful appendix which added nothing to the substantive arguments.[9] In other words, a typical BSR report on an issue of social or political significance appeared to have been assembled from the opinions of experts in a relevant field (provided their views were essentially part of the liberal mainstream), reached conclusions which could have been arrived at by the leader writer of a broadsheet newspaper, and included a theological chapter which might, or might not, include significant perceptions but which had not noticeably affected the recommendations of the report. Any recommendations were likely to be characterized by a slightly defensive moderation: the voice of the Church of England as a lowly courtier daring to suggest to government that some political decisions might be capable of improvement.

If this is an exaggeration for effect, it is nonetheless recognizable to many. The contribution of the Church and of theology to public life at a time of social conflict ought, it was argued, to be capable of passion and partisanship. Cautious moderation no longer addressed the crises of the times. The difficulty

---

[8] Henry Clark, *The Church Under Thatcher*, London: SPCK, 1993. p. 1.
[9] See: Michael Banner, 'Nothing to Declare', *Church Times*, 16 June 1995.

was that the political right and the political left both courted the Church's endorsement and were outraged when it failed to offer it.

Faith in the City and the crisis in theological method

Of all the Church's reports, *Faith in the City* of 1985 best epitomizes the problem and the shift of emphasis.[10] The whole project had been conceived as a classic middle-axiom exercise, somewhat on the lines of a royal commission, seeking to distil all kinds of wisdom which could address the problems of Britain's inner cities. But although the working party was made up, in time-honoured fashion, of the somewhat great and modestly good, its conception of 'expertise' extended well beyond the academy to include those whose expertise stemmed from their experience of the problems under scrutiny. Preston's last description of the middle-axiom method, quoted above, was actually the first to include a definition of 'expertise' which explicitly included the expertise of direct experience. Second, the theological chapter of *Faith in the City* took its cue, not from the pragmatic Christian realism which had characterized earlier reports but from the liberation theology tradition, then flourishing in Latin America and appearing to offer just the kind of righteous partisanship for the poor that a response to the divisive social policies of the Thatcher regimes appeared to demand. It was this espousal of liberation theology which won for the report the epithet 'pure Marxist theology' from a Conservative minister, and thereby (unintentionally) boosted its sales and its significance.

Faith in the City was something of an exception. Many other BSR reports of the time found the achievement of consensus impossible. A short report, *Perspectives on Economics* (1984), which set out to arrive at some shared Christian thinking about the contentious approaches to economics adopted by the Thatcher governments, frankly admitted that positions around the table were irreconcilable, and had to satisfy itself with publishing a short collection of essays on the theme of economics and faith which, taken together, were flatly contradictory. Although short, and largely forgotten, *Perspectives on Economics* was significant for its implicit acknowledgement that the BSR's classic methodology could not cope with fractious times and that the Board might be on safer ground confining itself to reports which set out a range of Christian thinking rather than coming to a (provisional) God's-eye view or at least some reasonably authoritative guidance for the Church. Liberation theology's overt partisanship was never likely to catch on in a national Church which crossed party political boundaries in the way the Church of England has usually managed.

But it was neither liberation theology nor neutrality that was to provide the most serious challenge to the classic middle-axiom approach to public

---

[10] Archbishop of Canterbury's Commission on Urban Priority Areas, *Faith in the City: A Call for Action by Church and Nation*, London: Church House Publishing, 1985.

theology. The fundamental assumption that Christian theology and other disciplines could converse unproblematically no longer seemed tenable. The role and task of the theologian had to be reconceived if the objective of serious engagement between faith and social affairs was to be achieved. What emerged was a sharper awareness of the disjunctions between theology and other modes of thinking. If belief in God makes a difference to how people work with evidence and argument, then it is not self-evident how a meaningful dialogue can take place with other forms of knowledge and expertise where the transcendent dimension is not automatically factored in. Conceiving theology as a slightly apologetic commentator on discussions happening largely outside its own boundaries was insufficient to make belief in God add up to any worthwhile difference.

One response from theology is to seek to re-establish itself as the foundational discourse which makes sense of all other knowledge. This is, as we will see in the next chapter, the project which has emerged since 1990 as 'Radical Orthodoxy'. Ronald Preston, who towards the end of his life often noted history's tendency to repetition, was among the first to spot the similarities between Radical Orthodoxy and the Christendom movement of the 1930s. Both, he believed, were insufficiently alert to the necessity for theology to sit humbly before practitioners of other disciplines whose work immensely expanded our understanding of the created order without, necessarily, undermining the perspectives of faith. Nonetheless, Radical Orthodoxy has done the Church a great favour by re-emphasizing the profound 'otherness' of God-talk in a social context where faith has been privatized and made marginal – or even incomprehensible – to daily existence. In the next chapter we will look at two major contemporary theologians whose work, while starting in different places, has shifted Christian ethics away from the assumptions of the middle-axiom approach and towards a much greater emphasis on the uniqueness and counter-intuitiveness of the Christian message.

As has been noted by John Atherton, the mood of theological engagement with non-theological knowledge takes different turns, reflecting the contingent and ambiguous place of 'today' in salvation history.[11] Middle axioms and the heyday of the BSR characterized what Atherton calls the Age of Incarnation – a period of history when, perhaps reflecting the largely progressive, optimistic and consensual politics of the time, it felt natural for Christians to reach for the doctrine of the Incarnation as the basis for understanding how world and Church relate. Christ has hallowed the world by becoming incarnate among us, so Christians can welcome human progress as, ultimately, leading towards the kingdom, optimistic that God is working his purposes out in the realm of politics, science and human development. But as Atherton observes, the social optimism of the post-war decades is not

---

[11] John Atherton, *Marginalization*, London: SCM Press, 2003.

wholly typical of human experience, and we may have entered a new Age
of Atonement – one in which the disjunction between heaven and earth,
between the things of God and the ways of the world, is more characteristic
of the way faith informs life. Here, there can be no easy accommodation
with disciplines which have no intrinsic space for transcendence; no assumption that the solution to sin and finitude lies in the political sphere, or that
a touch on the rudder by good people prompted by a concerned Church
will keep us on track for a kingdom come on earth.[12]

Along with the creativity of the Radical Orthodoxy movement, much thinking about Christian ethics now takes a stronger cue from the Germanic school
of Karl Barth in which the particular, indeed peculiar, nature of God's self-
revelation to the world in Christ is so central. The voices of Barth and Temple
had, for a long time, seemed to belong to estranged traditions.[13] Temple and
Preston stood for a Church and a theology which could be modestly at ease
as one of the 'estates of the realm' somewhere at the heart of nation and
citizenship. True, Temple's classic book, *Christianity and Social Order*, had
bemoaned the modern heresy that faith and politics don't mix, but his argument was precisely that this *was* a heresy – an aberration which those committed to the Good Society should not allow to be perpetuated. Barth's
theology is for a Church which knows itself to be profoundly at odds with
the culture around it. We cannot attempt to summarize the whole of Barth's
monumental *Church Dogmatics* here. Yet if the Christian faith can no longer
be assumed to be the default moral position for British people, Barth's work
may speak to our times. The detachment of culture from Christianity has
advanced to the point where Christian ethics is no longer the guiding hand
on the tiller but one of a number of hands contesting the right to determine
our cultural direction. This is not the territory in which the Church of
England's established approaches to social ethics were formed. The question
then arises: does the Church of England's historic relationship with the state,
and its concern for the spiritual welfare of all the people, prevent it from
simply tearing up its past methods and practices of social witness and entering the open market of religious voices competing for public attention – or
can the virtues of its tradition of engagement be harnessed afresh for a new
context in which there are no precise historical parallels to inform us? This
is what we will consider when we assess the possibility of Christian ethics
regaining a coherent public role in a profoundly plural social context.

---

[12] It is possible that a new Age of Incarnation may already be emerging. In the Church of England
at least, there seems to be a new energy behind evangelical social action projects which draw,
sometimes explicitly, on an incarnational theological model. Street pastors, working to ease tensions and social problems late at night on the streets of city centres, are a case in point.
[13] See: Peter Sedgwick's rejoinder to Michael Banner: 'Refusing to Despair over Families', *Church Times*, 30 July 1995.

Further reading

For more on William Temple, including a thorough analysis of the ethical tradition for which he stood, see: Alan M. Suggate, *William Temple and Christian Social Ethics Today*, Edinburgh: T&T Clark, 1987. For a symposium, both supportive and critical of the tradition as exemplified by Ronald Preston, see: Elaine L. Graham and Esther D. Reed (eds), *The Future of Christian Social Ethics: Essays on the work of Ronald H. Preston, 1913–2001*, New York and London: Continuum, 2004.

For an American perspective, see: J. Philip Wogaman, *Christian Perspectives on Politics*, Minneapolis: Fortress Press, and London: SCM Press, 1988.

For an assessment of how the tradition of social Christianity encountered political change in Britain after 1979, see: Henry Clark, *The Church Under Thatcher*, London: SPCK, 1993.

6

Ethics and ecclesiology

As we have seen, the tradition of Christian social ethics built around the middle-axiom method, and sustained in the writings of Ronald Preston, characterized the ethical engagements of the Church of England and some other denominations for most of the post-war period. Its weaknesses became increasingly apparent as the post-war consensus gave way to a more confident plurality and an increasing marginalization of the Churches from places of power within public life. Yet the eclipsing of the middle-axiom approach has been due as much to movements within the Church and academic theology as to changing cultural factors. Indeed, Ian Markham (who has had important secular experience as a member of governmental bodies such as the Advertising Standards Authority) notes that the approach of Oldham, Temple and Preston – carefully weighing evidence, conscious of the autonomy of different disciplines and alert to the pragmatics of implementation as well as abstract ethical principles – is still the way in which ethics is practised in most contexts outside the Church.[1] Something has been going on within the Churches in the last thirty years or so to generate a serious loss of confidence in this long-established method of social ethics and to elicit new and radical emphases drawing upon other strands within the theological tapestry. A recurring theme in this book is the need for corrective influences as ethical responses to social trends emphasize, at first helpfully and later excessively, particular theological themes and motifs.

Political and social change on the one hand, and the desire to correct a theological over-emphasis on the other, seem to be at work in the challenge to middle-axiom approaches within Christian ethics. Both point to the need to conceive afresh the place of the Church in ethical thinking. The Church's position alongside power, exerting influence through networks of influential people, has certainly become more marginal. At the same time, theologians have rediscovered a vision of the Church as a unique community, the first-fruits of God's kingdom and a prophetic presence on the edges, rather than at the centre, of the social mainstream.

The two main figures to consider here are the American theologian Stanley Hauerwas (whose influence in Britain continues to grow) and the British academic John Milbank (who has also worked extensively in the United

---

[1] Ian S. Markham, 'Ronald Preston and the Contemporary Ethical Scene', in R. John Elford and Ian S. Markham (eds), *The Middle Way: Theology, Politics and Economics in the Later Thought of R. H. Preston*, London: SCM Press, 2000, p. 257.

States). Hauerwas and Milbank are, in many ways, contrasting figures, yet they can be seen as different aspects of a single trend and they have, on occasion, collaborated together.

The superficial differences between them are acute. Milbank is an Anglican from the Catholic wing of the Church, refers to himself as a socialist (although of a somewhat unconventional sort) and writes in a dense and deeply erudite style which can be daunting to the reader. Hauerwas is denominationally footloose, but influenced most profoundly by the Mennonite tradition in a distinctively American context. He writes in a highly accessible style, often preferring to publish sermons and essays or to collaborate with others in writing books. As Robert Jenson put it somewhat waspishly, 'Linear exposition of a system has not to date been Hauerwas's greatest contribution',[2] although that view might need to be modified since the publication in 2002 of Hauerwas's substantial Gifford lectures.[3] But what brings Milbank and Hauerwas together is their common opposition to liberalism and their shared conviction that it is the theology of the Church which provides the key to Christian ethics and not some agenda thrust on the Church by secular society. If the Christendom movement exemplified the doctrinal union of Church and state, and if the ethics of Temple and Preston echoed the position of a humble yet still influential national Church, Hauerwas and Milbank alike seek to stress the Church's unique vocation and the impossibility of reconciling its world-view with that of Enlightenment liberalism. Both, in different ways, build a theological edifice upon MacIntyre's philosophical foundations.[4]

An introduction to Hauerwas and Milbank also allows us to dig more deeply into the problems of liberalism in theology, and to consider its alternatives more fully. In particular, it will rapidly become clear that, while both Milbank and Hauerwas are constant critics of liberalism, the liberalism they oppose is not quite (or not just) the popular version of liberal Christianity which takes predictable stances on contentious contemporary moral issues and is generally located slightly to the left of the political centre. Nor is their counter-blast to liberalism described in the simple epithet 'conservative'. Indeed, their work shows that a dichotomy between liberals and conservatives can be simplistic, inaccurate and unhelpful in understanding the currents and conflicts within Christian ethics today. The central themes of both Milbank and Hauerwas are captured in the word 'communitarian', which we have already examined.[5] Liberalism, conceived in quite specific terms associated

---

[2] Robert Jenson, 'The Hauerwas Project', *Modern Theology* 8.3 (1992), p. 289.
[3] Stanley Hauerwas, *With the Grain of the Universe: The Church's Witness and Natural Theology*, Grand Rapids, MI: Brazos Press, and London: SCM Press, 2002.
[4] For an attempt to use MacIntyre's work to examine the relationship between liberal and communitarian ideas in theology, see: Malcolm Brown, *After the Market: Economics, Moral Agreement and the Churches' Mission*, Bern: Peter Lang, 2004.
[5] The liberal/communitarian distinction is not confined to theology or Christian ethics. An excellent analysis of liberalism and communitarianism in their political modes can be found in Stephen Mulhall and Adam Swift, *Liberals and Communitarians*, 2nd edn, Oxford: Blackwell, 1996.

with modernity, plurality and the Enlightenment project, is challenged by a new focus on communities as places of moral formation, where traditions develop, narratives inform identity and practices of virtuous living evolve. MacIntyre's conclusion to *After Virtue* argues that liberalism faces a crisis comparable to the last days of the Roman empire. Some realized, then, that the *imperium* was unable to sustain the virtues of civilization and that the alternative might lie in other forms of community within which 'morality and civility might survive the coming ages of barbarism and darkness'; hence MacIntyre's proposal that we need another St Benedict.[6] Hauerwas and Milbank go further than MacIntyre in explicitly identifying the Christian community as the only worthwhile example of the kind of hopeful communitarianism which MacIntyre seeks.

Stanley Hauerwas

A Southern Methodist from Texas, acknowledging the influence of the Anabaptist/Mennonite tradition epitomized by J. H. Yoder, and sustained, for many years, within a Roman Catholic university before, more recently, associating more with Anglicanism, Hauerwas is not an easy person to pigeon-hole. In a splendid review article, Stephen H. Webb refers to Hauerwas as 'a voice cursing in the wilderness', and notes his pithy teaching style and his love of provocative and playful exaggerations to make his points.[7]

Underneath the comedy and the delight in poking fun at authority and received wisdom, Hauerwas's driving concern is the Christian commitment to peace. Violence and militarism are the antithesis of all the Christian community stands for. Not for nothing is one of his best-known books entitled *The Peaceable Kingdom*.[8] For Hauerwas, it is modernity's easy tendency to settle differences through war and violence that betrays its distance from the dispensation ushered in with Christ and being brought to completion in the kingdom of God. The calling of the Church is not to compromise with conflict or to give its backing to the kind of *realpolitik* which accepts war as a consequence of sin. Rather the Church is here to witness to the kingdom that is coming; to look first to its own faithful witness and not to pretend that it is somehow there to underpin the social fabric, liberal democracy or market capitalism. As a number of commentators have noted, Hauerwas rejects the whole entanglement of Church, state and culture that has existed since Constantine. In a neat phrase, Webb characterizes Hauerwas as a thinker who is 'interested in what American Christianity could be, if only it were not so American'.

---

[6] Alasdair MacIntyre, *After Virtue: A Study in Moral Theory*, 2nd edn, London: Duckworth, 1985, p. 263.
[7] Stephen H. Webb, 'A Voice Cursing in the Wilderness', *Reviews in Religion and Theology* 10.1 (February 2003).
[8] Stanley Hauerwas, *The Peaceable Kingdom: A Primer in Christian Ethics*, Notre Dame, IN: University of Notre Dame Press, 1983, and London: SCM Press, 1984.

Hauerwas's project is driven by his opposition to liberalism in politics and theology, and the attempt to counter this with a teleology of Christian virtue. As he put it:

> We are trying to reclaim Christian virtues in a context in which people assume that what it means to be a good Christian is little different from what it means to be a good liberal.[9]

Two concerns are central in Hauerwas's work: first, that the Church, as the community which embodies Christian virtue, is pivotal in any Christian ethic and, second, that the key to Christian virtue is the commitment to non-violence. Hauerwas sees narrative, with the scriptural narrative being normative, as the source of identity for the community which, in its common life, continues to develop the story.

In *A Community of Character*, Hauerwas outlines his approach to the Church's social role in 'Ten Theses Toward the Reform of Christian Ethics'.[10] He stresses the centrality of narrative; the Church's task of 'being itself'; the importance of the gift of relationship and the family. He also expresses two central motifs of his position: that the Church is, rather than has, a social ethic, and that the Christian community should deliberately dissociate itself from liberal positions, including the liberal narrative of democracy:

> In our attempts to control our society Christians in America have too readily accepted liberalism as a social strategy appropriate to the Christian story . . . The church does not exist to provide an ethos for democracy or any other form of social organization, but stands as a political alternative to every nation, witnessing to the kind of social life possible for those that have been formed by the story of Christ.[11]

Hauerwas's theology is clearly addressed specifically to contemporary North America, and this influences his polemical tone. While this creates problems in translating his theology to other contexts, the 'liberal' Church he describes is recognizable from a European viewpoint: 'the church is too often justified by believers, and tolerated by non-believers, as a potential agent for justice or some other good effect'.[12]

---

[9] Stanley Hauerwas and Charles Pinches, *Christians Among the Virtues: Theological Conversations with Ancient and Modern Ethics*, Notre Dame, IN: University of Notre Dame Press, 1997, p. xv.

[10] Stanley Hauerwas, *A Community of Character: Towards a Constructive Christian Social Ethic*, Notre Dame, IN and London: University of Notre Dame Press, 1981, pp. 9–12.

[11] Hauerwas, *A Community of Character*, pp. 11–12.

[12] Hauerwas, *A Community of Character*, p. 1. Alan Suggate distinguishes Hauerwas's account of the American Churches' capitulation to liberalism from the very different European history: 'Hauerwas is gunning for those many Christians in suburban America who blissfully fuse faith and American culture in a latter-day Christendom' (Alan Suggate, 'Whither Anglican Social Ethics?', *Crucible* (April–June 2001), p. 109). However, in a global economy increasingly dominated by American versions of capitalism, this may not be such a uniquely American phenomenon. For a striking analysis of Hauerwas's work in the context of British, and Anglican, church life, see: Samuel Wells, *Transforming Fate Into Destiny: The Theological Ethics of Stanley Hauerwas*, Carlisle: Paternoster Press, 1998.

Nevertheless, what Hauerwas describes as the Church's captivity to liberalism does need some translation before it can be made to fit a British context in recognizable form. One can gain a good sense of what Hauerwas means by 'liberalism' by examining what he is against. He mocks the idea that gay people should be regarded as a threat to military discipline: in his view, Christians should be far more suspect.[13] So he is not one of those Christians who regards attitudes to homosexuality as the touchstone of liberalism on the one hand and Christian orthodoxy on the other. His liberalism is not so much a distinct set of beliefs and values as the subordination of Christian belief to a higher commitment – the belief in 'America', or 'democracy' or 'capitalism' – to which the Church must always bow the knee and suppress the critical elements in its own tradition. Despite the cultural warfare in America, Hauerwas characterizes American society as essentially liberal in the most profound sense. That is, it is committed to some version of ethical pluralism and allows Christian faith to flourish only insofar as it bolsters the basic premises of liberal pluralism (not least the market economy) and the overall political objectives of the state (including military power). Expressed in this way, Hauerwas appears less as a warrior in the sterile argument between 'liberals' and 'conservatives' than as an analyst of the extent to which Christian faith has allowed itself – in the West, at least – to become the handmaiden of ideologies and attitudes with (in Hauerwas's view) only the most tenuous ancestry in the Christian story.

Hauerwas is explicit about the connection between liberalism in politics and contemporary liberal theology. Both are characterized by the separation of self from story; by the equation of freedom with transcendence of tradition; and by obscuring the fact that liberalism is itself only one narrative among many:

Liberalism, in its many forms and versions, presupposes that society can be organized without any narrative that is commonly held to be true. As a result it tempts us to believe that freedom and rationality are independent of narrative – i.e., we are free to the extent that we have no story. Liberalism is, therefore, particularly pernicious to the extent that it prevents us from understanding how deeply we are captured by its account of existence.[14]

and:

The great self-deception is in thinking that the tradition of liberalism gives us the means to recognize that it is indeed a tradition.[15]

The service that the Church offers to the world is to be a contrast model, but not to offer concrete alternatives to public structures or policies since

---

[13] Stanley Hauerwas, 'Why Gays (as a Group) are Morally Superior to Christians (as a Group)', in John Berkman and Michael Cartwright (eds), *The Hauerwas Reader*, Durham and London: Duke University Press, 2001, pp. 519–21.
[14] Hauerwas, *A Community of Character*, p. 12.
[15] Hauerwas, *A Community of Character*, p. 83.

any alternative in the public realm may be no less oppressive than what it replaces. The Church offers the world its commitment to non-violence (a theme developed in greater detail by Hauerwas in *The Peaceable Kingdom*).

Beyond the central focus on non-violence which must, he argues, pervade all the Church's internal and external relationships, Hauerwas's key area for counter-cultural witness is the family.

> The family is a crucial focus for Christian social ethics, not in the hackneyed sense of being the 'bedrock' of society, but because the kind and form of family created by the church is one of the most telling marks of the church's social significance.[16]

We shall consider Hauerwas's approach to the family and children further in Chapter 11.

When it comes to the question of how different traditions are to communicate with each other, Hauerwas is not easy to interpret. On the one hand, he holds that in such a situation 'our common historical nature means it is very likely that we will find we share something in common'.[17] On the other, he understands the Church's task as 'witness' rather than making judgements about other traditions. Witness is the invitation to 'look what manner of life has been made possible among us by the power of the Cross and resurrection of Christ'. Hauerwas sees the Church holding up its story within a plural world and seeking to attract converts from other traditions. Indeed, he is claiming further that

> what allows us to look expectantly for agreement among those who do not worship God is not that we have a common morality based on autonomous knowledge of autonomous nature, but that God's kingdom is wider than the church.[18]

And yet it is not entirely clear whether Hauerwas is talking about the real, contingent Church or its uncompromisable calling. Radical critiques of secular polity surely require that the Church in the world be subjected to an equally radical critique. It is not always clear whether, or when, he is referring to the Church-as-it-is or the Church-as-it-is-called-to-be. So while it is possible that, in an encounter with another tradition, the Church-as-it-is may find that it has something to learn and to gain,[19] no such possibility seems to be open to the Church-as-it-is-called-to-be since the Christian narrative is that which gives meaning to the whole world. Dialogue beyond the tradition is not apparently an essential element of the Church's true nature,

---

[16] Hauerwas, *A Community of Character*, p. 5.
[17] Hauerwas, *A Community of Character*, p. 103.
[18] Stanley Hauerwas, *Christian Existence Today*, Durham, NC: Labyrinth Press, 1988, p. 17.
[19] '[T]he church will often learn from different cultures what is and is not essential to its own life', *A Community of Character*, p. 105.

which is, as he says, to 'become a real option and a real confrontation for others'.[20]

One interesting question here is whether Hauerwas holds the Christian tradition to be one – a tradition founded in a single narrative and embodied in one community – or to be composed of different and distinctive narrative strands within a wider Christian tradition. He clearly recognizes different historical strands of tradition or he could not describe his own ecclesial allegiances as he does. Yet when he writes of the Church's calling and of the Christian narrative there is no suspicion of tension or dialogue between strands. Thus his assault on liberal theology is, by implication, about replacing bad, heretical theology, which has swallowed the myths of secular liberalism, with a single, truthful, Christian narrative. Indeed, he sometimes writes of 'Christians' and 'liberals' in ways that imply that the idea of a Christian liberal (or a liberal Christian) is, by definition, impossible.[21]

An important criticism of Hauerwas is that his critique of liberal institutions, and his refusal to allow the Church to bolster them, is conducted from the safety of one of the world's great plural democracies in which the freedom to live according to a variety of traditions and narratives is enshrined by the constitution and protected by precisely those liberal institutions about which Hauerwas is so scathing. The Church in places where the institutions of government and security are more fragile, or non-existent, may not be able to take so high-minded a stance. But it is worth remembering that Hauerwas seems less interested in a comprehensive and systematic theological account of what the Church should do than in the role of the Church as a contrast model: an example of how things might be, rather than a fully-worked out programme for saving this world. As such, it is precisely when security and prosperity conspire to enlist the Church in support of deeply flawed and compromised human institutions that the Church is called to stand in another place. It is not surprising that Hauerwas holds a deep antipathy for the work of Reinhold Niebuhr. Advising how those with power should use it is irrelevant for a Church that does not measure its influence by proximity to power, and so the Church is absolved from having a political programme of its own.

Webb concludes that, for all his difficulties with America as it is, Hauerwas is 'proto-typically American in [his] quirky ambivalence about authority' and in his paradoxical longing for a time when the Church set the rules. Webb wonders whether Hauerwas's Methodist background has something to do with this, observing that, 'Methodists began by trying to revolutionize American society, compromised with running it, and ended up just going along, all the while distancing themselves from their revivalist roots.' It is easy to identify loose ends and apparent contradictions in Hauerwas's work but, strangely

---

[20] Hauerwas, *A Community of Character*, p. 105.
[21] See, for example, Hauerwas and Pinches, *Christians Among the Virtues*, p. 67.

perhaps, that does not significantly diminish his impact. 'Perhaps', says Webb, 'that is what I like most about Hauerwas: of all the great theologians he is the one who seems to be having most fun.'

John Milbank

Milbank is best known for his monumental work *Theology and Social Theory*,[22] which is a complex book with a 'brilliantly simple thesis'.[23] Indeed, that thesis can be most easily discerned from an earlier essay with the typically Milbankian title, '"Postmodern Critical Augustinianism": A Short *Summa* in Forty-Two Responses to Unasked Questions', which opens thus:

> 1 The end of modernity, which is not yet accomplished, yet continues to arrive, means the end of a single system of truth based on universal reason, which tells us what reality is really like.
> 2 With this ending, there ends also the modern predicament of theology. It no longer has to measure up to accepted secular standards of scientific truth or normative rationality. Nor, concomitantly, to a fixed notion of the knowing subject . . . This caused problems for theology, because an approach grounded in subjective aspiration can only precariously affirm objective values and divine transcendence.
> 3 . . .
> 4 The priority given to structural relations allows theology to make a kind of half-turn back to pre-modernity.[24]

In the light of what we have already considered in terms of modernity and what may follow it, this is a very clear manifesto for theology and Christian ethics. The 'half-turn back to pre-modernity' indicates the debt Milbank owes to Christendom thinking, though he offers something richer, denser and more challenging. Nevertheless, the pull of Christendom as a half-imaginary era, when all power and politics was ordered under God through the mediation of a faithful and authentic Church, is tangible in Milbank's work and in the wider movement known as Radical Orthodoxy, in which he is a leading figure. Because *Theology and Social Theory* generated such interest, several symposia of essays analysing and critiquing its arguments appeared soon after its publication, and we shall consider Milbank's theology in dialogue with some of those critics.

The project, then, is to re-establish the possibility of a Christian grand narrative as a response to postmodernity. Theology, for Milbank, is not to be separated from the social sciences, since the latter are (unconsciously) riddled with quasi-theological assumptions about the nature of the world. Theology, indeed, offers a superior social theory: superior to liberalism, positivism,

[22] John Milbank, *Theology and Social Theory: Beyond Secular Reason*, Oxford: Blackwell, 1990.
[23] Fergus Kerr, 'Simplicity Itself: Milbank's Thesis', *New Blackfriars* 861 (1992), p. 305.
[24] John Milbank, 'Postmodern Critical Augustinianism', *Modern Theology* 7.3 (April 1991), pp. 225–37.

dialectics and the 'difference' of relativism. And Christian theology character-istically rejects an 'ontology of violence' – no solution to humanity's woes is to be found in a dialectic of conflict and counter-conflict – promoting instead a teleology of peace. Milbank is concerned, therefore, to stress the strangeness and surprise of Christian theological perspectives.[25] He is not concerned to bridge any 'gap' between theology and the secular world since at the heart of his thesis is the argument that no such gap exists. Milbank argues against theologians who have allowed autonomy to secular reason, and have thereby sought to position theology within an essentially atheistic social theory.

Whereas MacIntyre sets out to argue against aspects of secular reason (in its plural, liberal forms), for Milbank, the mode of encounter between tradi-tions is for the 'better' narrative to overcome rival, inferior narratives:

> *my* case is rather that it [secular reason] is only a *mythos*, and therefore cannot be refuted, but only out-narrated, if we can *persuade* people – for reasons of 'literary taste' – that Christianity offers a much better story.[26]

MacIntyre points forward to 'new forms of community', but Milbank is more specific: only the Christian community (and the Christian account of virtue) is adequate. MacIntyre remains within a dialectical mode of enquiry; Milbank stresses instead the centrality of rhetoric. He identifies erroneous 'liberal' concerns as far back in the historical narrative as Aristotle, at the point when philosophy began to part company with religion and to ask questions about 'the good' for humanity in general.

Such a question, Milbank believes, can only be met with a general, liberal, response, and thus one is led inexorably into a misleading universalism. Only through faith, he claims, can virtue be generated, and faith is to be engendered through persuasion, which Milbank interprets as rhetoric.

So whereas MacIntyre argues for 'virtue', Milbank pleads for 'Christian virtue'. Where MacIntyre argues for tradition-constituted enquiry, Milbank preaches the centrality of the Christian narrative, the Christian tradition and Christian practice. MacIntyre portrays tradition-constituted enquiry as a practice that can be worked out in a variety of traditions and as a process which allows the critical encounter between traditions and 'translation' between them. Milbank maintains that there is such radical incommensurability between traditions that knowledge from 'inside' can never be properly apprehended from 'outside'. Translation is impossible, only conversion remains.

Milbank has been widely criticized for the intolerant social implications of his theology. Graham Ward asks, 'Without further clarification might not Milbank's Christian story become a Christian imperialism that polices the sublime?'[27] Yet Milbank's claim for Christian distinctiveness is that it is

---

[25] Milbank's 1997 collection of essays is entitled, significantly, *The Word Made Strange*.

[26] Milbank, *Theology and Social Theory*, p. 330 (Milbank's emphasis).

[27] Graham Ward, 'John Milbank's *Divina Commedia*', *New Blackfriars* 861 (1992), p. 317.

unique in refusing ultimate reality to all conflictual phenomena . . . By comparison, all the other myths, or narrative traditions, affirm or barely conceal an original primordial violence, which a social order merely restrains.[28]

Milbank's replacement of dialectics with rhetoric (out-narration), which appears intolerant and potentially conflictual, sits uneasily with his rejection of the ontology of violence and his vision of the peaceful (Christian) kingdom. It is not easy to discern how Milbank avoids the implication of violence which lies behind his commitment to 'persuasion' – persuasion combined with power can slip easily into violence. Nicholas Lash points out that Milbank locates Christian theology 'on the far side of the cross', where, in Milbank's words, 'the absolute Christian vision of ontological peace now provides the only alternative to a nihilistic outlook',[29] and that this leads to a discipleship along the lines adopted by

> innumerable Christian groups and individuals from the desert fathers to the Amish . . . It is, however, a construal requiring, for its own integrity, the continual corrective pressure of another reading, a reading which would place us still . . . on *this* side of the Cross, set in Gethsemane; a reading which demands appropriate engagement with destructive violence, the strenuous exercise of a kind of power set to the service of a kind of politics, construction of the kind of culture of reconciliation . . . which might embody, sustain and publicly communicate the announcement of God's peace.[30]

This is a most helpful insight. The implication is that while Milbank's theology requires the corrective of a theology from the other side of the cross, theologies that have focused too exclusively on the engagement with destructive violence, politics and so on may need the corrective of Milbank's perspective. Lash finds Milbank's focus on the Church at times misplaced, requiring differentiation from the idea of the kingdom:

> That would remind us that, though Christ has come, although salvation has occurred, the classic Christian grammar of these things requires us also to say: salvation is occurring now and is still awaited, eagerly, in hope.[31]

It is this theology of the interim, this aspect of 'classic Christian grammar' which Milbank rejects in his fundamental opposition to dialectics and which leads him into a similarly lopsided view of the Church in society.

In fact, Milbank's theology of the Church, like his thesis itself, is hard to critique as argument, since he presents his theology explicitly as rhetoric, as self-consciously a story, and as the performance of narrative. He presents this as a case against theology's acceptance of, and subordination to, the autonomy of secular reason, and this makes it difficult to fault him on grounds

---

[28] Milbank, *Theology and Social Theory*, p. 262.
[29] Milbank, *Theology and Social Theory*, p. 433.
[30] Nicholas Lash, 'Not Exactly Politics or Power?', *Modern Theology* 8.4 (1992), p. 363.
[31] Lash, 'Not Exactly Politics or Power?', p. 362.

of inadequate adherence to the categories which secular reason erects. As Milbank himself says:

> Explication of Christian practice, the task of theology, tries to pinpoint the peculiarity, the difference, of this practice by 'making it strange'... Unless it reflects upon the singularity of Christian norms of community, theology has really nothing to think about.[32]

This vision of the Church as a unique, distinctive community, characterized by the peaceful acknowledgement of difference within '*absolute* consensus' about the nature and *telos* of the community itself, lies at the heart of Milbank's project.[33] The Church represents in its being all the things that nihilistic secular society is not. Yet the connection between this Church and any real community of Christians is problematical. 'How does the image and idea of the Church relate to contingency of churches and sects and even other faiths?' asks Graham Ward.[34] Rowan Williams takes the point further, saying, 'What I am concerned to keep in view is the danger of setting the common life of the Church too dramatically apart from the temporal ways in which the good is realized in a genuinely contingent world.'[35] And Kieran Flanagan similarly observes that, 'A question is continually begged as to which Church does Milbank have in mind?'[36]

Milbank himself retorts that

> it was not the purpose of *Theology and Social Theory* . . . to imagine the Church as Utopia. Nor to discover in its ramified and fissiparous history some single ideal exemplar.[37]

But this is because he does not envisage the Church in terms of a human institution at all. Rather, 'the Church is first and foremost neither a programme, nor a "real" society, but instead an enacted, serious fiction'. The Church is to be found 'on the site of the eucharist',[38] and, 'the church is present as much in an obscure but precise act of charity as in the deliberations of epochal councils'.[39] Elsewhere he suggests that 'the church is that paradox: a nomadic city', which misunderstands itself when it tries to secure peace by drawing boundaries around itself in the manner of 'most politics and most religions'.[40] This is important, since Milbank's romantic focus on the Church as the place where the peaceful community is realized is easily taken to imply

---

[32] Milbank, 'Postmodern Critical Augustinianism', p. 228.
[33] Milbank, 'Postmodern Critical Augustinianism', p. 228.
[34] Ward, 'John Milbank's *Divina Commedia*', p. 316.
[35] Rowan Williams, 'Saving Time: Thoughts on Practice, Patience and Vision', *New Blackfriars* 861 (1992), p. 323.
[36] Kieran Flanagan, 'Sublime Policing: Sociology and Milbank's City of God', *New Blackfriars* 861 (1992), p. 336.
[37] John Milbank, 'Enclaves, or Where is the Church?', *New Blackfriars* 861 (1992), p. 341.
[38] Milbank, 'Enclaves, or Where is the Church?', p. 342.
[39] Milbank, 'Enclaves, or Where is the Church?', p. 343.
[40] Milbank, 'Postmodern Critical Augustinianism', p. 229.

exclusivity. Yet Milbank can point to the nature of the Church's calling, but not to any priorities and stances that it may take in the contingent world. 'What is in danger of dropping out of view here', says Gerard Loughlin, 'is the *tension*, the difference, between the exemplary and the yet-to-be-fully-realized story of Christ.'[41] His ethic of the Church gives no hints about engaging with the world within which it is set. Echoing Hauerwas, Milbank asks only that the Church gets on with being the Church – performing its narrative. Nor does his commitment to out-narrating other narratives require a theology of engagement. But as long as the Church remains a contingent community whose members inhabit other, secular, and equally contingent communities, Ward's and Williams's reservations hold. Indeed, Williams adds:

> the Church's peace is a healed history not a 'total' harmony whose constructed (and thus scarred) character doesn't show . . . the peace of the Church *as an historical community* is always in construction.[42]

Ward goes further, reminding Milbank that, in assuming too readily the identity of the Christian story as the sole metanarrative which denies the possibility of there being more than one narrative strand within the wider Christian tradition, he is, in a sense, writing from the perspective of God himself.[43]

Not surprisingly, given his assault on liberalism, Milbank is no friend of market economics. In the early pages of *Theology and Social Theory* he sketches out a history of political economy which links the economic concerns of Adam Smith to a profoundly militaristic understanding of society. Economic growth enabled the military strength of the nation-state to develop. Milbank thus manages to associate the emerging 'science' of economics not only with the liberal tradition of the autonomous self, but with a social analysis based on violence and opposed to the peaceful kingdom. He makes the important link between market economics and an assumption of plurality, and opposes this with the narrative of Christendom and the exemplary community of the Church with its 'consensus' around the peaceful embracing of difference. Competition and violence are, for Milbank, hallmarks of an economy in a modern pluralist society in which tolerance means no more than using market mechanisms to manage the violence endemic in individualism. Milbank's alternative is a 'Christian socialism' which can critique the secular logic of capitalism.[44] But this is a socialism practised within and by the Church, and only a programme for the rest of society insofar as Christian rhetoric is able to re-establish Christendom. Milbank envisages the Church's political calling in terms of being a paradigm community, disclosing the possibility of

[41] Gerard Loughlin, 'Christianity and the End of the Story, or the Return of the Master-Narrative', *Modern Theology* 8.4 (1992), p. 379.
[42] Williams, 'Saving Time', p. 322.
[43] Ward, 'John Milbank's *Divina Commedia*', pp. 316–17.
[44] Milbank, *Theology and Social Theory*, pp. 195f.

alternative approaches. But for Milbank, such lessons cannot be learned piecemeal. One is either in the community and able to understand its practice from within, or not.

In 'making strange' the word, and out-narrating other narratives, Milbank offers interesting ethical dimensions to his theology. A central idea here is that of gift-exchange, which Milbank sees as a practice reflecting the Christian experience of God's gifts and grace freely given. Yet again, though, gift exchange only makes proper sense as a practice within a community. Outsiders may fail to understand how the reciprocation of obligation works – like foreigners in an English pub unsure when to buy their round. As Christian practice, gift exchange emphasizes an understanding that all gifts, all resources, have their origin and end in God. It also reflects the notion of the abundance of God's love and grace over against the economists' paradigm of scarcity. The emphasis on gift is an important step in constructing theological points of resistance to the commodification of the human person, a constant challenge in contemporary medical ethics.

Yet if we go too far towards a Milbankian emphasis on gift exchange, and seek to make a paradigm of abundance replace the economists' fundamental paradigm of scarcity, we hit other problems. Absolute scarcity is a factual condition for some resources in a contingent and finite world, and relative scarcity, as reflected in the economists' concept of opportunity cost, is a perennial problem of all societies. These ideas may be associated with the fallen nature of our current condition rather than the divine dispensation to come, but that does not mean that they cease being problems for any person who seeks to live well and to do justice. We find again that Milbank's work makes most sense as a corrective to theological imbalances. In relation to market economics, he aids balance with the concept of gift exchange, although he fails to engage with the way economists themselves understand scarcity. But criticism of part of Milbank's argument need not bring collapse of the whole. This is theology as story, as rhetoric and as drama:

> if we accept the correlation between our knowledge and our stories and that this book is a story, an invention, then there is no position available from which to claim that this story is right or wrong. We can only tell the story differently.[45]

The Church as the focus of Christian ethics

Milbank and Hauerwas alike, then, seek to free the Church to be a unique and counter-cultural community, released from subservience to the narratives of secular liberalism and striving to live out its vocation to bring the kingdom of God closer to fulfilment by living as if the kingdom were already fulfilled. In terms of an approach to ethics – to articulating a narrative of the good

---

[45] Ward, 'John Milbank's *Divina Commedia*', p. 315.

and of justice – this is a crucial response to MacIntyre's devastating analysis of the confusions and dead-ends of liberalism. By stressing, with MacIntyre, the vital role of communities of tradition in the whole ethical enterprise, Milbank and Hauerwas are driven, quite naturally, to a strong vision of the Church as the community which, above all others, has the potential to fulfil the role of preserving and promulgating civility and virtue in an uncomprehending cultural context. But the emphasis on the Church, as we have seen, creates problems as well as opportunities. It requires, as Ward, Williams and Flanagan note so clearly (but as Hauerwas and Milbank do not) a much more clearly articulated understanding of how the Church as a theological construct connects with the empirical Church with all its human flaws and wounds. Underlying this question is the important reminder which Lash poses to Milbank, and which could be put with equal force to Hauerwas: if the classic vocabulary of Christian orthodoxy stresses the both/and (this side of the cross, with the necessity of power and politics, and the other side of the cross where such things have been subsumed into God's transcendent goodness), is it not misleading to emphasize one side of the equation over the other and not to strive much harder to keep the both/and aspects of Christian theology simultaneously in play?

So we return to the question of corrective viewpoints. If we take the middle-axiom approach of Temple and Preston as representing – unwittingly, perhaps – a classically liberal retreat from the notion that Christian theology can offer the best, most beautiful and comprehensive framework within which to locate all human knowledge and endeavour, then the communitarianism of Hauerwas or Milbank appears to dispose of many of the problems associated with that method. The claim is that, by trying to affirm the good when found outside the Church, liberal Christian ethics loses the compass that indicates what the good might be. These confessional communitarians, with their insistence on the Church as the community with special access to the good, remind us that an abstract commitment to 'the good', without a narrative of how the good may be recognized, can lead straight into the trap of moral relativism. But when the question arises of how the good of my community can encounter the different good of your community without provoking bloodshed, it is not so clear that Hauerwas and Milbank, for all their insistence on the cardinal virtue of peace, can offer sufficient guidance. It is not, after all, only the warlike whose blood gets shed in war. In the end, their response to plurality is to assert the superiority of one tradition, one set of narratives and one community's practice. But while that may work, as Lash notes, for some isolationist sects like the Amish (at least up to a point[46]), it is not clear how it can be viable in settings where members of diverse

---

[46] For a reflection on the practical limits of separatism, see: Donald B. Kraybill, 'Amish Economics: The Interface of Religious Values and Economic Interests', in Donald A. Hay and Alan Kreider (eds), *Christianity and the Culture of Economics*, Cardiff: University of Wales Press, 2001, pp. 76–90.

communities have to rub along together. What is more, most people are members, not of one single community but of many. It may be proper to stress the primacy of our religious identities above all others, but our forma- tion as moral beings is rarely so sharply defined. Indeed, it is surely in the encounters with difference and otherness experienced from early childhood (even though we may not grace the experience with such terminology) that we grow to understand that goodness, justice and obligation have to make sense in a plural context or they lack meaningful content as we struggle to be citizens. Ethics in the tribal culture is barely a concern at all since there is nothing to argue about when no challenge has been perceived to inherited tribal wisdom. This may be close to Hauerwas or Milbank's ideal construct of the Church, but the very nature of their argumentative prose makes it very clear that there still is something worth talking about in terms of ethics.

So there is a necessary and timely corrective, found in communitarian Christian ethics, to the problems of liberal theology. But it is a pity that neither Milbank nor Hauerwas's writing style suggests that they recognize such a corrective role for themselves or others. Their intention is to expose the vacuity of liberalism and declare its obsolescence, not to correct its malformation. Nor, of course, do either give the slightest hint that the despised liberal tradition may have any corrective role for them. But if an Age of Incarnation has been overtaken by an Age of Atonement, and if this is not a once-for-all but a repeating pattern, then the gaps in communitarian thinking – principally, perhaps, around the question of how traditions are to encounter one another peaceably – may suggest that a 'liberal' corrective to Milbank and Hauerwas might be a next step to contemplate. To be sure, this next phase of liberalism will not look like the old version. Too much has changed in the social context of the Churches and too many of the communitarian's criticisms have been well-founded. But Hauerwas himself has hinted at the possibility of liberalism's virtues becoming separated from liberalism's hubristic claim to have transcended tradition.

In the next chapter, we will look further at the possibility that a public theology for plural times might be capable of reconstruction, attempting to harness the strengths both of the communitarians and of the liberal theological tradition.

Further reading

Stanley Hauerwas is a prolific author and all his books are worth reading. The collection in *The Hauerwas Reader*, noted in the chapter above, is an excellent introduction to the range of his work. A very good collection of essays, engaging with Hauerwas's work from a variety of perspectives, can be found in: Mark Thiessen Nation and Samuel Wells (eds), *Faithfulness and Fortitude: In Conversation with the Theological Ethics of Stanley Hauerwas*, Edinburgh: T&T Clark, 2000. For an extended reflection on what a Hauerwasian ethic might look like in the practices of real life, see: Charles R. Pinches, *A Gathering of Memories: Family, Nation and Church in a Forgetful World*, Grand Rapids, MI: Brazos Press, 2006.

The following journals have devoted whole issues to a consideration of John Milbank's theology: *Modern Theology* 8.4 (1992), and 15.4 (1999); *New Blackfriars* vol. 73, no. 861, 1992. Milbank's ideas are taken further in: John Milbank, Catherine Pickstock and Graham Ward (eds), *Radical Orthodoxy: A New Theology*, London and New York: Routledge, 1999.

7

The possibility of a public theology

The previous chapters have been leading up to this question: Where is the proper location for Christian ethics? Should we conceive Christian ethics as the private conversation of the Church about the nature of the good and the Church's internal conception of justice? Or is Christian ethics also a discipline with a public dimension? In other words, is Christian ethics about the lives of Christians as church members or their lives as citizens? Is it an internal language intelligible only to believers or can Christian ethics enable believers to collaborate with others for the common good?

The twentieth-century inheritance, within the Western Churches at least, is of a very public role for Christian ethics as the Churches have striven to make their moral engagement with wider society a central justification for their existence. For all the weaknesses of the middle-axiom approach, the expectation that the Churches will continue to talk about ethics in public remains strong, both within the Churches and beyond them.

Of course, the context has changed since the 1940s. Temple began *Christianity and Social Order* with a reminder that the common assumption (even in 1942) that religion and politics should not mix was a very recent heresy not borne out by the history of Church and state. We can see now that, while Temple was not himself convinced by the romantic mediaevalism of the Christendom movement, his own thinking nevertheless reflected the enduring legacy of Christendom as a concept. The fact that a presumption of separation between church and political life is a recent phenomenon is, in one sense, neither here nor there. Hauerwas, in particular, would regard such a connection between Church and state as a wrong turning taken back in the fourth century from which it is still not too late for the Church to recover. His vision of what the Church should be in relation to politics and the public sphere is poles apart from Temple's. It is worth at this stage asking which of them (given that they were writing forty years apart) has an ecclesiology which offers the best 'fit' for the Church of today.

Britain and America: perspectives in tension

Here, the differences between an American and a British perspective are significant, especially for English Anglicans who are still part of an established, state Church. This is not the place to go into the arguments for and against establishment, although the fact that England is a monarchy and that the monarch is titular head of the Church suggests that the Church is deeply embedded in the constitutional life of the nation, and that unpicking establishment would mean a radical rethinking of Crown, Parliament and the English version of democracy. Nevertheless, something approaching a 'free market' of faiths on a model familiar to Americans is perhaps closer to the way religion is perceived in Britain from the point of view of the average citizen. The assumption that Christian ideas should take a public role in shaping social behaviour and laws is far from universally held. Indeed, in a culture which has a very sketchy understanding of history (a lament of Temple's at the time of *Christianity and Social Order* but far more obviously the case today), the fact that Christian ideas actually do stand at the heart of many of the country's social institutions and structures of government hardly enters the public consciousness. But because the Church has a long history of public ethical engagement, and is widely expected to go on doing so (even when people choose not to listen to it), adopting a more Hauerwasian indifference to public life would mean a conscious decision to abandon a great deal of ecclesial history and practice.

For the British churches, and especially the Church of England, much turns upon the answer to a fundamentally political and cultural question. Britain has often been characterized as a country which does not know whether to look across the Channel or across the Atlantic to find its identity and destiny, and this ambivalence about things American and things European crops up constantly in cultural and public life. Historically, Britain and continental Europe are interwoven at innumerable levels, despite deep-seated antagonisms and major fractures such as world wars. In church terms, that is reflected in the continued existence of state churches in Germany and the Nordic countries, along with the persistent influence of 'traditional' churches – Catholic, Lutheran or Reformed – in countries which have to a great extent separated Church and state. The problem, as the British sociologist of religion Grace Davie has pointed out very clearly, is that it is precisely in Europe that the decline of churchgoing has appeared to validate the secularist's theory that religion inevitably withers in the face of modernity's technological and material progress. This, she argues, is almost exclusively a European phenomenon: in other continents, religion in general and often Christianity in particular continue to flourish in defiance of the secularist's expectations.[1]

So it is not surprising that, as an antidote to decline, Christians in Britain are frequently attracted to the religiosity of America. Of course, the attraction of American culture and social institutions – even envy of them – extends well beyond the sphere of religion. The USA has, from its foundation, maintained the separation of Church and state, and although this is under attack from some quarters, it is a separation which has done much to

---

[1] Grace Davie, *Europe the Exceptional Case: Parameters of Faith in the Modern World*, London: Darton, Longman and Todd, 2002.

mould the unique shape of Christian allegiance and observance in America today.

In America, public theology and Christian ethics are often conducted in a confrontational, culture-wars, style in which Christians portray themselves as the beleaguered underdogs oppressed by the liberal majority. At the same time, Christianity claims to be a dominant force which sets the cultural rules, and this is reinforced in the impossibility of conceiving an electable presidential candidate who lacks a very public display of Christian commitment. The attempts, during the 2008 presidential contest, to portray Barack Obama as a Muslim (a ploy which, according to a poll by the University of Texas, convinced 23 per cent of Texans)[2] bear witness to the importance of Christian identity in the politics of a nation that still prides itself on being a melting-pot of races and beliefs. As we have seen, it is this close identification of being Christian with being American that agitates Hauerwas and drives him to conclude that distinctively Christian ethics are the casualty of such an alliance.

Approaches to theology in public: liberals and communitarians

We can therefore discern a variety of possible stances for doing Christian ethics in the public sphere.

First, we have the Temple/Preston option – building on whatever is left of the Church's standing as part of the fabric of national life and trusting to the enduring possibilities enshrined in the liberal vision of universal reason which, however partial and flawed, could still form the basis for a worthwhile conversation between Christian ethics and other understandings of the good.

But we have already seen some of the weaknesses of this tradition in practice – not only weaknesses caused by the shifting position of the Church in society but intrinsic weaknesses which constrain the ability of this method to offer the kind of challenge to conventional thinking that the gap between Christian perceptions and secular ones seems to demand.

Second, there is the approach which treats Christian ethics as the narrative of the Church's own life, grounded in the specific stories and traditions of the Christian community and essentially impenetrable to those who are not already steeped in those traditions. To understand Christian ethics one must simply assent to the faith of the Church and understand from the practice of Christians, rather than from propositional knowledge, what they conceive to be the good. Hauerwas is the great champion of this mode of Christian ethics and, despite the essentially American context within which he writes,

---

[2] *The Guardian*, 31 October 2008, p. 23.

his ideas have been explored very suggestively by the English priest and scholar Samuel Wells.[3]

This approach becomes more problematic when it is suggested that most people operate as moral beings in a whole range of cultural communities as well as the Church. How are the moral perceptions from church life to be translated into the context of, say, the workplace or the political party? Or if they are not to be so translated, how is a person to live a life of moral integrity without confining his or her activities solely to transactions between Christians? Indeed, it is not at all clear how Hauerwas is able to have any real ethical engagement with the market economy which so dominates everyone's life across the world. As we shall see in Chapter 10 when we look in detail at ethics and market economics, the market is predicated upon an agreement about means rather than ends, and might, in theory, be a system which Christians and all faiths could endorse since it does not require them to abjure their fundamental beliefs. But the market's outcomes do not invariably accord with Christian ideals, for while many churches live comfortably in a market economy and many of their members are articulate supporters of market principles, few in the Churches have really given up on the idea that ends matter and that there are principles of justice – including distributional justice – which are non-negotiable and grounded in Christian narratives. To engage ethically with the market, Christians and others must address the question to which the market is part of the answer: How are peoples of diverse moral traditions to agree on questions of value? Milbank's half-turn back to pre-modernity and Hauerwas's indifference to dialogue across diverse traditions do not begin to meet this point. So treating the market economy, for a moment, as a test case for Christian ethics, some form of ethical discourse beyond the 'household of faith' seems unavoidable. The communitarian tradition in Christian ethics, while certainly addressing weaknesses and failings within liberal approaches, does not quite supply the tools for Christian ethics to do what Christians and the Church often want it to do.

The Christian right

Third, there is the approach to Christian ethical engagement in the public sphere adopted by the conservative Christian right – and not only in America, for the style and content of this approach are becoming part of the landscape in most parts of the world, although not always with the same political profile. This approach is not a major type of Christian ethics in an academic sense, but it nonetheless manages to combine the overt intention to address and

---

[3] Samuel Wells, *Transforming Fate into Destiny: The Theological Ethics of Stanley Hauerwas*, Carlisle: Paternoster Press, 1998.
  Mark Thiessen Nation and Samuel Wells (eds), *Faithfulness and Fortitude: In Conversation with the Theological Ethics of Stanley Hauerwas*, Edinburgh: T&T Clark, 2000.

transform the public and political spheres of life with the 'closed' account of dialogue with other traditions which characterizes the communitarians.

The Christian right mode of ethics is not easy to categorize theologically. It appears to start with a strong commitment to particular political programmes which are then justified on theological or biblical grounds, although the use of theology and Scripture may be selective and pre-critical. An interesting case study might be made of the vice-presidential campaign run by Sarah Palin for the Republican Party in 2008. The right-wing commentator and 'shock jock' Rush Limbaugh summed up Palin as standing for 'Guns, babies and Jesus' – a frightening combination of ethical stances for most Europeans. But behind those three words stands a perfectly comprehensible political programme, if one which contains interesting potential contradictions. Guns are the symbol of rugged American individualism, the right to bear arms reflecting the historic suspicion of federal government and making the self-reliant individual the key to understanding moral agency. This individualism can be seen to be one of the bedrocks of liberalism, despite the contempt with which that word is treated by the right. The focus on babies – that is, opposition to abortion – places the individual moral agent within a system of patriarchy in which the concept of a woman's 'right' as an individual to choose whether to continue a pregnancy is circumscribed by her subordinate role as childbearer (of course, there are other arguments against abortion, but my point here is the understanding of moral agency). In this restricted under-standing of human rights, the liberal individualism of the Christian right is incompatible with the individual moral agency of women. Commitment to Jesus locates Palin on the side of a particular brand of religion which validates and blesses the whole right-wing programme of free markets, individualism and military strength, and which simultaneously renders non-believers and Christians of other traditions as essentially 'other'. Indeed, one motif of Palin's campaign speeches was the constant implication that those who disagreed with her were part of another America, or even anti-American in their values. In all this, the inherent and unexplored contradiction is between the celebration of the individual and the essentially communitarian framework of a tightly controlled brand of religiosity. Is the Christian right's primary building-block the self-reliant individual and his family, the Church as a community of virtue or the nation as a potential theocracy? It is hard to tell, but reconciling the liberal strand of individualism and the communitarian strand of authoritarian ethics is always a juggling act for any political party which seeks social control alongside unregulated markets.

Inconsistencies of this sort do not fully explain the ethical approach of the Christian right – and at this point we come up again against the complex ambiguities of the word 'liberal'. Almost nothing could be less 'liberal', in the sense of tolerant, comfortable with ideas of human progress and willing to compromise with others, than the political programme of the Christian right. Yet precisely because it is a movement founded on a political programme, to which a comprehensive theology, a non-selective reading of Scripture and a concern for doctrinal consistency come a good way second, it has all the hallmarks of those liberal theologies which constantly make theological insights subordinate to a prior commitment to some political programme. If we are seeking a truly theological Christian ethic which can still engage in dialogue with other traditions, this is not the place to look.

It is a moot point whether the ethical stridency of the American Christian right should be called counter-cultural. Insofar as American (and European) societies are essentially pluralistic, committed to equality of races and sexes, and maintain some separation of politics and religion, the Christian right poses a significant challenge to the prevailing culture. Certainly, the claim to be that paradoxical thing, a beleaguered majority, is central to their campaigning stance. But in their uncritical enthusiasm for an unfettered market economy, for military power and for freedom conceived in a very individualistic yet patriarchal way, we are looking here at the dominant culture writ very large.

Finding a way forward in public Christian ethics

Are the approaches just outlined above our only options? Are we to be caught forever between the risk of theological vacuity associated with liberal ethics, and the insularity of a Church which treats its ethics as incomprehensible to outsiders, with only strident assertion of an authoritarian political programme as a third way? In other words, is there a coherent way of bringing together liberalism's commitment to dialogue and contingency (which reflects a concern to keep the theological interim in view) and communitarianism's deep engagement with the Christian tradition in all its surprising uniqueness?

If the liberal tradition was so concerned for relevance that it had nothing left to say about God and Christ, and the communitarian tradition is so concerned with Christian distinctiveness that it is incomprehensible to those beyond the household of faith, maybe an examination of words like 'relevant' and 'distinctive' can help us see what is at stake here.

Relevance is a weasel word, defying clear definition. If I am in a foreign country and about to drive the wrong way down a one-way street, the advice I receive from a passing policeman may be incomprehensible to me but is certainly relevant to my condition. Similarly, if I, a Christian, am in conversation with a hedonist libertine, I will surely believe that my attempts to convert him to a different way of seeing the world are entirely relevant to his well-being even though he may neither share my belief in God nor understand how anything I may say could be of use to him. Too often, the search for relevance fails to ask who determines the criteria against which the irrelevant can be discarded – and in terms of Christian ethical encounters in public, it frequently hands the control of criteria almost unthinkingly to others.

Nevertheless, the search for relevance can be interpreted as the attempt to find just enough common ground to support a connection. Relevance, in this sense, is a mutual thing – it is not about the relevance of what I want to say in terms of your ability to hear it, but the relevance of our respective frames of reference to one another. In terms of Christian ethics, it may be the first step towards communicating the concerns of one community in the context of another – a first step towards the possibility of a public theology.

The word 'distinctive' is easier to handle. My position can be said to be distinctive if no one else shares it. Christian ethics is distinctive, in this sense, if it is an ethic derived from Christian theology and no one who does not share the foundational narratives of the faith can arrive at the same position. One can see hints of this sort of distinctiveness when Christians use the concept of sanctity in relation to human life. Others might have some sense of what they mean but cannot penetrate the reasoning processes by which life is said to be sacred since the Christian concept of sanctity derives directly from the nature of the Christian God. You have to believe – or at least start to grasp – the theology before you can understand the ethics.

Two questions remain. First, is the Christian narrative in fact so private to the faithful that it cannot communicate to others with any meaningful content? Second, is the whole idea of Christian distinctiveness actually so important to a theological approach to ethics? Here, the British theologian and ethicist Nigel Biggar has some useful things to say.

Biggar is especially interesting because he stands within the Barthian tradition of Christian ethics in which the deductive approach is paramount. In other words, Biggar is concerned that Christian ethics should be constructed on the basis of God's unique self-revelation in Christ as mediated through Scripture, and is suspicious of the liberal tendency to start with other foundations and see whether a Christian edifice can be built upon them. So Biggar, coming out of this stable and a self-professed conservative in theological terms, might be expected to place a heavy premium on the distinctiveness of Christian ethics.

However, Biggar is also concerned that Christian ethics should play a part in public discourse. He is not willing to sacrifice either the foundation of the Christian narratives or the obligation of Christian ethics to attempt to shape the world around it. To allow these two concerns to be addressed together, he makes the interesting move from distinctiveness to authenticity as his central term. What matters, he argues, is not that Christians should hold ethical positions which no one else can hold, but that the positions they do hold should be arrived at theologically.[4] Thus, Christians and others may find themselves on the same side of the moral barricades from time to time, although they may have arrived there via quite different arguments based on

---

[4] Nigel Biggar, 'A Methodological Interlude: A Case for Rapprochement between Moral Theology and Moral Philosophy', in Mark Bratton (ed.), *God, Ethics and the Human Genome*, London: Church House Publishing, 2009.

greatly varying premises which will not be held in common. Nevertheless, the very fact of sharing moral convictions opens the door to the possibility of dialogue and the hope that the reasoning of members of differing traditions may not be totally opaque to one another.

This position places Biggar at odds with Hauerwas's confrontational stance towards liberalism. In an extended essay on this theme, Biggar starts with the impact of 9/11 and the London bombings of 7/7 – incontrovertible evidence that 'there are theologies that are frightful enemies of public reason in an ideologically plural society' – and draws the conclusion that, in the face of this kind of religiously inspired extremism, even those who retain serious doubts about some aspects of liberal culture are nonetheless committed to a liberal culture of some sort.[5]

Biggar goes on to examine the theological arguments which he himself deploys in his earlier book about euthanasia, and explores the potential for members of other ethical traditions to share moral ground with him.[6] We will return to arguments about euthanasia in Chapter 9; what matters at this point is to note that Biggar's arguments are thoroughly theological in the sense that they are 'shaped by theology at every appropriate point and in the appropriate manner'.[7] He goes on to suggest, not that secularists or members of other traditions will agree with his conclusions, but that they may recognize the role which belief in God and commitment to Christian narratives play in his arguments, and those arguments will not necessarily be opaque to them. So, for example, the humanist who holds that the value of a human life is supreme may come to recognize that this very principle can be affirmed and flourish within a theistic framework. They may even come to agree with the Christian that it is precisely in the context of belief in God that the equal yet supreme value of human lives can be secured. Even the acknowledgement by non-believers that a theologically informed contribution to ethics is capable of arriving at conclusions with which they may engage fruitfully can be worth having.

So, Biggar goes on, the humanist or secularist may share with the theist a belief that there are serious limits to consequentialist arguments. For the theist, the grounds for suspicion of consequentialism may be that, as God's will is not fully known, and as God is active in the world, it is not for human agents to say with confidence what the consequences of their actions will be. But even without belief in any god, there might be agreement that attempting to predict consequences is often hubristic because it demands greater knowledge than any person can lay claim to. (That, after all, is one of the key arguments for market economics: the attempt to secure particular outcomes is frustrated by the impossibility of predicting the collective

---

[5] Nigel Biggar, 'God in Public Reason', *Studies in Christian Ethics* 19.1 (2006), p. 9.
[6] Nigel Biggar, *Aiming to Kill: The Ethics of Suicide and Euthanasia*, London: Darton, Longman and Todd, 2004.
[7] Biggar, 'God in Public Reason', p. 13.

outcome of millions of individual transactions.) And while the Christian may be sceptical of the ability of laws, conventions and regulatory bodies to maintain ethical boundaries, on the grounds that human sin constantly erodes the common good in the name of sectional advantage, the secularist might make a careful appraisal of modern history and draw a similar conclusion on the basis of the demonstrable fragility of human civilization.

From these arguments, the idea of a public theology may be less of a dead-end than Hauerwas likes to think. The main difference between Hauerwas and Biggar is not that one is a communitarian and the other a liberal – both draw upon a similar strand of deductive, deontological ethical reasoning which is well outside the liberal tradition. But whereas Hauerwas is Cassandra-like in his despair at the direction of (American) liberal society, Biggar is moved by the implications of violent religious separatism to argue for an account of liberal virtue, focusing especially on the commitment to dialogue. This is not merely a theological or philosophical position. Biggar is arguing, not only against the religious extremism that led to 9/11 and 7/7, but also against the secularist and humanist reactions to those events which rapidly characterized all religious intervention in the public sphere as invalid. Since the most publicly prominent manifestations of religion entering the political arena were terrorist outrages on the one hand and the know-nothing stridency of Christian fundamentalism on the other, and with the memory of the Niebuhr or Temple traditions already fading in a culture that sits light to its own history, many pundits and commentators see religion only as irrational, impenetrable and potentially violent. According to this parody, religious people believe their ethical decisions are dictated to them by an imaginary, all-powerful being in the sky, whose followers exploit human dissatisfactions and the power of irrationality and strive to bring the whole world under their ideological control. Religion, in other words, is fascistic totalitarianism with the added ingredient of blatant mediaeval superstition.[8]

The difficulty is that there is enough of that sort of religion around for the secularist parody to have some purchase on the public imagination. The collapse in confidence of the liberal theological tradition, and the consequent retreat of theological argument from the public sphere, has left the field open to annexation by the kinds of religion which have no truck with plurality or with reasoned argumentation but which resort to violence (verbal, as well as physical or military) as an early gambit to protect their cultures. The trend in academic theology to spurn the tradition-transcendent pretensions of liberalism and concentrate upon the distinctiveness and counter-cultural nature of the Christian narratives has, perhaps, reinforced the perception that faith is an impenetrable mystery to those who remain outside its communities. Of course, where Milbank and Hauerwas part company with the jihadists and

---

[8] This theme recurs in the work of Richard Dawkins, Christopher Hitchens and Polly Toynbee. See: Dawkins, *The God Delusion*, London: Bantam Books, 2006; Hitchens, *God is not Great*, New York: Twelve Books, 2007; and the journalism of Toynbee in *The Guardian* newspaper.

Christian extremists is in their foundational commitment to the concept of peace and non-violence as the heart of the Christian story. But their weakness, as we have seen, is their lack of interest in negotiating shared positions with traditions beyond their own, and their indifference to the political structures which, by maintaining a plural culture, paradoxically preserve their freedom to dissent from pluralism. For Biggar, the alarming implications of religious separatism and intolerance are sufficient reason to seek some rediscovery of the liberal virtues that have created the political climate within which Christian faith and practice have flourished.

Piecing together a moral dialogue

But can we take matters further than the almost accidental sharing of ethical positions, arrived at through varying processes of narrative and argument, which Biggar describes? Are there elements within a Christian account of the world and of being human which might reinforce the Church's commitment to wider dialogue and give it some indication of what kind of dialogues might be fruitful? By fruitful, I mean not only dialogues which might promote the validity, beauty and completeness of Christian accounts of the good, but which might enable the Church to understand its own traditions better through an encounter with others. Here, I shall draw first on the work of two British theologians, Andrew Shanks and Peter Selby.

Andrew Shanks on civil religion

Proper attention to Christian identity, the freedom and tolerance entailed in dialogue, and the choice of dialogue partners, come together in Andrew Shanks's exploration of civil religion.[9] Civil religion, he says, is about exploring the connections between one's role as a member of the confessing community and as a citizen of a wider society.

> All religion is about the definition of social identity – but which identity? . . . confessional religion (i.e. religion shaped by confessional theology) takes shape as a meditation on the identity deriving from the worshippers' membership within the worshipping community itself . . . Whereas by contrast, civil religion is a meditation – within the context of otherwise confessional worship – on the worshippers' other identity as *citizens*.[10]

Crucially, then, Shanks sets out to offer a theology underpinning social engagement through a Church living within a plural civil society. This is approached, not through the suppression of Christian identity in order for the Church to take its place within liberal discourse, but by understanding that identity entails membership and participation in society and politics as well as in the (counter-cultural) Church. Shanks is therefore another critic

---

[9] Andrew Shanks, *Civil Society, Civil Religion*, Oxford: Blackwell, 1995.
[10] Shanks, *Civil Society, Civil Religion*, p. 2.

of the 'closed' accounts of disagreement offered within the confessional/ communitarian theological traditions (seeing Barth's confessionalism as preventing him from expressing solidarity with the Jews under Hitler), without making recourse to liberal assumptions about transcending the particularities of tradition.

Shanks codifies three key sets of virtues for a theological/religious involvement in civil society:

- *solidarity of the shaken*: solidarity on the basis of a shared commitment to anti–ideological thoughtfulness and the values of *isonomy* (direct spontaneous participation in public affairs) ...
- *the virtues of sanctity*: living a life which perfectly embodies the values of one's own culture ...
- *the virtues of transgression*: crossing over the boundaries between one's own culture and other cultures, in order to interpret each to the other, as effectively as possible.[11]

What Shanks calls the virtue of sanctity is a mark of his attentiveness to the question of Christian distinctiveness. In a plural context, embodying the values of one's own culture is the antithesis of liberal normlessness – it entails the exploration of the practice (in the MacIntyrean sense) of living in a tradition-constituted community, and involves an account of the virtues.

However, the virtues of sanctity are balanced by the virtues of transgression. This is how Shanks encapsulates the principle of encounter and dialogue between traditions and, in focusing on the interpretation of one to another, assumes the possibility of translatability. Whereas Markham sees dialogue as intrinsic to Christian theology (although abused and misunderstood by the Churches), Shanks, understanding dialogue to be no less intrinsically Christian, sees a deeper conflict between authentic Christian practice and the institution of the Church. It is not just a matter of ignorance or error that the Church has preferred closed, confessional accounts of difference, but of the history of the Church itself, dominated by a 'pastoral monoculture' evolved in the face of persecution and clung to in a 'neurotic' manner long after the circumstances that gave it birth have ended.[12] Thus, crossing the boundaries between the Church and other traditions is perceived as transgressive – but Shanks affirms and celebrates this as a part of Christian identity equal in importance to the virtue of sanctity. However, he goes beyond Markham's focus on dialogue to set out terms for choosing the dialogues we take part in:

> the question of theological method is, very largely, a question of *with whom* one chooses to be in dialogue, and on what terms. The Barthian approach dictates that the theologian is chiefly in dialogue with his or her fellow church

---

[11] Andrew Shanks, 'A Theological Context for Urban/Industrial Mission', privately circulated paper, 2006, p. 3. These ideas appear in a less succinct but more fully developed form in *Civil Society, Civil Religion*.

[12] Shanks, *Civil Society, Civil Religion*, p. 91.

members, and only very secondarily, or incidentally, in dialogue with any part of the outside world.[13]

Shanks is here setting out his case against the communitarian confessionalism of Barth and of Milbank. The 'solidarity of the shaken' (the term is taken from Jan Patočka) is about 'solidarity among those "shaken" by the loss of ahistorical meaning, hitherto inherent in the apparent naturalness of moral and religious custom'.[14] It is thus part of Shanks's response to the position of religion within the crisis of liberal modernity, but extends beyond the particular crisis of liberal theology to explore commonalities with other groupings and traditions who share a sense of crisis. This is about solidarity among those who share the very predicament with which MacIntyre opens *After Virtue* – people brought together in a highly diverse grouping, 'united not by any common political ideology or orientation, but solely by a common concern for the moral quality of public life in their country'.[15]

While Shanks draws expressly on his own extensive experience in the Czech Republic, before, during and after the end of Communism, a possibly more trivial but revealing example from Western politics might be taken from the rise of the environmental movement and its ability to transcend old boundaries of class and economic interest through a shared sense of 'shakenness'. I recall a telling moment on British radio during the 1990s when the controversial second runway at Manchester airport was under construction and various groups of environmentalists were engaged in direct action to disrupt the project. Many of the activists were young eco-warriors, veterans of several such campaigns and unafraid to dig and occupy tunnels under the workings or to build encampments in trees scheduled for felling. Their lifestyle was that of the hippy communes and their attitude to authority confrontational. But the second runway was also opposed by the wealthy communities of nearby Cheshire settlements like Knutsford and Wilmslow (the latter town renowned for having the most lucrative Porsche dealership in Britain). It transpired that the residents of the neighbouring villages were clandestinely crossing security lines to take provisions to the protesters and welcoming the latter back to their immaculate homes for baths and respite – all this involving a certain risk and defiance of the law. On the BBC, one woman resident of Knutsford was moved to proclaim loudly that those taking direct action were 'People like us!' – and I reflected at that moment on the power of 'shakenness' to create this level of fellow-feeling across social boundaries which would, in other circumstances, tend to provoke disdain rather than a common sense of identity. Nor was this just a case of temporary shared self-interest, for the eco-warriors and the local residents had both been

---

[13] Shanks, *Civil Society, Civil Religion*, p. 83.
[14] Shanks, *Civil Society, Civil Religion*, p. 115.
[15] Shanks, *Civil Society, Civil Religion*, p. 116.

dismayed at the way in which the decision to build the runway had been steamrollered through, and both groups perceived very clearly that the assumptions about democracy, due process, respect for diverse opinions and so on were not as they had once assumed them to be. A superficial example, perhaps – but one which fleetingly demonstrated that shared perceptions of shakenness, in Shanks's sense of the term, hold potential to enable communicative dialogue across seemingly unbridgeable social gulfs.

Shanks expresses the limitations of confessional communitarian theologies in terms of their inability to enter genuine dialogue. He is not sympathetic to communitarian trends in theology, yet in his concentration on identity questions, and in his analysis of the crisis of modernity, he is no straight-forward liberal. He draws attention to Bonhoeffer's gradual movement away from Barth's exclusive confessionalism – and this is significant, because Bonhoeffer also provides the foundations for Selby's approach to the questions of identity, dialogue and solidarity which bears some resemblance to Shanks's, yet draws more strongly communitarian conclusions.

Peter Selby on Christ for us today

Peter Selby takes Bonhoeffer's Christological question, 'Who is Jesus Christ for us today?'[16] and analyses it in three parts as: the question of identity (Who?), the challenge of discernment (Whose 'today' is it to be?) and the question of solidarity (Who is 'us'?).[17] This exploration of Christology leads not only towards the distinctive nature of the Christian community, but to the question of which alliances that community will make and for whose cause it will stand. By stressing the immediacy of 'today', Selby introduces an explicit contextuality – Christian identity leads into alliances and solidarities that are not detached from the contingent and finite nature of concrete situations.

> The claim to know what today is, its cultural shape and character, is ultimately a claim to prescribe the framework into which Christ must be fitted. The claim is inevitably patrician: the today that is being referred to is the today of those in power today, those who form the culture of today. Theirs will not be the descriptions of the today of the dispossessed . . .[18]

The question of identity (Who are we? – the 'we' who ask the question) is for Selby the central issue of Christian distinctiveness and, in common with Hauerwas as well as Shanks, he understands the question to be espe-cially pressing in a period when old understandings are decaying and new

[16] Dietrich Bonhoeffer, *Letters and Papers from Prison*, ed. Eberhard Bethge, London: SCM Press, 1971, p. 279.
[17] Peter Selby, *Grace and Mortgage: The Language of Faith and the Debt of the World*, London: Darton, Longman and Todd, 1997, pp. 10ff., 119.
[18] Selby, *Grace and Mortgage*, p. 20.

frameworks only tentatively emerging: 'the question of identity, ours and Christ's, arises with special force in a world where *religious* identity and identifiability can no longer be assumed'.[19]

Selby also sees solidarity beyond the Christian community as inseparable from the community's own identity, understanding engagement with wider society to be intrinsic to the Churches' task. Again, this is more than a general disposition towards dialogue: 'the question of "us" is the issue of the boundaries of our solidarity, the territory beyond which all we see is "just a bunch of strangers"'.[20]

So the choice of allies, or dialogue partners, is crucial, and more than a matter of pragmatism since it must reflect 'Christ's refusal to accommodate to any self-chosen "us"'.[21] In other words, the choice of allies and partners takes place in the context of a continuing reflection on the Christological foundations of our own identity.

Selby's work is especially interesting because he applies his analysis of theological method to questions of the economy – specifically, the nature of debt and indebtedness within the local, national and global economies of today.[22] His exegesis of Bonhoeffer's question is therefore specifically tied to this issue:

> asking who Christ is means asking who *we* are *economically*: debtor? creditor? disciple seeking a community of jubilee? So too the economy obliges us to ask who is the 'us' we mean when we speak of 'Jesus Christ for *us* today': with whom do we locate ourselves in a world of injustice – with those who have or those who have not? And we are asked too, whose 'today' we have in mind – the today of those who have control of the economy and who decide its timetable, or of those who juggle their debts . . .[23]

Whereas Shanks's theology points towards alliances of those shaken by the loss of frameworks of meaning, Selby is led by a similar process towards choices of alliances grounded in economic experience – not poverty as such, but the dependency of indebtedness. By his analysis of the social pervasiveness of debt, Selby avoids any simplistic notion of 'the poor'. In the end, the contradiction between the logic of debt and the message of the gospel is too great for compromise. Only a confessional stance, emphasizing the nature of freedom in Christ, is adequate to resource the requirements of solidarity, and at the centre of this counter-cultural stance is the life of the Christian congregation.

---

[19] Selby, *Grace and Mortgage*, p. 18.
[20] Selby, *Grace and Mortgage*, p. 22.
[21] Selby, *Grace and Mortgage*, p. 23.
[22] At the 1998 Lambeth Conference, Selby led the sessions on global debt, thus seeking to put into practice his commitment to a theological engagement with political and economic realities through the mobilization of the confessional community (or at least its bishops).
[23] Selby, *Grace and Mortgage*, p. 143.

The similarities between Selby's and Shanks's methodologies suggests that here are the beginnings of an approach that can bridge the dichotomy between 'more liberal' and 'more communitarian' theologies.

This is not all that can be said about the emerging new model for public theology. With Markham, we have seen that the liberal values of tolerance and dialogue can begin to be justified on theological grounds. Biggar has explored the case for maintaining a public dimension to Christian ethics which must draw from the liberal tradition at least a basic commitment to dialogue while remaining resolutely theological. Selby and Shanks suggest something of what such a process might look like. What more might we say, then, about the content of a public theology? At this point we introduce two further voices from contemporary Christian ethics: Duncan Forrester and Jeffrey Stout.

Duncan Forrester and 'theological fragments'

Forrester (who seeks to bring communitarian perspectives into a critique of middle axioms) maintains both an attentiveness to the Christian tradition and an openness to dialogue by confining his discussion of content to the idea of 'fragments'.[24] In this, he draws on MacIntyre, noting that the 'apocalyptic' opening of *After Virtue* corresponds with the experience of practitioners on the ground trying to make a coherent engagement between theology and public life. But the fragments of moral insight, which are all that remain, are not negligible – indeed the understanding that there are no complete systematic theories to be had is a reflection of the theological interim in which there is no complete certainty at all. So 'when a fragment is recognized as in some sense true, one should expect an interest in its provenance, in its embeddedness in a broader truth'.[25]

Thus, on questions of social justice (the concept that Hayek, for example, rejects as completely meaningless) Forrester brings to bear a fragment from the Judaeo-Christian tradition to the effect that justice is best understood in relational terms (between God and humanity and between human beings) and is thus expressed in the obligations and responsibilities that tie people together in society. The covenant relationship (which Forrester brings forward as the fragment informing the idea of social justice) places limits on the exercise of self-interest, and such limits are set by the obligation of care towards those who cannot contribute directly towards production.

Forrester's introduction of the fragments of a tradition into a wider social debate makes sense in terms of MacIntyre's idea that 'the good' is best expressed as *the quest* for the good. If, with MacIntyre and Forrester, we accept that, in the current condition, fragments of moral discourse are all we have, and accept in addition a degree of translatability between even fragmentary traditions,

---

[24] Duncan Forrester, *Christian Justice and Public Policy*, Cambridge: Cambridge University Press, 1997, pp. 193ff.

[25] Forrester, *Christian Justice and Public Policy*, p. 203.

then an emerging shared moral language becomes possible. Because (even on MacIntyre's terms) the users of moral fragments still believe themselves to be working with moral concepts, and even those who recognize the fragmentary nature of their discourse still want to be able to debate morality, the struggle for understanding and dialogue remains essential. As Stout puts it:

> If we want to understand our fellow citizens – whether they be Dorothy Day, Martin Luther King Jnr., Jerry Falwell, the Roman Catholic Bishops, Mario Cuomo or Elie Wiesel – we had better develop the means for understanding the moral languages, including the theological ones, in which they occasionally address us and in which their deliberation is couched.[26]

Jeffrey Stout's moral bricolage

The process of working among fragments is described by Stout as *moral bricolage*:

> The process in which one begins with bits and pieces of received linguistic material, arranges some of them into a structured whole, leaves others to the side, and ends up with a moral language one proposes to use.[27]

So fragments of the (Christian) traditions may, if in dialogue with other fragments of tradition, lead not only in the direction of their provenance in the deeper tradition (Forrester) but towards the discovery of common elements and themes in a useable, and essentially new, moral language (Stout).[28] But have Stout and Forrester assumed too quickly, with MacIntyre, that fragments are all we have? Might it be possible to rebuild from the fragments something more like the substantive tradition from which they came?

An example of such an attempt is offered by Nigel Biggar and Donald Hay (interestingly, addressed to the question of social security provision), who set out to argue, *contra* Preston, that the fragments which together make up a biblical tradition on economics can be of direct application to contemporary economic problems. This is not to suggest that a biblical ethic can be 'lifted intact' from its scriptural context:

> Rather, it necessarily involves the *construction* of a coherent ethic out of biblical bits and pieces – although, to be sure, this construction is not a *creatio ex nihilo*, but is beholden to the truths that the Bible discloses.[29]

Biggar and Hay establish the important point that the process of constructing a moral narrative from fragments may be pursued within a tradition as well

---

[26] Jeffrey Stout, *Ethics After Babel: The Languages of Morals and Their Discontents*, Cambridge: James Clarke, 1988, p. 188.

[27] Stout, *Ethics After Babel*, p. 294.

[28] Stout goes on to describe the stages of reconstructing moral language from fragments as moving from *moral pidgin* to *moral creole* (i.e. developing over time the richness to be used as a language of reflection) but stopping short of the unrealistically optimistic *moral Esperanto*.

[29] Nigel Biggar and Donald Hay, 'The Bible, Christian Ethics and the Provision of Social Security', *Studies in Christian Ethics* 7.2 (1994), p. 45.

as between traditions. Biggar's work with Hay shows that, even before 9/11 pushed him to suggest that 'we are all liberals now',[30] he was alert to the need for Christian ethics to maintain its voice in the public realm, but it is in his later work that he focuses more explicitly on how the process of exploring the tradition from within goes on to engage with those beyond.

So it appears that confessional communitarians like Biggar can move beyond the closed account of Christian ethics, which can only be understood from within the Christian community, to a position which accepts the necessity of dialogue with other traditions and is comfortable that this is possible without privileging some liberal account of universal reason and subordinating all that is particular to the Christian story. It is equally clear that theologians starting out from a more liberal perspective, like Shanks and, to some extent, Selby, nonetheless draw upon the Christian story very strongly in order to, first, underpin the necessity for dialogue and, second, to discern how and with whom dialogue can take place. The apparent stand-off between liberals and confessional communitarians is not necessarily irreconcilable.

The shape of a renewed public theology

There is still a great deal of work to be done before all this emerges as a robust practice of public theology. But the outlines are in place as a preliminary guide to how the Churches might pursue a public dialogue in a plural society without abandoning all that connects them to the traditions in which they were formed. After careful consideration of the weaknesses of the liberal theological tradition and the difficulties of bringing the confessional communitarian tradition into dialogue beyond the internal conversation of an idealized Church, and with the work of Biggar, Shanks, Selby, Forrester and Stout to guide us, we can begin to set out the characteristics of a renewed public theology through which Christian ethics might take its place in the shaping of communities and structures in the wider world.

First, the case for dialogue beyond the tradition must be made from within the tradition itself, not from an appeal (covert or overt) to the liberal ideal of universal reason, or to a grand narrative which transcends the particularities of real, living traditions. As we have seen, a rich reading of the Christian tradition points towards something more than 'making people become like us' – that is, to the immanence of the God who is always greater than the Church, and the truth that God's people discover God and themselves in encounters with others. It is because the Church is the kind of community it is, drawing on its particular narratives, that it is called into wider dialogues. A relational God points us not only to relationships of

---

[30] Biggar, 'God in Public Reason', p. 9.

kin and kind but to relationships which embrace radical otherness. It might be added that, in Catholic social teaching, there is a strong insistence on the common good — that the Church seeks the welfare of all because that is intrinsic to the Christian vocation. The concern for the common good extends well beyond Catholicism, as the Church of England's form of intercessions at Holy Communion bear witness.[31]

Second, it remains that the steps towards a renewed public theology require some of the 'liberal' virtues of tolerance and awareness of contingency — but these must be located *within* the traditions, not imported via an assumption of liberal universalism.

Third, public theology will most probably be marked by provisional alliances rather than positions unique to Christians or the political dominance of the Church's viewpoint. The latter is long gone in Western countries, despite the implied desire of the Christian right to establish some sort of theocratic state. However, contemporary Western society is in some danger of falling for the secularist myth that religious opinions are, by their nature, irrational and therefore impossible for outsiders to engage with. A renewed public theology can expect to find itself in ethical alliances with various other groups at different times, to the extent that they share a scepticism about theocracy on the one hand and secular reductionism on the other, but probably with no other group all the time. This is a consequence of looking within the tradition for authenticity and yet not being so hung up on distinctiveness that sharing common ground with others is perceived as selling out our Christian uniqueness. It also challenges the confessional insistence that the Christian tradition is fundamentally incomprehensible to those outside the household of faith. It acknowledges our membership of 'overlapping communities' but seeks an authentic integrity rather than a piecemeal 'ethical mobility'.

Stances for the Church

Now, perhaps, we can trace the options open to the Church in terms of the public dimension of its ethical reasoning. These are not offered in any historical order or according to their significance — they are all positions that continue to shape debate about the role of the Church and Christian ethics in public policy debates today.

One option is to accept the default position of any voluntary association in a liberal democracy and join the cacophony of voices vying for attention and influence. On the whole, such associations carry weight in proportion to the number of their members, and attempts to speak for 'silent majorities' or to claim large nominal memberships are dismissed as misleading. This was very much the attitude to voluntary associations held by the governments of

---

[31] See: *Common Worship*, London: Church House Publishing, 2000, p. 281.

Margaret Thatcher which, starting with the trade unions, effectively outlawed the notion that social significance, long histories or mere worthiness were qualifications to take part in public debate. The idea that authority comes only with the numbers who can be turned out to the ballot box has penetrated British culture deeply.

A second option is to see the Church as the body which, as it were, 'holds the ring' while rival viewpoints argue their case. There is some suggestion of this approach in William Temple's *Christianity and Social Order* and in the way he arranged and managed the various big conferences on Church, community and politics between the 1920s and Malvern in 1941. The problems with this approach in a self-consciously plural society, where the tenets of Christianity are not only doubted but often dismissed out of hand, are obvious. But it has not totally vanished, as is seen at election times when, in English constituencies, it is almost invariably the Churches which arrange, host and manage panel discussions between the rival candidates. The way such hustings are set up makes it more difficult for the Church to take a public stand on a disputed question of the day, but assumes that the Church can be the 'honest broker' precisely because it does not, as a body, have partisan political views.

Perhaps this is not so very far from a third approach which one might term residual Christendom thinking. One still hears quite often the view that it is the role of the Church (especially an established Church) to be the 'moral conscience of the nation'. The difficulty here is that a plural society can, by definition, have no one moral conscience. Where this principle is invoked, it almost invariably disguises a belief that the Church should agree with the moral convictions of the speaker. A frequent reaction to this is the belief, widely held in the Churches, that when they incur the wrath of the political right and the political left at the same time, they are more or less in the correct place. There is, of course, no guarantee that such a middle position (in the trivial sense) has anything to do with any version of a Christian ethical tradition.

A variant of the previous position, held more often in America than in Britain, is that Christian theology's role is to act as a bulwark for a political or economic structure which is deemed to be good in and of itself. Thus Michael Novak (of whom more in Part 2) offers a series of theological arguments which support his notion of democratic capitalism, although he judges this state of affairs to be good on purely pragmatic grounds. From the political left, others such as Ronald Thiemann want Christian theology to support their commitment to a softer and more humane kind of democracy – but, again, this seems to reflect a prior commitment and not an argument from an authentic Christian foundation.[32] The Novak / Thiemann approach is about

---

[32] See: Michael Novak, *The Spirit of Democratic Capitalism*, London: Institute of Economic Affairs, Health and Welfare Unit, 1991; Ronald Thiemann, *Religion in Public Life: A Dilemma for Democracy*, Washington, DC: Georgetown University Press, 1996.

the Church underpinning specific means – the market or democracy – in a very clear echo of Hayek's definition of a liberal 'Great Society'.

None of this allows much room for the Church to connect its public ethic to its own traditions, narratives and practices. Hence the reaction – or corrective principle, if you will – which takes the Church out of the public arena altogether, rather on the lines of Milbank or Hauerwas's theology. We have already looked at this option in some depth and concluded that it not only leaves little room for a public theology but expressly regards such a venture as undesirable and even impossible. We have also considered the strange amalgam of confessional ethics in an individualistic liberal market economy which is the approach of the Christian right.

What remains is the kind of approach which has been sketched out in this chapter. A juggling act, perhaps, between liberal and communitarian ethics, and one which, being conscious that different positions within the Christian ethical tradition should act as correctives one to another, must retain the awareness that it will itself require corrective interventions. If such an approach is characterized by provisional alliances, it may also be noted for its ability to frame the ethical questions in new ways. As we will see more than once in Part 2, the state of ethics in our culture is at least as disordered as MacIntyre describes it in the opening chapter of *After Virtue*. The degree of sterility is considerable, with false polarizations constantly reducing every issue to a simple either/or – are you with me or against me: in tune with the media version of the politics of 'Left or Right?' Our culture is so used to seeing moral choices as simple bifurcations on the road that the question is rarely asked whether we are on the right road in the first place. One major contribution of Christian ethical thinking in public moral debate is its ability to introduce unexpected categories and new ways of looking at things, frequently exposing the thinness of the secular liberal assumptions which pervade public life and yet accessible, and even enlightening, to many who would not share the foundational beliefs of the Christian.

And there is one more point to be made in support of the project to reconstruct public theology and the public voice of Christian ethics. If Christians believe in an active, immanent, God who continues to be at work in the world, and are equally aware of the human limitations which prevent us from knowing the mind of God fully, some kind of dialogic openness must be essential if we are not to close down the possibility that the revelation of God's self may be happening in the events around us. Yet because we have already a revelation of the nature of God in Christ, the Holy Spirit among us and the guidance of Scripture, our humility in the face of God's work in the world does not silence us or leave us with nothing to say: rather the contrary. As Andrew Shanks says,

> there is a revelatory quality to certain aspects of twentieth-century experience which – if properly attended to – ought to compel confessional theology to drop its defences in this regard. If ever God has spoken, historically, this must

be one of the clearest cases. Yet, far from reinforcing the importance of confessional orthodoxy, of any sort, the revelation in question tends on the contrary to relativize its pretensions.[33]

Further reading

An excellent collection of essays, put together as a tribute to Duncan Forrester, gives a broad view of the topic of public theology: William F. Storrar and Andrew R. Morton (eds), *Public Theology for the 21ˢᵗ Century*, London and New York: T&T Clark/Continuum, 2004.

For a substantial monograph, drawing largely on Augustinian theology, see: Charles Mathews, *A Theology of Public Life*, Cambridge: Cambridge University Press, 2007.

For a very accessible discussion of the topic, see: John Atherton, *Public Theology for Changing Times*, London: SPCK, 2000.

---

[33] Shanks, *Civil Society, Civil Religion*, p. 5.

Second interval: 'eating people is wrong'

As one passes the mid-point of a two-semester course in Christian ethics, there is a pressing need for a change of tone. There has been much to take in and not all of it will have been easy to follow or remember. Seeking to present ideas afresh in a different medium can be a helpful mnemonic devise. Time, then, to dig out the CD player and take a musical trip back to the humour of an earlier decade.

Sometimes, one can discover ethical profundity in unlikely places. Readers with long memories, or who have a penchant for the English humour of the 1950s, will need no introduction to Michael Flanders and Donald Swann, whose songs emanate from a more gentle age than our own. In their day, they were a great hit with American audiences too, and they may, for all I know, continue to be popular in that cultural setting just as the more dangerous, transgressive and startling comic songs of Tom Lehrer from the same period retain a devoted following in Britain. Their greatest works were performed in concerts entitled *At the Drop of a Hat* and (inevitably) *At the Drop of (Another) Hat*. Both offer rich pickings for the student of social and ethical mores. The song which, in a way, could be the theme tune for this book appeared in the first collection and is the Flanders and Swann immortal number, 'The Reluctant Cannibal'.[1]

Sadly, or perhaps mercifully, this is not an audio book. Readers who have not heard the song could easily (and cheaply) download it from the internet or can imagine the riotous dialogue which forms the central lyric of the song. Of course, the last half-century has undermined the myths of cannibalistic tribes which inform the song but, although the song is set in a tribe, the satire is aimed at the much more familiar institutions of the modern West. The premise of the lyric is simple enough. A comedic tribe of cannibals is about to settle down to feast upon 'roast leg of insurance salesman' when Junior 'pushed away his shell, got up from his log and declared, "I want no part of it! ... I won't let another man pass my lips!"' He has become convinced that cannibalism is wrong and the ensuing duet consists of an angry exchange with his father, who rehearses all the arguments he can muster in favour of cannibalism only to meet the stonewalling retort that 'eating people is wrong'.

The point of unearthing this example of British whimsy is that the various arguments, offered by the father against his son's assertion that eating people is wrong, reflect many of the different kinds of moral reasoning already alluded to in the previous chapters. Thus:

---

[1] 'The Reluctant Cannibal' reproduced by permission of the Estates of Michael Flanders and Donald Swann 2009. Any use of Flanders and Swann material, large or small, should be referred to the Estates at <leonberger@donaldswann.co.uk>.

'But people have always eaten people – what else is there to eat? If the
ju-ju had meant us not to eat people, he wouldn't have made us of
meat!'

What is this but a splendid example of natural law reasoning with a touch
of natural theology? Because something is the case, it is reasoned that it also
ought to be the case. People are made of meat: meat is nutritious and good
to eat. The ju-ju intends our flourishing – therefore it follows that eating
people is OK. A parallel has been observed at times during the vexed debate
about homosexuality in the Church of England in recent years. An Anglican
bishop was even heard on the BBC claiming that, because it was self-evident
that the male penis was designed to penetrate the female vagina, and equally
self-evident that the anus was intended for the passage of waste material,
it followed that anal intercourse was, equally obviously, wrong. But this is
surely to mistake custom and usage for divine intention. A woman, com-
menting privately on the bishop's interview, reminded me that the vagina
serves purposes other than the reception of the penis (childbirth and men-
struation), and of course intercourse is only one function of the penis itself.
Introduce these considerations, and the bishop's assertion of what is 'natural'
and intended by God begins to look more contentious. His equation of
apparent intention with moral validity is a good example of assuming that
'is' always equals 'ought' before having a full account of what is. Perhaps the
bishop was a Flanders and Swann fan, overly influenced by the arguments
against the reluctant cannibal.

'Do you realize if this were to catch on it could ruin our entire
internal economy?'

Now we are into the realm of consequentialist arguments. A particular
practice is deemed to be good because, regardless of any intrinsic qualities it
might have, it is felt to bring about desirable outcomes. As with so many
'slippery slope' arguments, which are wary of one change because of
the greater changes it is supposed to imply, there is a strong sense here that
it is conventional wisdom, rather than any actual outcome, which is under
threat. Economies, internal or otherwise, are complex and adaptive structures.
Radical changes in human behaviour can, indeed, blow them off course,
but a well-ordered economic system is designed to accommodate change.
Economics is a good example of the practical limitations to consequentialist
thinking. Beyond the local, even tribal, economy, economic relationships
extend far beyond what any one person can grasp. It is a fundamental
principle of market economics that no one can know the ultimate consequences of his or her own transactions. Consequentialism, then, assumes a
higher degree of human understanding than most societies can ever offer the
individual.

Nevertheless, the thought of major economic change is unnerving, not
least because people who are already on the margins can expect to be the

ones to bear the brunt of disruption. It is not surprising that what is perceived as economic necessity has a strong influence on what is perceived as right or wrong. What works, economically, is often taken to be self-evidently right and good. Anything which threatens economic disruption must therefore be an offence against morality. Needless to say, the fate of the tribe's internal economy does not dissuade the reluctant cannibal from his conviction that eating people is wrong.

'Here am I, Chief Assistant to the Assistant Chief.'

Where does authority come from? One interpretation of obligation suggests that the reason to do something is because it is required by someone in authority. But personal authority is a synergy between the one with authority and those over whom authority is exercised. When authority is challenged from one quarter it can be weakened in another, which is why powerful people in public life can be embarrassed so easily by the exploits of their children. Authority may be precisely defined and constrained within clear parameters, but those with authority frequently regard it as seamless – authority spills over from one sphere of life into every other aspect of existence.

The father's appeal to his authority reveals its precariousness. Being Chief Assistant to the Assistant Chief is a fair way from the source of power itself. The point at issue here is reflected opprobrium: the sins of the son rebounding upon the father, and implying, perhaps, some inherited unsoundness. The fact that this implication is so clearly recognizable suggests some of the limits to the notion that the autonomous individual is the fundamental building-block of social ethics. Just as MacIntyre succinctly defines humanity as 'dependent, rational animals', so the father's pompous appeal to his status and authority reveal that the son's moral actions are not merely his own autonomous affair.[2] It is an example of the difficulties that arise when autonomy and a particular sort of rationality are elevated to become supreme moral categories – the impact upon others who live by more communitarian codes can be acute and, unless some means of establishing dialogue can be found, a much wider set of relationships (such as the father's position with the Assistant Chief) can be damaged. Personal moral autonomy is never just personal.

'You've been talking to one of your mothers again!'

The son has come under the influence of the 'wrong sort' of authority and the moral question boils down to which source of authority is to be trusted. This may exemplify MacIntyre's point in *After Virtue*[3] about the

---

[2] Alasdair MacIntyre, *Dependent Rational Animals: Why Human Beings Need the Virtues*, London: Duckworth, 1999.
[3] Alasdair MacIntyre, *After Virtue: A Study in Moral Theory*, 2nd edn, London: Duckworth, 1985.

interminability of moral disagreement when protagonists argue from distinct and incoherent moral traditions.

The question of moral authority is worth opening up a little here. It has been said that the most common expression of a moral principle encountered in British soap operas (*Coronation Street*, *EastEnders* and so on) is the expression, 'Do what you think is best'. In other words, the autonomous individual is the ultimate source of moral authority. No one can tell another person what is the best course of action, or what constitutes justice, and so on. While appearing to affirm the individual as a moral creature, the ultimate message is that, in the end, you are on your own.

But having listened to a few soap operas with the specific intention of discovering the truth of this assertion, I did detect a couple of other implicit moral principles below the surface of the script.

One is, 'Do this because I say so' – in other words, the appeal to recognized (or recognizable) authority. In 'The Reluctant Cannibal' it comes down to, 'obey me, not your mother(s)'. In the soap opera version, it may be a parent speaking to a child, or a bully speaking to a weakling, but the appeal to personal authority needs, apparently, to be backed up by implicit threat. In the context of Christian ethics, it is worth reflecting on the extent to which this principle remains covertly active, whether in claims by a residually powerful Church harking back to the Christendom image of temporal power submitting to spiritual authority; in a clerical elite seeking to control the conduct of the laity; or as an image of an all-powerful God imposing morality through threats of vengeance.

Another moral attitude, sometimes discernible in soap opera plots, is more distinctly communitarian. 'Do this because that's the sort of thing people like us do.' To behave otherwise would be to stand outside the community itself, to transgress the moral codes which are taken for granted yet which bind the community together. When, in the song, the father says, 'Going around saying "Don't eat people"! – That's the way to make people hate you', he is expressing precisely this fear. In Christian ethics, the whole thrust of Hauerwas's or Milbank's work is to emphasize the role of the Christian community in moral formation: we act like this because that is how people formed by the narratives of faith behave.

All three of these moral approaches – each rendered down to their most rudimentary form in the scripts of contemporary soap operas – are discernible in comic form in our Flanders and Swann song.

'You're just a yellow-livered coward. You wouldn't mind eating people if you weren't afraid of ending up in the pot yourself.'

The appeal to self-interest is a frequent interloper in moral argument. Altruism itself has been portrayed as a selfish impulse through which individuals seek to control others. The reductionism which understands all human behaviour in terms of a pseudo-Darwinian primeval urge to survive and dominate has been much popularized in recent years, notably through the work of that arch-atheist Richard Dawkins.[4] On this principle, an apparent concern for the welfare of others – including the notion that eating people is wrong – boils down to nothing more than a selfish predisposition to enhance one's own interests.

In the end, this kind of scientific reductionism is hard to refute except by appealing to the aspects of human life which seem not to fit the theory. As with many closed accounts of meaning, reductionists can deal with appeals to things like poetry, aesthetics or altruism, which seem to carry meaning beyond a genetic calculus of personal and species survival, by denying that these things convey anything 'more' than their simple meaning. In other words, the theory of genetic predisposition cannot be falsified since elements of experience which don't fit are reinterpreted and ruled to be mistaken or filtered erroneously through culture. MacIntyre makes just this point in respect of 'degenerate traditions', such as astrology, one mark of which is that 'it has contrived a set of epistemological defences which enable it to avoid being put in question or at least avoid recognizing that it is being put in question by rival traditions'.[5]

It remains that the reduction of all morality to the question of genetic advantage and species survival seems to leave out a considerable range of human existence. It may be that all our talk of ethics relates to an outmoded way of understanding humanity – an understanding superseded, if we could but see it, by a properly scientific world-view. One can only retort that, so long as a very large number of people believe that they possess moral volition, and that questions of ethics are worth pondering as if they meant something more than applied selfishness, there is scope for books like this. In Christian ethics, a focus on narrative makes the central story of the cross inescapable. Adducing the crucifixion as a retort to Dawkins is, of course, fruitless, since he explicitly rejects any religious premise. But if ethics grounded in story-formed communities is, indeed, more promising than the ethic of atomized, autonomous individuals, as Hauerwas and many others suggest, then it is not only the Christian story which suggests a central role for altruism, unconnected with 'scientific' accounts of selfish urges.

In another line of the song, the father asserts that, 'You can't change human nature.' The Christian ethicist has to ask whether the gospel story of salvation is precisely a contradiction of that view, all about changing human nature through the intervention of God in Christ. Whether the gospel is about changing human nature, or about revealing human nature in its true character, is a discussion for another day. The fact remains that human nature has first to be defined before any assertion of its unchangeable nature can be

---

[4] Richard Dawkins, *The Selfish Gene*, Oxford: Oxford University Press, 1976.
[5] Alasdair MacIntyre, 'Epistemological Crises, Narrative and the Philosophy of Science', in Stanley Hauerwas and L. Gregory Jones (eds), *Why Narrative?: Readings in Narrative Theology*, Eugene, OR: Wipf & Stock, 1997, p. 147.

made – and a reductionist version of science is only one among many stories (including Christian theology) which has something to say about the nature of being human.

'Communist!'

The single word is delivered as an expletive. This is nothing to do with any implicitly communitarian ethic but is simply the label of 'wrong-headed and threatening outsider'. Capturing 'good' words for one's own moral position, and ensuring that 'bad' words are applied to others, is a standard rhetorical manoeuvre which is often (as here) so blatant that the retreat from argument to name-calling is obvious. But the approach can be more subtle, and it is a gambit often encountered in Christian ethics. One need look no further than the usage of the highly loaded word 'orthodoxy' in the more rancorous debates within the Churches. The question of what is orthodox and what is not requires a great deal of exploration rather than simple assertion. The tradition is too complex, woven out of numerous strands, to reduce to a single, obvious, orthodoxy. In some Churches, orthodoxy boils down to authority – this is the teaching of the Church, I/we determine it and those who disagree are heretics or in need of correction. In a more conciliar Church, the appeal to orthodoxy may be more problematical – it is certainly not the case that members of the Church of England, for example, are bound either by synodical votes or by the pronouncements of archbishops, although both offer points of guidance. Often, the claim of 'orthodoxy' seems to be a covert appeal to majoritarianism – in other words, this is what the majority of Christians, across the world and through the ages, believe. But if the beliefs of Christians across the centuries are determinative of orthodoxy, then there is little scope for the workings of the Holy Spirit to correct the limitations of human understanding. The whole idea of Christian orthodoxy is, simultaneously, deeply important (although, as we shall see, appeals to authenticity may be more fruitful and able to handle difference through dialogue) and deeply problematical. Nevertheless, the claiming of words like 'orthodox' for oneself, without further analysis of the meanings in play, amounts to little more than a claim to authority based on power.

> 'You see a man sitting in a pot and you think he's suffering. It's not like that at all. He's just had an invigorating chase through the forest. He's sitting there in the nice warm water, with all the carrots and dumplings and things, and he's thinking "Oh the pleasure and happiness I'm going to give to a whole heap of people!"'

We must not try to milk the ethical potential of a single comic song beyond what it will bear, but the above quotation does offer a chance to comment briefly on the problem of perceiving the moral interests of others with clarity. The rise of perspectival theologies, mentioned in Chapter 5, emphasizing the different interests and understandings of people in poverty, women, black people and so on, has helped demonstrate the ability of those who hold power to shape 'common sense' in their own interests and to render all other understandings deviant. While the song is a clear parody of some of the arguments made in favour of fox-hunting, the wider point is that moral judgements made on behalf of others are always suspect. Liberation theologies have taught us to apply 'ideological suspicion' whenever truth is being claimed for a position which, in practice, benefits some over others.

The need for ideological suspicion arises frequently in discussions of sacrifice and suffering. It arises in arguments about homosexuality, and in the wider discussions about celibacy and chastity. If renunciation of physical intimacy is indeed an act of sacrifice, the imposition of that sacrifice on those who do not feel themselves called to renunciation becomes suspect. It is a commonplace that disadvantages and sufferings one may choose for oneself are more extensive than one can legitimately impose on others. But on the other side of the equation looms the spectre of individualism and autonomy as ultimate values. If the principle is taken too far – to the point where no one may comment on the ethical choices of another and the individual is bound by nothing more than his or her own conscience – we are back in the moral Babel described earlier. This is one good reason why the debate about sexuality is being fought out in the Churches, since the role of the Christian community and Christian narratives is a fundamental corrective to the individualizing tendencies of our culture.

And finally, what of the son's rejoinder to all these arguments? In fact, it amounts to no argument at all; just to a repeated assertion: eating people is wrong. No more eloquent example of a deontological principle could be offered. Eating people is wrong because . . . eating people is wrong!

Part 2

8

From meta-ethics to concrete cases

Thus far, we have been dealing largely with the conceptual groundwork upon which approaches to Christian ethics can be constructed. There is certainly a kind of logic in starting in this way with meta-ethics, but it remains that ethical issues only become really problematic when they take concrete form in contested ways of understanding the good or of interpreting the demands of justice. In the contested public forum we actually inhabit, ethics becomes problematic precisely because of the need to choose between rival versions of who we are, what we should do or what positions we should espouse. Without a grasp of meta-ethics, we lack the tools to unravel such questions profitably, but we only know our need of the tools because a contested question has arisen.

The chapters that follow draw on the preceding consideration of meta-ethics to address a number of pertinent questions and problems which, in various ways, test out the themes in Christian ethics which we have considered so far. I have tried, however, to avoid any implication that ethical reasoning is about confronting a set of dilemmas in which one horn of the dilemma represents an authentic Christian position in a way in which the other does not.

Instead, as we saw earlier, it is often more fruitful to apply MacIntyre's question: Of what story or stories do I find myself a part?[1] Although our subject is Christian ethics, to ignore the 'stories' which form the general ethical attitudes of our culture seems to me to drive too hard a wedge between the Christian and the 'secular'. First, Western 'secularism' still carries within itself the ghosts of Christendom, obscured and distorted though they may be. The historical lineage of secular liberalism includes what one might call a 'Christian gene', and the gulf between faithfulness and secularity can be over-emphasized. Second, MacIntyre is surely right to include the possibility that the stories we are part of can be plural as well as singular. Even if the Church ought to be the be-all and end-all of social existence for Christians (and, in a missionary Church, that is disputable), the fact is that Christians usually play a part in stories from beyond the Church which are no less morally formative than the stories from within the Church. Sometimes, being part of more than one story can mean an irreconcilable contradiction, but if we retain any understanding of natural theology and natural law, we will not

---

[1] Alasdair MacIntyre, *After Virtue: A Study in Moral Theory*, 2nd edn, London: Duckworth, 1985, p. 216.

rule out the possibility that God may speak to those outside the Church through the ethical fragments which they regard as morality. As Ronald Preston once said, 'men and women who are wise will think rather of their resemblances to their fellow human beings than of their differences from them'.[2]

Of the five topics considered in the following chapters, two – perhaps three – fall within the class of question which 'ethics' is usually supposed to address. Questions around the beginning and end of life – including, of course, abortion and euthanasia, but in fact much wider than these specific issues – and questions of sexuality, are the kind of thing that Christians are supposed to get hot under the collar about and where Christian opinion is often expected to stand over against the dominant secular culture. Certainly it is true that whenever moves are made in Parliament to adjust the legal time limits to abortion, or when attempts are made to legalize assisted suicide, the question is often portrayed as the Churches (sometimes 'the religious lobby') versus the 'rational' rest. And it is notorious that opposition to homosexual rights, homosexual practice and homosexuals in general is popularly perceived to be intrinsic to Christian belief. In both cases, popular perceptions are misleading. Bills to relax the abortion laws or to promote assisted suicide have been defeated in Parliament without the intervention of the Church of England bishops (or even the known Christians) being decisive. And the very fact that churches are struggling over issues of sexuality gives the lie to the idea that all Christians think the same on that topic. When we look at these issues more thoroughly, it will not be a matter of outlining a secular argument and a Christian one so that an orthodox line can be established and Christians reassured that they are right and the world wrong. I hope instead to open up the questions in ways that suggest a much greater richness within Christian ethical thinking than popular impressions allow for.

The third topic which may sit within a popular view of Christian ethics is that of war and armed conflict – and the role of Christian pacifism. Although this is a topic which most people, if asked, would concede to be part of the proper ethical business of the Churches, it has had a much lower profile in public debate than questions of medicine and sex. This is despite the high-profile public controversies about recent and current armed conflicts in Iraq and Afghanistan, and the so-called 'War against Terror'. The most recent controversy concerning an ecclesiastical intervention on the ethics of war may even be the famous sermon of Archbishop Runcie at the service commemorating the end of the Falklands War, when he incurred the fury of Prime Minister Thatcher for daring to articulate the Christian view that the dead Argentinian servicemen should be remembered alongside the fallen British. Views on the ethical implications of war are probably distorted by

---

[2] Ronald Preston, *Church and Society in the Late Twentieth Century: The Economic and Political Task*, London: SCM Press, 1983, p. 47.

history – on both sides of the Atlantic. In Britain, it is hard to escape an interpretation of the Second World War which stresses the motif of 'Britain against the rest' and offers the reasonable, if somewhat *ex post facto*, rationale that it was a just war against genocide and totalitarianism. The spirit of 1940 colours most perspectives on war and military matters in Britain. In the USA, since 2001, the trauma of the terrorist attacks on the World Trade Center and the Pentagon seem to have hardened the national expectation that America must wield its unique military might, not only in the cause of world peace but, more overtly than ever, to defend its national interests through military interventions around the globe – although public opinion about overseas conflicts can be fickle. In neither case is there much public moral debate into which the Churches can enter and, on the whole, the Churches have not been especially active in trying to generate one – despite some interesting theological reflection on war directed mainly to church audiences. We shall look at some of those arguments, and the Churches' historical contribution to the ethical analysis of war, in Chapter 12.

Questions relating to medicine tend to reinforce the idea that Christian ethics is primarily about personal conduct and especially those areas of life connected with sex. The long and profound tradition of Christian reflection on war and conflict, and the strong and enduring tradition of pacifism within the Churches, means that the ethics of war are widely assumed to be a proper Christian concern, even if the Churches are not expected to rock the national boat. In all these topics, the Christian does not need to make excuses for being interested and articulate. It is another matter when the topic under consideration is one like the market economy.

The relative absence of economic questions from the popular conception of what the Churches care about is surprising. My standard quip to students was that I had reached the age when I was more interested in money than in sex, and so our seminars would spend more time looking at the market than at the traditional issues of personal ethics – but even the students of my age and older usually preferred to consider the ethics of sex. I suspect that this largely reflected their roles within the Church. The popular impression is that the Church is counter-cultural about sex, so ministers feel the need to be well-versed in the arguments. But I also wonder if the relative lack of interest in the ethics of the economy is partly about a sense of being implicated too deeply to risk raising difficult questions. It is possible to conceive of purity in sexual and personal terms in a way which is impossible in terms of economics, since all of us are inextricably part of the world of money, labour and consumption. Moreover, the market economy has been promoted so assiduously through the slogan, 'There is no alternative', for over thirty years that serious alternatives, or even adequate critiques, are quite hard to conceive. When we dig deeper, it is to discover that market theorists reject the very idea that markets are about morality at all – on the contrary, it is claimed that markets are amoral and cannot be judged against concepts like justice, or the good, at all. Cold War propaganda also juxtaposed the market economy with 'Godless Communism' in a way which implicitly identified markets uncritically with godliness. All these factors, I think, conspire to push the ethics of the market economy out of sight and to make any ethical critique of the market feel like a kind of subversive act against an institution upon which all depend. It seems vital, then, that a theological consideration of the market – its strengths as well as its weaknesses – should be integral to any study of Christian ethics. Apart from the intrinsic interest of the topic, it is important to address ethical issues in which one is, oneself, implicated, as well as those which can comfortably be regarded as other people's business upon which we can opine from outside.

As for the fifth topic in this section, human rights are essentially an Enlightenment concept but have only really come to prominence as a foundational legal and political concept since the Second World War. They are therefore a relatively new topic for Christian ethical concern. The Universal Declaration of Human Rights was adopted and proclaimed by the United Nations in 1948 and the European Convention on Human Rights adopted by the Council of Europe in 1950. The rise of human rights legislation as a major tool of domestic social policy in Britain is an even more recent phenomenon, mainly associated with the Blair and Brown governments after 1997. As a question for contemporary Christian ethics, human rights is especially interesting because it exemplifies the way in which secular ideologies can work towards practical goals which most Christians would support, yet in a way which, some argue, forces a Christian understanding of being human off the agenda. Christians are therefore placed in a tricky position. They can accept, and seek to work with, the human rights agenda for the sake of its good objectives and, in the process, risk the further marginalization of a Christian understanding of why such objectives are good. Or they can stand apart from the language and politics of human rights, and risk being identified with those who oppose human rights from a desire to abuse other humans. They may also face the charge of failing, in practical political terms, to strive against the abuses which human rights legislation seeks to outlaw. Having already considered the possibility of Christian ethics working authentically in concert with others from differing ethical traditions in order to bring about good ends which may be shared for varied reasons, we shall look at human rights as an example of how this approach can introduce significant (though not necessarily insuperable) tensions.

There are, of course, many other topics which could have been chosen to illustrate the themes from Part 1, and a large number of other ethical issues which may be regarded as no less pressing or problematical for Christians and the Churches today. I have not given specific attention, for example, to the environment, genetics or punishment, each of which has a good claim to be the topic of the moment. Indeed, I have tried to avoid the implication that Christian ethics can be reduced to a series of topics as if each could be handled in isolation from the others. My hope is that Part 2 of this book will expand upon and illuminate Part 1 such that the reader will grow in confidence to apply ideas and approaches to topics of all kinds. But students need to care about the themes through which they learn to be ethicists so, in the meantime, there are some suggestions below for further reading on other themes and topics in Christian ethics.

Having worked through Part 2, the reader may conclude that the topics I have covered now appear to involve many more questions and few firm conclusions. But this is where we return to the idea that one viewpoint requires the corrective reading of another, equally authentic, theological perspective. As I hope Part 1 has shown, the tensions within Christian ethics may not be completely irreconcilable, but reconciliation is usually less illuminating than dialogue if it oversimplifies or excludes valid stances. If this ends up producing more questions than answers, it is nonetheless an important staging-post on the road to competent ethical analysis.

Further reading: on four other ethical themes

Environmental ethics

Not surprisingly, there is a growing literature on theological approaches to the environment and the pressing issue of climate change. Michael Northcott is a leading figure in this work and there is much useful material in both the books listed here. The first is a passionate and accessible study, covering the ground very widely; the second takes the arguments further in theological terms. Meanwhile, Celia Deane-Drummond's book explores the wider issues of ecological ethics:

Michael Northcott, *A Moral Climate: The Ethics of Global Warming*, London: Darton, Longman and Todd, 2007.
Michael Northcott, *The Environment and Christian Ethics*, Cambridge: Cambridge University Press, 1996.
Celia Deane-Drummond, *A Handbook in Theology and Ecology*, London: SCM Press, 1996.

Genetics and bioethics

The rapid growth of knowledge concerning biology and genetics – human and otherwise – raises many new questions for the ethicist, not least because these issues often achieve prominence in the media. The topic is a good example of how Christian ethics must grapple with the detail of other disciplines in order to get behind superficial reporting and make ethical judgements on the basis of what is really happening. The following books offer helpful ways into the subject:

Neil Messer (ed.), *Theological Issues in Bioethics: An Introduction with Readings*, London: Darton, Longman and Todd, 2002.
Robert Song, *Human Genetics: Fabricating the Future*, London: Darton, Longman and Todd, 2002.
Stephen R. L. Clark, *Biology and Christian Ethics*, Cambridge: Cambridge University Press, 2000.

Crime and punishment

What is the place of punishment in a Christian dispensation which emphasizes God's mercy? The historical concern of Christians for the condition of
prisoners, prompted, often by Luke 4.18, has a new significance as prison
populations soar in Britain and the USA. Criminal justice is a good example
of an ethical issue which is illuminated by a theology of the interim. The
following books all give useful insights into the theme:

T. J. Gorringe, *Crime*, London: SPCK, 2004.
Christopher Jones and Peter Sedgwick (eds), *The Future of Criminal Justice:
Resettlement, Chaplaincy and Community*, London: SPCK, 2002.
T. Richard Snyder, *The Protestant Ethic and the Spirit of Punishment*, Grand
Rapids, MI and Cambridge: Eerdmans, 2001.

Managers and managerialism

Innumerable areas of human activity are now organized according to theories
of management. MacIntyre calls the manager one of the foremost characters
of modernity, since the manager professes to possess instrumental skills which
are divorced from practical wisdom – as in the many cases where managers
from (say) private industry are enlisted to run healthcare provision. Reflection
on management in the light of Christian ethics is a fairly new development,
and here are two contrasting approaches. Higginson seeks to align management ideas with Christian themes; Pattison suggests that managerialism behaves
rather too like a religion for comfort:

Richard Higginson, *Transforming Leadership: A Christian Approach to Management*,
London: SPCK, 1996.
Stephen Pattison, *The Faith of the Managers: When Management Becomes Religion*,
London and Washington, DC: Cassell, 1997.

9

The beginning and end of life

The beginning

During the American presidential election campaign of 2008–9, the candidates attended a staged debate at a well-known evangelical mega-church. To the question, 'When does life begin?' Barack Obama quipped that the question was 'above my pay grade'. His Republican rival, John McCain, answered straight back: 'At conception'.

In the context of American cultural conflicts, the question was loaded with not-so-hidden agendas and McCain had read his audience well. The question was designed to tease out the candidates' position on abortion and, by articulating what we shall identify as the 'precautionary principle', McCain probably expressed the views of many present. Obama, in contrast, appeared to duck the question, although he may just possibly have been hinting at a profound respect for the mysteries of the deity. Perhaps Obama intended to suggest that the definition of when life begins lies in the mind of God alone – a subtlety that (if intended) was probably lost on his audience. The candidates epitomized two positions in the strident debate about abortion – not, on this occasion, the divide between 'pro-choice' and 'pro-life', but the divide between simple certainty and a more hesitant complexity. As we shall see, questions of the beginning and end of life do involve complexity, although that does not entail that ethical responses cannot be, in the final analysis, quite simple.

But was the question to the candidates well put? Was it, in moral rather than political terms, the right question? 'Life' is a word that covers so much – including vegetable matter as well as the animal world – that some further qualification seems necessary. And while 'When does human life begin?' may be a well-formed question, in the context of the disputed issue of abortion the more apposite question might be 'When does human personhood begin?', since the question at issue is not the fact that the embryo consists of living tissue but whether, or to what extent, the embryo should be considered as a person.

In order to consider this question more fully, it helps to move away from the emotionally charged arena of the abortion 'debate' – if such a dialogue of the deaf can be dignified with the word. The question of where human life, or human personhood, begins is equally present in other issues such as the permissibility of experiments on embryos conceived *in vitro* (that is, in a laboratory dish). It is worth remembering, though, that a definitive answer to the question (assuming such an answer is to be had) does not, in itself, justify any particular set of practices, whether therapeutic experimentation or abortion. Indeed, we will go on in this chapter to use questions of the beginning and end of life to illustrate the difficulties of arguing from a consequentialist or a deontological position. But let us start with the vexed question of when personhood can be said to begin.

To that question, the short answer is simple — we don't know. We don't know, that is to say, in the way we might be said to know other facts which are susceptible to empirical measurement. I can know with a degree of certainty (if I bother to look) when the first white hair appeared on my head. Personhood is not susceptible to that kind of verification. Personhood is important because it is the criterion upon which rests a considerable raft of moral meanings. If I am deemed to be a non-person, others will assume they can do things to me that would be forbidden were I a person. That takes us to the heart of the matter. Personhood is conferred socially rather than measured empirically, even when, as Rowan Williams suggests (see Chapter 13), personhood is seen as an attribute of embodiment. Societies have existed (and not so far back in history either) in which certain groups of human beings were deemed to be less than fully persons, with the consequence that slavery, genocide and other great evils were construed as acceptable. The moral status of personhood is a vital safeguard against the repetition of appalling events — but this ensures that it has a social and political dimension as well as an ethical one.

So a degree of human agency enters into the question of personhood. We can say with empirical clarity where life begins, although the word 'life' in that context conveys no great moral content. Personhood is something most people would recognize as a morally significant concept, but defining it is another matter and it is important to remember that understandings of personhood can be deeply coloured by the culture within which they are formed.

Most cultures, including Christian ones, have distinguished between the primitive embryo at the moment of conception and the foetus approaching its term in the womb. Personhood appears to pertain to the latter in ways which seem inappropriate to confer on the former. Nor is this a singularly modern issue. The problem of when 'quickening' took place was considered by Augustine, drawing on what was known at that time about the gestation process. At some point between conception and the later stages of pregnancy, the foetus acquires the characteristics of a person and, as personhood is a construct, different answers about timing will follow from different social priorities, even when there is a considerable degree of agreement about what a person is.

We can illustrate this by considering the significance of autonomy in a definition of personhood. Despite its many drawbacks as a key to understanding the human, autonomy may plausibly be one element in a definition of personhood, but is it a defining factor? A culture which places a high premium on autonomy in understanding what it is to be human will be less favourably disposed to regard those who lack autonomy as fully human. Autonomy can be interpreted as the ability to sustain life outside the womb, in which case a foetus of around 20–24 weeks' gestation has autonomy, since it is likely to survive if born at that moment. But a foetus of under 20 weeks' gestation has the *potential* for autonomy, provided it is allowed to develop for a further period. Here we get into the problematic area of realized qualities versus potential. But, sticking with the question of autonomy, it is clear, as we have seen, that an emphasis on human autonomy is likely to be a characteristic of a liberal culture, and especially of a consumer economy in which the exercise of independent choice is regarded as a defining criterion of personhood. There are, of course, serious inadequacies in the consumerist account of being human, but in terms of the beginning of life, the key point against making autonomy too central is that dependency is as much a characteristic of being human as autonomy. The corrective emphasis on dependency, no less a characteristic of being human than autonomy, helps to extend the question of personhood back into the gestation period. If dependence on others is part of what it means to be human, then the inability to exist outside the womb ceases to be the chief defining attribute of personhood. Moreover, by reminding ourselves of the connection between assumptions made about autonomy and consumerism, we can see how attitudes which are sometimes seen as mere common sense are brought into question, since they are revealed to be culturally relative – and part of a culture which, on many grounds, is widely understood to be less than perfect.

Can our growing scientific knowledge help here? We know that the fertilized ovum passes through many stages to become the viable foetus, and that each stage marks a further step towards the embryo becoming recognizably a human person. We know that, in the early days after fertilization, a very high percentage of fertilized ova fail to implant in the womb and are lost. We also know that, at approximately 14 days after fertilization, the so-called 'primitive streak' is first detectable in the multiplying group of cells – the first sign of something other than randomness in their multiplication and, hence, arguably, the first intimation that the embryo is progressing towards human-ness. Fourteen days is also the point by which it will be known whether the embryo is going to divide such that it will become one, two or more persons – as in the case of monozygotic, or identical, twins. What significance does this knowledge hold for ethical judgements about personhood?

It is important to be clear what is at stake here. The question is whether the embryo can be treated as a 'thing' rather than a person. Something that is not a person may legitimately be destroyed, modified or experimented upon, if so doing will serve a greater good. Here we are dealing with a complex mixture of consequentialist and deontological arguments and it may help to try to unpick them as far as we can.

The influence of deontological thinking is seen in the widespread consensus that human life is in some way 'sacred' or of ultimate concern. This belief is not always expressed in terms of religious principles, although the use of the word 'sacred' hints strongly at the genealogy of the idea. Christians, indeed, often prefer the concept of life as a gift, which is held in trust and not to be discarded lightly. The prohibition on killing another human being, or experimenting on them in ways which do not benefit them or to which they have not consented, is widely abhorred, in and beyond religious traditions. But there is another, perhaps quite widespread, perception that the foetus or embryo somehow does not 'count' as a person – or at least does not count as much as people after they have been born. The fact that even the proponents of abortion on demand would shrink from infanticide, even if it could be shown to be beneficial for many other people, suggests the existence of a deontological principle that human persons are not to be wilfully violated. Yet, where the boundary between persons and non-persons is contended, consequentialist arguments are often wheeled in and abortion justified by the perceived good to the mother.

Similarly, embryo experimentation is often justified on the grounds of its therapeutic value, and the fact that it needs to be justified at all reveals that, even in a predominantly utilitarian culture, the moral status of the embryo is regarded as significant.

In the case of abortion, the consequentialist nature of many arguments is even more obvious. A foetus may be aborted (under British law) if carrying it to term would seriously damage the mother's health – damage, in this context, being construed in a broad way which, in effect, allows abortion on demand up to the legal time limit. That limit has, of course, been subject to considerable parliamentary jockeying, although no party has felt able to challenge the fact that some legal limit must be set. But in the case of embryo research, the legal time limit is very early indeed, and although there is pressure to relax it, it seems likely that a line will be maintained very near to conception. Here, consequentialist arguments have to make their case against a much stronger presumption of a deontological principle which seems to start from some notion of the special nature of the human embryo. What is going on here? Is it, perhaps, that the dilemmas facing the researcher are, to the average person (or, perhaps we should say, the average opinion-former) perceived as dubious and inhuman whereas the implications of an unwanted pregnancy are regarded as immediate and personal?

If the foregoing appears inconclusive and complex, it is partly because I have tried to avoid rehearsing the standard positions which emerge on either side of the ethical barricades whenever questions of the beginning of life are raised in public. MacIntyre, in *After Virtue*, uses the abortion question as an example of an interminable debate in which any rapprochement between the different sides is impossible, since both are arguing from incommensurate ethical traditions.[1] On the one hand, the notion of the sacredness of human life, however far back into gestation that sacredness is extended, draws on a religious, often Christian, tradition that the human person is always an end, and never a means for others to achieve their own ends. On the other hand, there is the tradition of human autonomy in which the freedom to choose and shape one's destiny is paramount. Because neither side recognizes that it is working with fragments of a once-comprehensive ethical tradition, the arguments pass by each other without being able to move either protagonist from their entrenched positions.

MacIntyre is using the abortion question to exemplify his ideas about the fragmentary and incommensurate nature of much that today passes for ethics. In practice, the abortion question is more complex, not least because the proponents of human autonomy and the right to choose continue to work with a version of the argument that human life is uniquely important – but without extending that sacredness backwards very far before birth. The question of when human personhood begins is the hidden step in their syllogism.

Secular reason does not necessarily lead to one conclusion only about when personhood begins, nor, of course, does 'religious opinion' always come out with an absolutist position. The emergence of abortion as the issue at the heart of American culture wars has provoked a degeneration of thought into sloganizing, on both sides, so that many fail to recognize their own position in the caricatures of pro- and anti-abortionists which fill the media. Moreover, the hardening of positions on abortion has introduced a similar slogan-ridden rigidity into other debates about the beginning of life, notably that on embryo research.

If we start from the observably true premise that Christian men and women find themselves on both sides of the abortion debate, the question then arises whether this latitude in ethical standpoint is justifiable within the Christian tradition of social ethics. One problem, as so often in ethics, involves the relationship of traditional teaching and doctrine to new forms of knowledge – in this case, not so much the new knowledge from medicine and the natural sciences as new perspectival knowledge which emerges when theology ceases to be done exclusively by men.

There is much biblical scholarship today which emphasizes the radical nature of Jesus' attitude towards women and the special place given to women as the first witnesses to the resurrection, very much in contrast to the prevailing culture of the times. From the perspective of today, therefore, the equality of esteem given to men and women appears to be attested biblically and doctrinally, although how that equality is embodied in practice is more contentious within the Churches. To contemporary eyes, the notion

---

[1] Alasdair MacIntyre, *After Virtue: A Study in Moral Theory*, 2nd edn, London: Duckworth, 1985, pp. 6ff.

that a Christian ethic on matters which intimately and uniquely affect women and their bodies could be defined solely from the point of view of men, seems more than a little deficient. This is not to suggest that all women regard the embryo or the foetus as having a greater or lesser moral standing than is accorded to it by men. It does mean that a woman's perception about what is happening to her own body is not a morally negligible factor in so far as experience is a source of moral insight. But the difficulty is that questions about abortion do not take place in a cultural vacuum. In a context where women have, historically, been granted far fewer opportunities to make active decisions about their lives compared to men, where exactly that kind of active choice is increasingly regarded as a sine qua non of full human living, and where the Churches have tended to collude with male constraint of female sexual and reproductive matters, then the question of who decides on doctrinal and ethical questions within the Christian community becomes highly contentious and cultural particularities may obscure ethical reasoning.

It remains that a Christian ethic on the beginning of life, and related issues such as abortion, needs to be grounded in Christian beliefs. That is not to say that only one set of conclusions can be authentically drawn. But arguments from Scripture and doctrine need to be clearly differentiated from arguments based upon the pastoral imperative of compassion or the culturally relative appeal to experience. Again, this is not to diminish the Christian vocation to act compassionately, but it takes us back to the point made earlier that ethics and pastoralia are not the same thing – and the observation that, very often, pastoral concerns driven by an aversion to suffering are allowed to trump the ethical question of what is right. We have already raised questions about the difficulties around consequentialist arguments, with their calculus of outcomes, in the context of a culture which is at odds over the very nature of the good.

So, accepting that it is easy to fall into the traps of patriarchal reasoning and of interpreting pastoral care through a religiously illiterate culture, how should we approach the questions of the beginning of life? Two points stand out: first that the moment when a group of cells become a person is not known, or empirically knowable. The best we have are hints that a new phase in the embryo's development has occurred and the inductive argument that, because this change usually occurs at, or by, a certain time, that time is highly significant. Second, questions about the beginning of life turn upon answers to a prior question about the purpose and nature of human life. Only when we can say what life as a person is for can we argue about what constitutes personhood. This is where a Christian perspective and much contemporary culture part company. For only in a religious (and, in our case, specifically Christian) dispensation does the answer come back that the purpose of human life is to glorify God. If this sounds too sweeping, consider the other possibilities, none of which go quite far enough to justify the assertion that human life is sacred, even in the residual ways in which that term is often used outside the religious framework. If the purpose of human life is to change the world, to be creative, or to *do* anything, then our existence is essentially utilitarian and a great deal of what is generally thought to be human life is diminished and devalued. If we say that the purpose of life is to love and be loved by others, life is still not being judged solely by its intrinsic qualities, of and for itself. But place the human person in relationship to the eternal God, and no life, however unproductive or unlovely, is valueless. This is not to say that non-theists cannot treat human persons with immense value – only that, without God, their value is dependent upon factors that are themselves fleeting and temporal, and it is difficult to establish in such a framework that human persons are intrinsically of ultimate value.

But does that get us very far in establishing the moral status of the embryo from conception to birth? In other words, is a newly fertilized ovum a person in God's eyes? Here, the 14-day point becomes significant. If it is impossible, prior to 14 days, to say whether the zygote will ensue as one, two or more persons, can it be, itself, regarded as a person? Given that a very high proportion of fertilized ova fail to be implanted – fail, in other words, to begin the specific relationship of dependency on the mother which will lead to birth – is it consistent with Christian understandings to regard God as so wasteful of human persons? More outlandishly, given the advances in cloning that appear to be on the scientific horizon, if a cloned being could be generated from a mere sample of DNA, does all human tissue take on the status of a potential other person, or is that a *reductio ad absurdum*?

The arguments for treating 14 days from conception as a significant moment in the move from a mere group of cells to a human person are quite strong. The suggestion that God is not wasteful is, however, more difficult to sustain. One key Christian principle is that God's love for his creation is abundant beyond our imaginings. It seems, at the least, rash to declare wasteful what God, for all we know, may regard as joyous abundance. It has been suggested that if all non-implanted fertilized ova are truly human persons, loved by God, then heaven is populated by many times more small cell clusters than fully grown human beings. To which, I think, the proper answer is, 'So what?' The nature of heaven is not for us to constrain with earth-bound rationality. Nevertheless, there is still something in this argument about wastefulness which seems hard to square with the notion of a purposeful creation, although the point is far from being a decisive one. More significant is the question of monozygotic twins, for identical twins are indisputably separate persons and so the zygote which has not yet divided (if it is going to do so) is not an indicator of the unique person or persons which may ensue, each loved uniquely by God.

It is this argument, coupled with the emergence of the primitive streak at around the 14-day mark, which has convinced many, including the Church of England in its official responses to the question, that therapeutic research on embryos *in vitro*, up to the 14-day point, is morally permissible (for certain purposes, determined on other moral grounds).[2] The obvious conclusion must be that, up to 14 days, the embryo is less than a human person. This is a position which draws both on theological perspectives and on contemporary scientific knowledge and has the integrity of not ignoring either.

Nevertheless, the 14-day principle is not without critics who base their case on a number of arguments. First, it is important to recognize that the figure of 14 days is not a precise description of what happens in the womb at that moment – it is a point by which certain changes will have happened if they are going to happen at all. This means that, in any specific case, 14 days may not be an accurate measure of what has, or has not, happened.

Second, it is argued that, because the concept of personhood is not a scientifically verifiable concept but a human construct, it is perfectly legitimate to endow with personhood every zygote from the moment of fertilization. This may be done on the grounds that, since God's views on the matter are not definitively known, we should err on the side of caution.

Third, since there is a long history of human beings making arbitrary judgements about other people, which are self-serving rather than objective, no boundary imposed by human law is likely to be observed scrupulously – once the principle that embryos can be tampered with for supposedly good ends has been established, the demand to tamper with them for less good ends will inevitably follow. This is the 'slippery slope' argument.

All these objections suggest that, on the grounds that human knowledge of God's will is limited and that human sin corrupts humanity's best intentions, any encroachment on the human embryo risks being an encroachment on a human person. Better, then, to deem that life and personhood begin at conception than to start down a slippery slope – even though the consequences may include an increase in human suffering because of the restriction on embryo research for therapeutic purposes and the human misery of unwanted children.

This precautionary principle has much to commend it. Perhaps the question turns on one's doctrine of sin. As Michael Banner has said, 'Christians have usually believed that sin is the deep explanation for how the world goes (though grace is finally the deepest).'[3] The precautionary principle seeks to hold a line because it is alert to the tendency of sin to breach any human-constructed boundary. The line which confers personhood at the moment of conception is not intended to be empirically grounded; it is based on a

---

[2] See the Church of England, Mission and Public Affairs Division response to the UK Government's Human Fertilization and Embryo Bill, 2007. <www.cofe.anglican.org/info/socialpublic/science/hfea>. Accessed 2 August 2009.

[3] Michael Banner, 'Nothing to Declare', *Church Times*, 16 June 1995.

judgement that an absolute line is more defensible in practice than one constructed on fallible human knowledge and perception. Those who are more inclined to see God's grace at work in human discovery may be more inclined to adopt the 14-day principle, and it is possible to see the disagreement here as being between different theological emphases (between a stronger emphasis on sin versus a stronger emphasis on grace) rather than a conflict between a Christian point of view and a secular one.

While this might get us somewhere in terms of embryo research, it has interesting implications for the debate about abortion. Even permitting interference with the embryo up to 14 days is of little help here, since at that point few women will be aware that they are pregnant. On the other hand, the so-called 'morning-after pill', normally taken within 72 hours of intercourse, would not entail ending the life of a person if personhood has not, at that point, begun. As we noted, the question of human personhood seems to be handled very differently in arguments about abortion compared to those about research. While the immediacy of the pastoral dimension obviously impinges on the abortion question, it is puzzling to find such disparate approaches to ethics operating simultaneously in public debate, with a presumption of personhood afforded to the embryo at an early stage in terms of research but a presumption of non-personhood until a late stage in the case of abortion.

The 'debate' about the permissibility of abortion has all the characteristics of an interminable dispute between incommensurable positions. Perhaps a better way is to ditch both the rights-based approach and the approach from sacredness, since neither is fully intelligible to the other side, and attempt to reframe the question in different terms. A promising example of this approach was made by Rowan Williams, writing as Archbishop of Canterbury in *The Observer* newspaper in 2007. Here, Williams characterizes in terms of tragedy every instance where the question of abortion arises.

He suggests that many of those who sought to liberalize abortion law in the 1960s were seeking practical answers to extreme situations, but that:

> legislation intended to deal with exceptions, intending to tackle tragic circumstances that offered no simple right answer, has in its outworking had the effect of shifting some basic assumptions. Many of the supporters of the '67 Bill started from a strong sense of taking for granted the wrongness of ending an unborn life – and the same was undoubtedly true of those who campaigned for changes in the law in other countries. What people might now call their 'default position' was still that abortion was a profoundly undesirable thing and that a universal presumption of care for the foetus from the first moment of conception was the norm.[4]

---

[4] Rowan Williams, 'Abortion: Fundamental Convictions about Humanity Need to be Kept in Focus', *The Observer*, 21 October 2007. <http://www.archbishopofcanterbury.org/1237>. Accessed 2 August 2009.

Now, however, across Europe abortion is commonplace and, as Williams notes, it is supported by a rhetoric of individual choice in which the idea that morally significant decisions need to be taken in the light of discussion and shared insight has vanished. But Williams also picks up one of the paradoxes of the culture of individual rights when he notes the emergence of a vocabulary of embryo rights in the context of whether a mother-to-be should smoke, drink or do anything else which might harm the foetus. There is, as he says, a lack of joined-up thinking in a society which can simultaneously curb a woman's personal rights for the good of the embryo, but which still treats the embryo as having no rights if the mother chooses to abort it.

Significantly, Williams avoids the notion that clear moral principles render hard cases easy:

> clear principles don't let you off the hook. There is no escaping the tough decisions where no answer will feel completely right and no option is without cost. But when do we get to the point where accepting the inevitability of tough decisions that may hurt the conscience has become so routine that we stop noticing that there ever was a strain on the conscience, let alone why that strain should be there at all?[5]

Williams offers a hand to the proponents of more liberal abortion laws by recognizing the seriousness of the compassionate impulses behind their stance. He does not shy away from this by arguing that what appears to be compassion is actually no such thing: he is arguing openly and from a Christian perspective for the realization that the world is complex. Although, in a newspaper article, he does not explore the theology overtly, he is arguing from within an understanding of the theological interim and the ambiguities and compromises that arise when trying to act with holy integrity in a fallen world. His argument focuses on the way in which compassionate steps to alleviate suffering in tragic cases can bring about a shift in perspective so that what was once perceived as tragic becomes understood as commonplace. In short, he is arguing that practical policies dealing with ethical questions are often specific to their time and place. Negotiating a way through the theological interim requires correctives – scope for greater compassion, perhaps, but at other times a reaffirmation of moral seriousness. The seeds of each imbalance lie in the previous act of correction. What allows us to hold the two together is, perhaps, the perception that all abortions are tragic, one characteristic of tragedy being that no course of action is ethically uncomplicated or uncompromised.

Williams began his argument with the observation that those seeking to liberalize abortion in the 1960s were often motivated by the need to respond to ethical hard cases. More generally, debate about abortion frequently proceeds from hard cases to general principles. Examples include cases where a choice must be made between saving the life of the mother or that of the

---

[5] Williams, 'Abortion'.

foetus, the case of pregnancy following rape, and so on. I have tried to avoid this approach as it can have an uncomfortably rhetorical flavour which smacks of winning arguments rather than reflecting upon principles. If abortion can be justified in a (perhaps hypothetical) hard case, then opposition to abortion in other cases is undermined. Similarly, the rhetorical trick of describing a hard case where abortion can seem a reasonable option, and then declaring with a flourish, 'Congratulations! You have just aborted Beethoven!' does not seem to me to fall within the category of responsible argumentation.

Many of these arguments take on a different character if we do not merely accept the fallen world as it is but seek to model a better kind of human existence. This is a response typical of Hauerwas's vision of the Church. Here, for example, the concept of the unwanted child is rendered otiose by the nature of the relationships and moral discourse within the alternative community. For Hauerwas, children in the Church are gifts to the whole community, not just to their parents, and the assumption is that, for the members of that community, no child is unwanted. But while there is something deeply attractive, and far from unachievable, about Hauerwas's Church, it remains that that Church exists within a wider society to which the Church is called to be a missionary presence. Has the Church nothing to say to the woman who is pregnant and alone outside its gates except 'Come and join us'? And while the American separation of Church and state allows Hauerwas to be blithely unconcerned about influencing the law of the land, that is not the historic position of the Churches of Europe, such as the Church of England, where it is still widely held that legislation (and moral life) is better if informed by Christian faith, however remotely.

The end

Turning now to the end of life, the question normally presents itself as the problem of euthanasia. When, if ever, is it permissible deliberately to end the life of someone who believes themselves, or is deemed, to be in insupportable pain, or whose life is, on other grounds, regarded as not worth living? There are many similarities here with the arguments surrounding the questions at the beginning of life, and this is not surprising since both turn on the ultimate purpose of life in different cultures, including Christian culture.

There is much that could be said about the different situations embraced by the blanket term 'euthanasia', but they are brought into sharp focus by an area of the debate with a high public profile today: the situation where someone decides that their own life is not worth continuing and wishes others – a physician or a family member – to take the deliberate step of ending their life for them. This is usually known as assisted dying or assisted suicide. The point here is not about withholding intrusive treatment or maximizing pain relief in the knowledge that, in consequence, life will be shortened – the principle of double effect which most Christian ethicists see as acceptable. The voices calling for people to be given the right to choose the moment of their own end are loud, frequent and often persuasive – not least to Christians who (in Britain, at least) seem to be divided on this issue – and since many will not be able to achieve their end without help, assisted suicide is high on the moral agenda. Again, the conflict between the perceived pastoral imperative and the demands of an ethical principle appears to be at the heart of this.

Another aspect of the argument, which we have also considered, is the anthropology which privileges autonomy and regards dependence as a diminution of full humanity. Frequently, the case for euthanasia is made on the grounds that a life heavily dependent upon others is undignified and implies that the person who once was is now appreciably diminished in personhood. It is worth saying again that it is not only the Christian tradition which treats dependency as a fundamental characteristic of being human – MacIntyre, for example, establishes his working definition of humans as 'dependent rational animals' without open recourse to any religious tradition (although, of course, the view is compatible with Christian and other religious anthropologies).[6] Paradoxically, assisted suicide intrinsically acknowledges that dependency is often inescapable, but makes dependency subservient to autonomy.

The Christian, naturally, will wish to introduce a particular understanding of the purpose of life – the end of life in the sense of life's *telos* rather than its temporal limit. Michael Banner offers some interesting arguments here, drawing on the Christian approach to martyrdom. Analysing the thinking of the early Fathers, especially Clement and Augustine, he summarizes thus:

> Too ready a relinquishing of life, amounting to a seeking of death, is incompatible with faith in the creator whose gift of life may be yielded in case of necessity, but not cast aside with an alacrity which renders one an accomplice to one's own murder. Too studied a refusal of martyrdom betrays 'an impious and cowardly love of life', and is incompatible with faith in the redeemer ...[7]

Banner's contention is that the practices of euthanasia are driven by a fear of death, but that martyrs live and die under Christ's command to 'fear not'. Martyrdom involves a death filled with hope, suffered rather than sought. The Christian martyr looks to a future of resurrection in Christ and not to a future wrapped in terror. Banner's arguments are worth much more detailed attention than I am able to give them here. They make a very clear case that seeking death, even *in extremis*, is a failure to see the promise of resurrection as a defining truth about human life under God.

But does the pastoral concern to alleviate suffering have no place in this argument? If the words of the early Church Fathers sound remote and

---

[6] Alasdair MacIntyre, *Dependent Rational Animals: Why Human Beings Need the Virtues*, London: Duckworth, 1999.

[7] Michael Banner, *Christian Ethics and Contemporary Moral Problems*, Cambridge: Cambridge University Press, 1999, p. 75.

austere to our ears, it must be recalled that the question of martyrdom was a great deal more immediate to them than to most of us. In our culture, we are bidden to take very seriously the voices of those who are actually experiencing a situation. Given that we are part of a global society, then the voices from both past and present who speak of the faith of the martyrs are not to be ignored since they too represent significant areas of human experience. But the voices of those today, experiencing an agonizing and lingering decline towards death, must be given due weight too.

The parallel between a person seeking assistance to commit suicide and the Christian martyrs is not a precise one. Because modern medical technology has enabled life to be sustained in ways that were not hitherto possible, even at the cost of grievous suffering for the patient, it is not unreasonable to argue that the obligation to sustain life as long as possible is no less frustrating to the will of God than deliberately ending a life that has no hope of improvement. This point, however, is also met by Banner's comparison with martyrdom. The Christian is called, not to avoid death until it cannot be resisted any further but to recognize that the moment of death is in God's hands. The obligation on those surrounding the dying person is to do all that can be done to ease pain, but not to take the irreversible step of deliberately bringing death about. Thus the objective of health care is not life at all costs but to sustain the possibility of life in a way which makes care for the patient the highest priority.

Living in a culture of atomized individualism – and, as we saw in Part 1, a culture in which the traditions of ethical reflection have deteriorated into a Babel where the views of the individual are not to be gainsaid – structures for placing other considerations over the primacy of personal choice are hard to sustain. Nevertheless, our culture does retain some notion of the common good as a defence against unrestrained individualism. Despite the attempt by some proponents of assisted suicide to attribute all opposition to 'irrational' religious traditions, there are many arguments from Christian belief which may also have a much wider appeal. Here, then, is a good example of Christian ethics sharing common ground with other positions, arguing authentically from Christian principles to conclusions which can also be reached by other routes.[8]

In *Aiming to Kill*, Nigel Biggar develops the argument that human life has both a biological and a biographical dimension. Human life is more than the reflex actions of breath and heartbeat, and entails a developing story in which a person contributes to, and receives from, the world beyond themselves. Biggar calls this a capacity to exercise responsibility, and while he makes it a

---

[8] As we have seen, this theme is worked out in detail by Nigel Biggar in his essay, 'God in Public Reason', *Studies in Christian Ethics* 19.1 (2006), pp. 9–19. Here, Biggar develops his theme by taking the arguments from his book *Aiming to Kill: The Ethics of Suicide and Euthanasia* (London: Darton, Longman and Todd, 2004) and showing how shared positions can be arrived at from within the Christian tradition and from secular starting-points.

theological construct, he is clear that the understanding of life in both biological and biographical terms can be appreciated without recourse to theology at all. In other words, an authentic theological argument may lead to practical positions which can be shared with others, arguing from very different principles.

It is not my purpose here to reproduce Biggar's arguments in full. But one argument has seemed especially telling in the public debate about assisted suicide and is simultaneously congruent with (though not exclusive to) Christian theology and an important challenge to the dominance of the consumerist motif of personal choice.

Sometimes the arguments for assisted suicide rest very heavily on the right to choose one's own end, and not to have that right removed on the grounds of a religious belief one might not share. Here, it is worth asking whether this expectation of choice and self-determination is a universal human attribute or a particular characteristic of some people in specific times and places. In other words, do the arguments based on the right to choose draw on a truth about being human or an accident of politics and history? The more one examines the image of self-determination as a key characteristic of being human, the less universal it appears. It may be that the ability to determine the course of one's life (and death) is a condition to which the world should aspire, but it remains that it is far from being an adequate description of many people's experience of choice. For many people, freedom of choice has been a virtue exercised by others which impacts on their lives in ways they did not choose. For many, in the so-called developed economies as well as in the more hard-pressed parts of the world, choice is perceived as threat and not benefit. One need only consider how 'choice' has been a mantra for market 'reforms' which have often closed down the options available to poorer people in order to expand the choices available to the rich and articulate. In the promotion of 'choice' in the National Health Service or in schooling, what people say they want is good health care and good schooling – but what they often get under the 'choice agenda' is what is left after the mobile, articulate and comfortable have taken what they want out of the system. Extend that experience to an even more unequal world, and the primacy of choice as a principle for being human begins to collapse. The ability to determine the time and manner of one's death may present itself as promise to people who are used to shaping their lives through the exercise of autonomous choice. But it may be perceived by others with different life experiences as another threat of being done-unto in the interests of others.

The point here is not to just to make the moral case against assisted suicide but also to call into question the assumed universalism of the particular construct of personhood on which the arguments for it are often based. My case flows directly from Christian understandings, even if it can also be widely shared, for it is central to faith that the gospel is good news for all and not only for those who are so happily placed that they can make it good for themselves. One grace given to the global Church is the perception that people are called to discipleship in many contexts, quickly relativizing the things that any one culture takes for granted. Freedoms and rights make sense not only in the context of me and my own life but in the context of what would be good for all if it was extended to them. The tradition of seeking the common good, so central to Christian ethical reflection, cannot be sidelined in the case of assisted suicide. Part of perceiving the common good is to attempt the imaginative exercise of asking how things we hope for would look to someone whose life experience was very different from one's own. It is surprising that, in a culture which is well used to acting inclusively in terms of ethnicity and gender, the diversity of experience between wealthy and poor, articulate and hesitant, confident and cowed, is so frequently absent from public ethical debate.

This point connects to the earlier remarks about the pitfalls of a therapeutic culture which privileges compassion over virtue. In the case of assisted suicide, it is notoriously difficult to untangle the wishes of the patient from those of others, including their family and the medical profession. It is a very strong reminder of how limited individualism can be in its ability to reflect upon the web of relationships within which moral decisions take place. The point is not just about inappropriate external pressure on the individual, but the individual's own difficulty in calculating the extent to which her decision is motivated by her own wishes or her sense of the interests of others, which may or may not be accurately calibrated. How far might my desire to avoid burdening my family affect my decision to have my life ended? Is my pain at their distress as they observe my suffering part of the equation? And is my evaluation of their distress accurate? The inscrutability of other people's values and motives comes sharply into focus – whose pain is being relieved here? One feature of many of the assisted suicide cases which have come to public prominence is the complexity and ambiguity of the love demonstrated between the patient and their family. 'For whom is this decision being made?' is hardly ever a straightforward question. Once more, the reflections on martyrdom are apposite, for martyrs do not hold their own lives cheap in order to lighten the suffering of others. But even without the specific Christian traditions around martyrdom, the secularist too can recognize the problem of human psychology. If I have spent my life putting others' interests before my own, how likely is it that my decision about the time of my death will be unaffected by a distorted form of self-sacrifice?

Finally, it is worth rehearsing the well-known slippery-slope argument, since it is often perceived as decisive by one side and irrelevant by the other when it comes to assisted suicide. As with the precautionary principle already articulated, it rests upon a suspicion of humanity's ability to hold lines which have been imposed on the basis of judgement rather than absolutes. Just as the precautionary principle demands that we should attribute personhood to the embryo from the moment of conception, since any other timing will be based on arguments which may be challenged or falsified, so it is argued that permitting assisted suicide on any grounds breaches the prohibition on taking life and makes any legal limit, or restriction to hard cases, open to later modification. Even the best motives, it is argued, are complex and may be self-deluding (the argument from original sin). Moreover, committing the protection of the vulnerable, whether the dying or the unborn, to governments and judges assumes a benevolence in such circles which may be justified now, in our peaceful liberal democracy, but which has proved extremely fragile over the longer view of history. Furthermore, we should note the tendency to move too quickly from the 'is' to the 'ought' with the argument that, because a procedure or practice is possible it therefore ought to be done. (There is a variant on this which argues that, because something can be done, if we don't do it someone else – without our scruples – certainly will.) All these things suggest that breaching an absolute position might very well mean embarking on a slippery slope, the trajectory of future developments being quite easily predictable. How many cases can be called to mind where a practice that has once been permitted has later been retracted? Some have – the time limit on abortions is frequently reopened in Parliament and has sometimes been reduced, but this is tinkering at the edges compared to the initial decision to permit the practice at all.

As we noted earlier, where one stands on this may reflect the relative theological significance given to sin and grace. However, the pessimistic secularist may share a similar analysis of the difficulty of defending a position once the absolute case has been abandoned. It is, after all, within living memory that some parts of Europe were torn apart by a creed which classed other human beings as less than persons and saw no objection to wiping them out on an industrial scale. The reaction against that era, and the determination that it should never be repeated, accelerated the ascendancy of a philosophy of human rights which has brought much good – but also many problems – into the world of ethics. A doctrine of human rights requires a prior clarity about what it means to be human – and that is where a real social consensus is, rather distressingly, absent still.

Further reading

For an evangelical approach to the question what it means to be human, see: Oliver O'Donovan, *Begotten or Made?*, Oxford: Clarendon Press, 1984.

It is well worth reading the papal encyclicals touching on this subject, since they are frequently referred to but less often read in full: Paul VI, Encyclical Letter, *Humanae Vitae* (1970), London: Catholic Truth Society, 1999; John Paul II, Encyclical Letter, *Evangelium Vitae*, London: Catholic Truth Society, 1995.

Perhaps the best recent book on the end of life is: Nigel Biggar, *Aiming to Kill: The Ethics of Suicide and Euthanasia*, London: Darton, Longman and Todd, 2004.

While most of the mainstream churches are against assisted suicide, some Christians are prepared to allow the case for compassion, and other arguments in favour of the practice, to carry more weight than official church teaching allows. Paul Badham is one theologian who is willing to argue that assisted suicide is compatible with Christian thinking in certain limited cases: Paul Badham, *Is There a Christian Case for Assisted Dying?*, London: SPCK, 2009.

10

The market economy

An examination of the market economy gives us a good opportunity to consider the liberal/communitarian dichotomy which was explored in Part 1.

Another reason for considering the market economy is that this is a somewhat neglected area of Christian ethics. True, there are a number of contemporary theologians working in this field, and at some periods in the past the subject has been of modest interest within the Churches. But on the whole the Church has not been particularly comfortable attempting to address economic issues.

In many ways this is surprising, since the market economy is not only a major influence upon how people understand value but epitomizes many aspects of the liberal culture which we have already considered. The market is all about human behaviour and is therefore a proper subject for the ethicist. One difficulty is, perhaps, that the market is about human action en masse and individual market actions can seem remote from their consequences. The great theorist of market economics, Friedrich Hayek, claimed that the market should be regarded not as something which could be influenced by human will but as something which simply *is*. He said that to protest about the outcomes of the market was as fruitless as protesting about the weather. But this seems counter-intuitive since market outcomes are the aggregation of millions of individual actions. The problem of relating individual action to remote outcomes is, of course, a problem faced by consequentialism in general – but there is a difference between 'hard to discover' and 'unknowable'. Moreover, judgement on individual moral actions is only one approach to a moral critique. Another is to question whether the conceptual framework of the market does justice to its moral significance. To do this, we need to consider the moral claims made on behalf of market economics, and for this a short excursion into relatively recent history may be helpful.

Western countries have, of course, worked with a market economy of some kind for a very long time. But from the Great Depression which began in 1929, successive governments saw their role as providing a framework of regulation which would moderate the tendency of markets to swing, often violently, between phases of prosperity and recession. Yet this principle was never the subject of a complete consensus. From the 1930s, the so-called Chicago School of economics, incorporating the work of thinkers such as Milton Friedman and Friedrich Hayek, had been developing a critique of government 'interference' in the free working of the market; a critique based on both economic and moral grounds.

By the 1970s, the thinking of the Chicago School had caught the imagination of Keith Joseph, a leading figure in Britain's Conservative Party, and Joseph found an enthusiastic supporter in Margaret Thatcher. With Thatcher's election victory of 1979, the policies of the Chicago School (which had been piloted in Pinochet's Chile but never before in a democracy) could at last be put into practice in a national economy of significant size. When the Reagan administration in the United States adopted similar policies in the early 1980s, it was not long before the work of Friedman and Hayek had become a new global economic orthodoxy.

While government regulation had sought to constrain the volatility of markets in order to protect populations from the impact of recession, the new orthodoxy argued that this had a stultifying effect which limited prosperity in general. The claims of social justice were declared to be illusory or even immoral and, while it was acknowledged that an unregulated market would increase the gap between rich and poor, it was claimed that, even so, the lot of the poor would be better than under a regulated system. The metaphor of the time was that of the rising tide which 'lifts all boats' – the fact that the tide lifts the dinghy and the liner by an equal amount was conveniently overlooked when a deregulated economy began to widen the gap between rich and poor.

Adjustment to the new orthodoxy inevitably created casualties, notably in rapidly rising rates of unemployment, often concentrated in communities which became economic deserts almost overnight. Here, the Churches in Britain began to become restive. When rioting broke out in a number of British cities, the then Archbishop of Canterbury, Robert Runcie, set up a commission to consider the state of the urban poor. The Commission's report, *Faith in the City*, of 1985, appeared to set the Church on a collision course with government.[1]

We have already considered briefly the content and theology of *Faith in the City*.[2] One reasonable criticism of the report, however, was its failure to see the moral case which the British government was making for a deregulated market economy. The tone of the report suggested only that the government had been ignorant of the human cost of its policies and that greater awareness and sympathy would lead to a change of course. This was to underestimate the government's belief that the unfettered market was not only effective but good. In the wake of *Faith in the City*, Raymond Plant,

---

[1] The Archbishop of Canterbury's Commission on Urban Priority Areas, *Faith in the City: A Call for Action by Church and Nation*, London: Church House Publishing, 1985.

[2] There have been a number of studies and theological reflections based on *Faith in the City* and its impact, notably: Anthony Harvey (ed.), *Theology in the City*, London: SPCK, 1989; Henry Clark, *The Church Under Thatcher*, London: SPCK, 1993; Peter Sedgwick (ed.), *God in the City*, London: Mowbray, 1995.

then Professor of Politics at Southampton University and a theologian, set out to convince the Churches that the moral case for markets needed to be understood if the human consequences of markets were to be addressed. The most accessible account of Plant's arguments is to be found in a short essay (modestly attributed to 'Raymond Plant and others') in Anthony Harvey's book, *Theology in the City*.[3] As this is out of print, a summary is appropriate here.

Drawing on Hayek, Keith Joseph and others, Plant's response to *Faith in the City* characterizes the case of the 'New Right' before proceeding to build the case against it. His first point is that, in Hayek's and Joseph's thinking, any concept of injustice requires that there be agency and intention. An unjust situation can only obtain as a result of an action intended by someone who has the agency to bring it about. The market involves millions of individual transactions, each characterized by agency and intention, but *collectively* the overall outcomes of these transactions are not – indeed could not be – intended, nor does anyone act with agency to bring them about. And so the outcomes of market processes cannot be unjust. Moreover, any attempt to modify the outcomes of market processes, for example by redistributing scarce resources, *will* be unjust since it would constitute coercion, thus infringing individual freedom. In a plural society how could principles of redistribution be arrived at? In the absence of widespread social consensus, redistribution must involve one sector of society imposing its beliefs and values (coercively) on everyone else – and this must be immoral.[4]

A comment on the centrality of the concept of scarcity in economics is apposite at this point. Scarcity, in its economic sense, does not just mean that there is not enough of a good to go around. The concept of relative scarcity means that a good may have a variety of alternative uses and, if it is used for one, it cannot be used for the others. This is closely linked to the idea of opportunity cost – the cost of the alternative which is forgone when a choice is made – which is an essential element in determining the market price of a good. Scarcity in its economic sense is thus a consequence of finitude, and making one person wealthier generally means that someone else has to forgo something.

The market, according to Hayek and the Chicago School, is a model for resolving the problem of distributing scarce resources in a condition of moral plurality. Tight-knit, or tribal, communities might form agreements about how wealth was to be distributed. But in a world where no one moral framework is universal, the only reliable method for distributing wealth is a structure where millions of individual transactions lead to unforeseeable outcomes and there is no external intervention. Thus all people can participate,

[3] Raymond Plant and others, 'Conservative Capitalism: Theological and Moral Challenges', in Anthony Harvey (ed.), *Theology in the City*, London: SPCK, 1989, pp. 68–97.
[4] See F. Hayek, *Law, Legislation and Liberty*, vol. 2: *The Mirage of Social Justice*, London and Henley: Routledge & Kegan Paul, 1976, pp. 31ff.

without 'coercion' by a dominant elite imposing its own distributive model on everyone else.

Plant concedes a good deal of this argument. In rebutting some of the claims of the market he accepts, for instance, that the appeal to community, as a mechanism for establishing shared values and priorities, is too 'slippery' to have much meaning.

Although Plant accepts that a descriptive meaning for community is conceivable, he argues that such a meaning would be so formal as to be of no use in social or political analysis. This is scarcely surprising since,

> The liberal tradition had its very origins in a *critique* of communitarian concepts and institutions ... This type of social theory sought the basis of human association not in tradition and habit but in the contract and consent of naturally free persons.[5]

This locates the market economy firmly within the liberal ethical tradition. It is important, though, to recognize that arguing for strong communities *or* atomized individualism as mutually exclusive does not describe any recognizable reality. Most cultures exhibit aspects of both, although the line between them can be hard to trace with precision. For example, in Britain (but not in America) the transfer of blood and human tissue is a sphere where the gift relationship is generally seen as preferable, and where social consensus regards markets as inadmissible. For this to be the case, there must be some sense in which it is possible to speak of 'the community' wherein these social priorities can be expressed.

Nevertheless, the ground for an appeal to community values is problematic, and this makes it difficult to address the distributional problem of scarce resources according to any given conception of social justice. There appear to be two possible responses to this situation. One is to argue that the inherent weaknesses of a market system are serious enough to invalidate such a system, to the extent that the countervailing anomalies of a different system appear preferable. The second is to argue that the notion of community may be less useless than Plant suggests, and that some construction of social bonds may be an achievable project that would act as a corrective in the processes of the market.

Plant contributes to the first argument. Drawing on the work of the economist Fred Hirsch, he seeks to show that at least some of the claims of market economics are fallacious – either because of internal inconsistencies or because, empirically, the economy does not function as market theory supposes.[6] The substance of his critique is that markets, with their foundation in liberal ideas of traditionless individualism, give an inadequate account of

---

5 See: Raymond Plant, 'Community: Concept, Conception and Ideology', *Politics and Society* 8.1 (1978), p. 82.
6 See Plant and others, 'Conservative Capitalism', and Fred Hirsch, *Social Limits to Growth*, London: Routledge & Kegan Paul, 1977.

reality because they ignore the socially formed nature of morality. At the heart of Hirsch's empirical analysis lies the concept of 'positional goods' – goods whose value decreases the more people acquire them. Hirsch's key examples are education – the more people have degrees the less valuable is *my* degree in securing me a better job – and mobility, where the 'open road' is available only to those who are first to own a car before motoring becomes a mass activity. As Hirsch puts it: 'to see total economic advance as individual advance writ large is to set up expectations that cannot be fulfilled, ever'.[7]

This is not, of course, a criticism of the whole of market theory, but it does fatally damage the 'trickle-down effect', which justified the enrichment of some and widening economic inequality on the grounds that all benefit as a result.

The case of positional goods is not the only way in which liberal market theory can be empirically questioned. The market's requirement for free competition may be jeopardized if there is nothing to stop monopolies defending their interests by preventing free entry to the market. In a system that is supposed to optimize outcomes by allowing all participants to follow the promptings of their own self-interest, the requirement to maximize competition is hard to sustain. The tendency for free competition and contestable markets to be eroded can only be countered by means external to the market process itself.

Plant adds a further point when he shows that market outcomes are not, in fact, unforeseeable, and therefore cannot always be regarded as unintended. It can be broadly foreseen that those who start with most resources will end up with even more while those who start with least end up with less. If outcomes are not unforeseeable then they become more clearly open to human agency and thus subject to moral judgement. So it appears that the market principle rests upon virtues and values other than the self-interest principle, even though these are hidden from view. As Hirsch puts it:

> Truth, trust, acceptance, restraint, obligation – these are among the social virtues grounded in religious belief which are now seen to play a central role in the functioning of an individualistic, contractual economy.[8]

Liberal capitalism is 'a system that depends for its success on a heritage that it undermines', and so, 'cannot be sustained on the record of its bountiful fruits'.[9] This is an extremely important point in considering the relationship of economics to Christian ethics. In short, markets can only work when there are broadly accepted moral foundations among the various 'players' in the market place – yet the individualistic assumptions of the market not only fail to reinforce those foundations but actively undermine them.

---

[7] Hirsch, *Social Limits to Growth*, p. 9.
[8] Hirsch, *Social Limits to Growth*, p. 141.
[9] Hirsch, *Social Limits to Growth*, p. 11.

These criticisms do not necessarily validate any alternative system. It may still be that the market is the least bad system around. Nevertheless, if the judgement that the market erodes its own moral foundations is correct, then liberal individualism is an inadequate ground for economic theory and the economics of market liberalism cannot deliver its promises. Even the advocates for markets have often recognized that 'laissez-faire' is an inadequate approach to certain areas of public life – at the least, to the maintenance of internal and external security. But these areas – and hence the requirement for interventions in market operations – have always been seen by market apologists as anomalous. In reality, according to Plant and Hirsch, the anomalies lie at the heart of the market mechanisms themselves. The problem is that 'the attempt has been made to erect an increasingly explicit social organization without a supporting social morality'.[10]

So the theory of the unregulated market economy contains flaws within itself. The idea that the outcomes of the market are neither moral nor immoral, since they are not intended by any moral agent, neglects the need for morality among market players and the inability of the market to sustain that moral foundation. But what of the claim, so central to the Chicago School and to the politicians of the Thatcher administrations, that the moral argument for the market turns upon the impossibility of modifying its outcomes without perpetrating injustice by coercing people to redistribute their wealth to others? The key point here is that the market not only promotes individualism, it also presumes that social plurality makes any moral agreement impossible.

Most people are in favour of equality – we just don't agree about what it is we want to be equalized. Equality of material wealth is not the same thing as equality of opportunity, and both are incompatible with equal freedom. The moral argument for unfettered markets turns upon the priority of freedom: because, in a plural society, there is no one version of justice or fairness, any attempt to overrule the workings of the market constitutes unacceptable interference with somebody's freedom. Thus, redistributive taxation involves coercing the rich to support someone else's version of social justice. Regulating the behaviour of entrepreneurs curtails their freedom in the name of some other end than profit. As we saw early in earlier chapters, the market is predicated on the idea that, in a plural society, there is no agreement about moral ends – the best one can hope for is agreement about means. That is what the market is – an agreement about the mechanism for social and economic exchanges which is designed to accommodate any number of individual objectives or ends.

We have also seen that the simplistic appeal to the virtue of 'community' is somewhat threadbare. Appeals to 'community' do sometimes imply covertly coercive attitudes. There is, for example, a particular brand of Christian

---

[10] Hirsch, *Social Limits to Growth*, p. 12.

radicalism which is fond of declaring what 'we' must do to become a more just society. At a conference about the British Churches' response to the recession of 2008, one speaker talked about the need to redistribute the housing stock so that good homes were available to all. The objective made theoretical sense from the point of view of managing scarce resources, but would no doubt be strongly resisted by many – not only those who lived in opulent mansions, but all those whose home held an emotional or family significance and was not just a utilitarian place of shelter. So how could this redistribution take place – except, perhaps, at the point of a gun? The illiberal implications of such a policy suggestion, voiced by Christians who would, in most circumstances, pride themselves on their liberality of mind, suggested that Plant's careful analysis of the case *for* a deregulated market economy had fallen on deaf ears.

This is one measure of the difficulty Christian ethics has had – at least in the so-called 'Christian' countries of the West – in adapting from a default 'Christendom' theology, as if the Churches and Christian theology were still able to speak with validity on behalf of all the people. Even if all Christians agreed on the right course of action, a plural context requires that the rightness of the action must be accepted by others also.

We will consider ways through this difficulty later in the chapter. Meanwhile, it is worth examining some of the arguments about Christian ethics and market economics offered from contrasting theological viewpoints. Both the enthusiasts for free markets, and their opponents, have representatives among serious Christian theologians.

Michael Novak and the spirit of democratic capitalism

The American Roman Catholic Michael Novak is a good example of a Christian market apologist. It is no accident that the British edition of his book, *The Spirit of Democratic Capitalism*, was published by the Institute of Economic Affairs, a think-tank which has fought a very able, but partisan, campaign on behalf of deregulated markets and right-wing social policies, not only through the Thatcher years but to the present day.[11]

Novak argues that the complementary structures of liberal democracy and the market economy are not themselves Christian in character, nor should they be, but that a theological rationale for their pre-eminence can be constructed. In parentheses, it is worth remarking here that, despite espousing policies which are generally associated with the political right, Novak is, theologically, very much a liberal in the sense that his 'project' is to offer a theological justification for a set of social institutions to which he is already committed rather than starting with theology to discern the proper shape of

[11] Michael Novak, *The Spirit of Democratic Capitalism*, Lanham, MD: Madison Books, 1982, and London: Institute of Economic Affairs, Health and Welfare Unit, 1991.

society. He is, in the terminology of our earlier chapters, arguing inductively and as a consequentialist, since his case is that democracy and markets
are good primarily because they lead to good effects. He insists that the
discipline of economics must be allowed its own autonomy and that Christians
must accept its wisdom without seeking some sort of theocratic economics
in its place. He allows human experience as a valid source of knowledge
about God, alongside God's self-revelation. And he holds that Christian
ethics must be constrained by contingency and the incomplete realization of
the kingdom of God – in other words, he expects ethics to accommodate
to the reality of sin. All these things show that Novak stands within the
liberal theological tradition and, incidentally, demonstrate that liberals are not
all on the political left.

Here, I want to focus on Novak's use of theology to set out the case for
the market economy. Whereas Hayek, Joseph and others made the moral
case for the market, Novak makes out the case in terms of Christian ethics.
His claim is that the market economy, political democracy and a plural
culture go together and support one another. Interestingly, Novak makes
this claim more by assertion than argument, and with some distinct sleights
of hand. For example, he claims that capitalism flourishes under democratic
regimes and implies a causal connection, but fails to mention that capitalism
can also flourish under non-democratic and illiberal regimes, as in the case
of Pinochet's Chile.

We are more concerned here with Novak's theological arguments; and
in many respects, his tone is surprisingly Protestant. His model of plurality
goes much deeper than merely the diversity of social, economic and gender
experience. It is closer to MacIntyre's conception of plurality, with the
difference that Novak celebrates what MacIntyre deplores: 'In a genuinely
pluralistic society, there is no one sacred canopy. *By intention* there is not.
At its spiritual core, there is an empty shrine.'[12] And however bleak, this is a
reflection of reality:

> Democratic capitalism not only permits individuals to experience alienation,
> anomie, loneliness and nothingness. Democratic capitalism is also constantly
> renewed by such radical experiences of human liberty ... humans are not,
> in the end, fully plumbed by the institutions in which they dwell. Each
> experiences a solitariness and personal responsibility which renders him (or
> her) oddly alone in the midst of solidarity. Conscience is the taproot of
> democratic capitalism.[13]

Conscience and the primacy of the individual, therefore, are at the heart of
Novak's Christian ethic. Elsewhere he talks down the significance of human
communities with the observation that, in the last analysis, we are judged by
God not as members of a community but stripped naked and alone. He does

---

[12] Novak, *The Spirit of Democratic Capitalism*, p. 53 (Novak's emphasis).
[13] Novak, *The Spirit of Democratic Capitalism*, p. 55.

not, however, dismiss the significance of community altogether since, he argues, the flourishing of societies and communities is best realized in freedom from coercion and state control, as modelled by democratic capitalism. Novak is concerned with processes rather than ends, and in that respect is again identified as firmly within the liberal tradition.

Novak calls upon six theological arguments (he calls them doctrines) to make the case for the compatibility of market economics and Christian faith – the Trinity, Incarnation, Competition, Original Sin, the Separation of Realms and *Caritas* (the word Novak chooses to circumvent the debasement of the word 'love').[14] Nowhere, however, does Novak explain how these six themes are adequate together in characterizing the Christian tradition – the omission of any focus on Christology or a doctrine of salvation being very noticeable.

The Trinity is offered as a model of pluralism-in-unity. The problem which this poses for democratic capitalism is how community can be constructed without damaging individuality. There is a lack of reciprocity in his handling of 'individual' and 'community' here. Versions of community – especially those promulgated by socialism – are characterized as threatening to individuality. But the threats to community posed by capitalist models of individuality are not explored. First, this reflects Novak's rhetorical approach – he is arguing *against* socialism. Second, his argument here demonstrates contentious empirical foundations – for in the end, whether individuality is under greater threat from community or vice versa is something only measurable against experience.

The Incarnation establishes Novak's emphasis on contingency and this-worldliness. 'The Incarnation is a doctrine of hope but not of utopia',[15] and 'The point of Incarnation is to respect the world as it is.'[16] Utopianism is, for Novak, one crucial source of societal coercion. Here his alertness to human sin is important. When human beings start to believe they can bring the kingdom of God to its fulfilment by their own efforts, human freedom is usually the first casualty (of many).

Competition seems an odd inclusion in a list of Christian doctrines and, interestingly, Novak does not try to attach competition to the doctrine of sin as if it were one aspect of the finitude and imperfection of the world. Instead, he sees competition as a positive virtue, obscured in Christian ethics because clergy and religious, unlike most people, are temperamentally 'passive, sweet and non competitive'.[17] Then again, 'The Jewish and Christian view shows that God is not committed to equality of results.'[18] The empirical and

[14] Novak, *The Spirit of Democratic Capitalism*, p. 337. After the 1982 edition, Novak added that, on reflection, he might have added 'Creation' as a seventh doctrinal heading (p. 419).
[15] Novak, *The Spirit of Democratic Capitalism*, p. 341.
[16] Novak, *The Spirit of Democratic Capitalism*, p. 341.
[17] Novak, *The Spirit of Democratic Capitalism*, p. 344.
[18] Novak, *The Spirit of Democratic Capitalism*, p. 345.

doctrinal arguments flow together because it 'would be odd if the virtues recommended by the Creator were *entirely* out of keeping with the laws of creation'.[19] So there is a kind of natural theology which supports the virtue of competition, but which has been occluded by the predispositions of religious professionals: 'to compete ... is not a vice. It is, in a sense, the form of every virtue and an indispensable element in natural and spiritual growth.'[20] Despite the deliberately provocative view of religious professionals, Novak has a point here. As Ronald Preston frequently pointed out, to the economist the opposite of competition is not, as the idealists would have it, co-operation, but monopoly. While Novak ignores the empirical evidence that unregulated markets often exhibit a tendency towards monopoly, he nonetheless scores a point against Christians uneasy with the principle of competition.

Original sin is another aspect of the nature of things which democratic capitalism, in its realism, must comprehend and embrace: 'Every form of political economy necessarily begins ... with a theory of sin. For every system is designed *against* something as well as in *favor* of something.'[21] Novak goes on to argue, from the principle of original sin, that the public display of vice which is often evident in capitalist economies is tolerable in a free society because such a society 'has confidence in the basic decency of human nature ... Belief in original sin is consistent with guarded trust in the better side of human nature.'[22] What is missing here is any sense that original sin not only affects individuals as moral agents but also corrupts the structures which people and societies construct to order their affairs. The market as an empirical reality can no more approach perfection than can the sinful individual. But Novak's liberal individualism prevents him from acknowledging this.

The doctrine of the separation of realms is crucial to Novak's pluralism as he argues that democratic capitalism cannot, in principle, be a Christian system. Thus 'Christian economics' is an impossibility since a market must be open to all, regardless of faith. All Christians do not follow their consciences to the same end – so, by implication, there is no single distinctively Christian account of 'the good'. But the separation of realms is also a safeguard against the distortion which sin introduces into systems. 'The perception of each of us is regularly more self-centered than our ideal selves can plausibly command.'[23] The separation of realms prevents our lack of objectivity from translating itself into self-interested coercion of others.

Finally, *caritas* is for Novak a deeper concept than the kind of individual charity which (in some right-wing understandings) takes the place of the state in caring for the unfortunate. The nature of divine love is that it values

---

[19] Novak, *The Spirit of Democratic Capitalism*, p. 346.
[20] Novak, *The Spirit of Democratic Capitalism*, p. 347.
[21] Novak, *The Spirit of Democratic Capitalism*, p. 350.
[22] Novak, *The Spirit of Democratic Capitalism*, p. 351.
[23] Novak, *The Spirit of Democratic Capitalism*, p. 353.

others as other. Novak then makes a significant move from theology to his economic case: 'In order to create wealth, individuals must be free to be other.'[24] That is, they are not to be understood as fragments of a collective. Virtues such as sympathy and co-operation are essential, but they are to be found in communities that are chosen, elected and contracted into. *Caritas* flourishes, according to Novak, not in the givenness of kinship or ethnic versions of community, but in the otherness of individuals within associational groupings.

Not only does Novak have little to say about salvation, he is also surprisingly hesitant about the promise of the *parousia*, allowing his 'realism' to create an unbridgeable gulf between the fallen world and the promised kingdom. As he puts it: 'The world is not going to become – *ever* – a kingdom of justice and love.'[25] So much for the Lord's Prayer.

It is worth noting, however, Novak's strong commitment to the material condition of the poor. It is, he says, the market that helps the poor to rise out of poverty. Here he draws on his own family's experience as immigrants to the USA and reaches the general conclusion that it is not redistributive socialism but democratic capitalism that has enabled immigrants to flourish in America. Novak's American identity is clearly of central importance in understanding his thinking: he does not attempt to justify his move from the particular US context to the general principle, and his examples of real forms of democratic capitalism are chosen very selectively. His general point about the efficacy of capitalism in alleviating poverty is just a version of the 'trickle down' theory that greater prosperity for the rich leads eventually to better conditions for the poor: a theory that relies on a benchmark of absolute poverty rather than any sense of social cohesion. If trickle-down doesn't work, then Novak's argument that free markets are good because they benefit the poor is fatally undermined, and here Hirsch's argument about positional goods is important.

Novak argues that we should evaluate societies by their fruits, but he does not, apparently, allow that people may choose different fruits from those which his version of capitalism bears – that is, disagreement about means may be as legitimate as disagreement about ends.

Finally, there is surprisingly little in Novak's writings about the Church. His focus on the individual, on choice and on freedom, and his horror of collectives, militate against a strong ecclesiology, and shared Christian principles or ways of life are not central themes. This neglect of ecclesiology shows how thin is his idea of community. He is thus unable, in the final analysis, to use Christian theology as more than a rationalization for a system chosen for other reasons.

---

[24] Novak, *The Spirit of Democratic Capitalism*, p. 355.
[25] Novak, *The Spirit of Democratic Capitalism*, p. 341.

Ulrich Duchrow and the *status confessionis* on the economy

Among the theologians who have directly addressed the ethics of the market economy, the German Lutheran Ulrich Duchrow could be said to be the polar opposite of the American Catholic Michael Novak. Duchrow's work has been closely associated with the World Council of Churches (WCC), who published his book *Global Economy: A Confessional Issue for the Churches* in 1987.[26] The use of the word 'confessional' in the title indicates the Christian communitarian direction of his thinking – the point of his argument is to establish what all Christians ought to believe about the global market economy. There are three characteristic features of his position.

First, Duchrow is profoundly shaped by the experience of his country under Hitler, and the emergence of the Confessing Church. Bonhoeffer is therefore a central influence. In response to the acquiescence of mainstream Lutheranism under the Nazis, Duchrow's doctoral thesis contributed to a radical reappraisal of Luther's theology in his work on the doctrine of the Two Kingdoms, reading this as a foundation for the Church's active involvement in political processes rather than a doctrine of separatism, which he sees as a nineteenth-century heresy. Duchrow's is therefore a theology of engagement with the secular, however distinctive the rationality and practice of the Christian community may be in the ways it makes that engagement.[27]

Second, Duchrow's theology starts from the condition of the poor under capitalism. The experience of marginalized people on the one hand, and the demands of God revealed in Scripture on the other, are of equal importance for his work. Unlike Novak, who sees the best hope for the poor to lie in the unfettered market economy, Duchrow is deeply influenced by the liberation theologies of Latin America and by the struggle against apartheid by the black churches of South Africa. Duchrow shares Bonhoeffer's insight that social theology requires an empirical analysis of society and politics, and this leads him into a respectful relationship with sociology and economics.

The third characteristic is related to the second: Duchrow is not very interested in plurality. His concern is material as well as theological – the exposure of an idolatrous economic system which oppresses the poor – and issues of plurality arise in his work only insofar as plurality is a challenge to hegemonic ideologies of power. Duchrow privileges the view from below rather than working with an assumption of a multiplicity of rival viewpoints. He is unashamedly on the political left, but is no liberal, in contrast to Novak who is a liberal of the political right.

---

[26] Ulrich Duchrow, *Global Economy: A Confessional Issue for the Churches*, Geneva: WCC Publications, 1987.

[27] There is a very helpful exposition of Duchrow's work in John Atherton's *Social Christianity: A Reader*, London: SPCK, 1995.

At the heart of Duchrow's position is the empirical observation that the global market economy is a force of oppression which bears intolerably on the poorest and most vulnerable and is thus, for Christians, an idolatrous creed which reverses the divine option for the poor. Explicitly, he compares the market with the apartheid system of South Africa – emphasizing in particular the structural nature, rather than the personal practices, of oppression. His second point of comparison is with the German Church under Nazism, where (in Duchrow's summary of events) the desire of the mainstream denominations to preserve themselves as worshipping communities allowed them to acquiesce in the oppression of others beyond their own membership. It is central to Duchrow's argument that the global market economy should be seen as no less idolatrous and no less devastating to human flourishing than Nazism and apartheid.

On two occasions during the twentieth century, first in the face of Nazism (by the Confessing Church) and later in response to South African apartheid, Churches have declared a particular ideology to be incompatible with Christian discipleship. Apartheid was declared a *status confessionis* by the Lutheran World Federation in 1977 and by the World Alliance of Reformed Churches in 1982. Rejection of Nazism and apartheid were deemed to be prerequisites for authentic Christian belief. No one could support those practices, or the regimes which upheld them, and remain within the Church.

Duchrow's call is for a similar *status confessionis* to be declared upon the global market economy. Supporting the ideology of the market and wilfully profiting from it should be declared incompatible with belonging to the Church. Following Bonhoeffer, the criteria for a *status confessionis* are: '1) When a socio-political institution notoriously fails to fulfil its God-given duty, 2) When it tries "too much" to be and to do, i.e., when it becomes absolute'.[28] The second criterion is a declaration against totalitarianism, but the global economy cannot be said to be absolute in this way, since countervailing economic models remain possible, if only on a small scale in 'closed' communities. In any case, the market celebrates plurality (even if it does so within a single ideology), so contains its own rebuttal of totalitarian ambitions. The first criterion is more problematic since it is framed in confessional terms. It requires an analysis of what the economy's God-given duty might be. Duchrow presents a lengthy analysis of biblical principles, and a comprehensive account of the market's failings. Just as he is clear about the fallen nature of the Church, and that it is called to continual repentance, so his demand from the global economy is penitence and reparation.

While the formal *status confessionis* is a rare event in church history, the idea that certain beliefs and practices are utterly incompatible with Christian belief is far from uncommon. But the key question is whether Christians

---

[28] Ulrich Duchrow, 'The Witness of the Church in Contrast to the Ideologies of the Market Economy', in *Poverty and Polarisation: A Call to Commitment*, Manchester: William Temple Foundation, 1988, p. 32.

may honestly and faithfully disagree on a particular point. Duchrow is forth-right in putting forward scriptural sources to justify his condemnation of the global market. His point is not that Christians should seek to be pure and to separate themselves from a sinful world but that they are called actively to resist the system under which they are forced to live, and to do so both for the sake of their own souls and for the good of the most vulnerable people of the world. Duchrow holds Christian ethics to be binding upon the faithful rather than a general social ethic based on Christian principles in which commitment to Christ is optional. He is impatient with the liberal's tendency to see complexity in everything to the detriment of clear principles and the campaigning stances which flow from them.

Duchrow sees liberalism both as the ideology responsible for the 'idolatrous' market system, and the movement within theology that has allowed Christian understandings to be co-opted in the service of capitalism. Like Milbank and Hauerwas, Duchrow accuses liberal theology of granting an unwarranted autonomy to economic and political matters, which has obscured the distinct-ive perspective of the Christian community. He maps out how 'a post-Constantinian version of caesaropapism' obscured the subtleties of Luther's position in the post-Reformation period, and how elements of Luther's concept of the Two Kingdoms were rediscovered in the late nineteenth cen-tury and used inappropriately to justify a hard division between the private and personal sphere of religion and the public sphere of politics:

> The intention of the late nineteenth-century liberal theologians, of course, was to defend the Christian faith as much as they could. All they managed to save was the inner faith, the inner attitude, the Sunday service, personal relationships.[29]

Duchrow goes on to note how this neo-Lutheran doctrine of the Two Kingdoms persisted even after the 'disaster' which overtook Lutheranism in the Hitler era – notably in South Africa as a justification for apartheid.

For Duchrow, Luther's theology points not to a separation of spheres but to the opposite – the necessity of Christian engagement with idolatrous power. So he is critical of theologies which interpret the biblical message in terms of 'common sense' (i.e. as a moral tradition shared widely with secular soci-ety). In common with other communitarian theologians, Duchrow is con-cerned to retell the biblical narratives in ways that draw out their strangeness and counter-cultural perspectives. While Milbank and Hauerwas perceive a principle of non-violence at the heart of the Christian tradition, Duchrow sees there a fundamental opposition to worldly power and the accumulation of wealth. Duchrow not only argues from the texts to the context but moves constantly between the experience of poor and oppressed people and a per-spectival reading of the texts of Scripture. This methodology has much in

---

[29] Duchrow, *Global Economy*, p. 10.

common with the so-called Pastoral Cycle model originating in liberation theology.[30] In contrast to Milbank in particular, Duchrow's use of Scripture focuses more on the Old Testament (especially Exodus and the prophets) and the dominical teaching of the Gospels (the Sermon on the Mount) than on a soteriology of the cross and resurrection.

The role of the Church as the community witnessing to radical alternative values is crucial for Duchrow. His is very much the flawed, contingent Church as it is. Despite the Church's stake in the capitalist economic system, and its social and political privileges, '[a]s long as the word of God is preached within it, the present empirical church is where the struggle for the true church of Jesus Christ is to be waged'.[31]

Yet for all the importance he places on the Christian narrative and tradition, exemplified in the Church, Duchrow is concerned to avoid narrow understandings of the boundaries of the community, and to avoid the legalism of defining who is within and who without. 'If boundaries are drawn, they are drawn by those who exclude themselves.'[32] This has two interesting consequences. First:

> the people of God is more than the church members who go to church on Sundays. It is about coming together with those who are trying to *do* the life-preserving and life-promoting will of God.[33]

So confessing the faith is not the only criterion for membership of the 'people of God' – rather, orthopraxis is the key: doing the right thing, rather than believing the right things. It is his conviction that the global economy is idolatrous and demonic, with its accumulations of wealth for the few and destruction for the many that leads Duchrow to declare that the crisis has been reached. His 'project' in response is the Kairos Europa movement 'for a socially just, life-sustaining and democratic Europe' which in 1998 issued a call

> to faith communities, trade unions and all movements and individuals that are working for social, political and economic change, to build coalitions to work for the liberation of society from the stranglehold of the deregulated global economy and its competitive culture.[34]

The Kairos principle is openly derived from the *Kairos Document* issued by the South African Churches in 1985,[35] and raises again the connection between Duchrow's work on the global economy and apartheid.

---

[30] See, for example, J. Holland and P. Henriot, *Social Analysis: Linking Faith and Justice*, Maryknoll, NY: Orbis, 1983, p. 8.

[31] Duchrow, *Global Economy*, p. 26.

[32] Duchrow, *Global Economy*, p. 127.

[33] Ulrich Duchrow, 'Let's Democratize the West as Well', in Christa Springe and Ulrich Duchrow (eds), *Beyond the Death of Socialism*, Manchester: William Temple Foundation, 1991, p. 80.

[34] Kairos Europa, *The European Kairos Document*, Salisbury: Sarum College Press, 1998, preamble.

[35] The Kairos Theologians, *The Kairos Document: A Theological Comment on the Political Crisis in South Africa*, 2nd rev. edn, London: CIIR/BCC, 1986.

But can the injustices of the global economy be treated as morally comparable to apartheid? Preston argues that, whereas apartheid 'could properly be called a heresy',

> it is extremely difficult to see other issues to which [the *status confessionis*] could apply ... It is much too blunt an instrument to cope with issues which need a closer analysis than the simpliste formulations on which the *status confessionis* concept relies.[36]

For Preston, the moral status of the economy is ambiguous in a way that apartheid is not. It cannot, therefore, be subject to the term heresy. On an issue like the economy it is impossible to reach a 'Kairos' moment, since questions of distributional justice remain intractable this side of the eschaton while the world is marked by sin and finitude. Preston argues that a *status confessionis* can work only where 'an ideology is totally false and the practice also corresponds to this ideology'.[37] Where Duchrow takes the institutions of the global economy to lead inherently to the abuses he describes, Preston's case is rather that the institutions are flawed, but that abuse is not of their essence.

Neither the liberal defence of the market by Novak nor the communitarian attack on market economics by Duchrow succeeds comprehensively. Novak's liberal approach causes him to make theology subordinate: the handmaiden of his prior commitment to the market and to liberal democracy. He is strong in his analysis of plurality but theologically somewhat superficial. For Duchrow, the idea that the market economy might be a response to the problem of ethical pluralism is an irrelevance. For him, the gospel imperative allows no truck with the amoral market mechanism and it is the role of the disciple to reject it and to respond in penitence to the fact that all are caught up in a global economic order. In Duchrow's ecclesiology, there is no room for debating the rights and wrongs of the market. If we find the outcomes of a global market economy impossible to square with the Christian vision of a just world, Duchrow offers a theologically grounded response which works, provided we ignore the problem of plurality which the market is concerned to address. The fact that market economics professes to be a system which avoids coercion forms no part of his thinking. The difficulty of applying Duchrow's ideas in a plural world, except by coercion, does not figure for him. For all his aversion to 'caesaropapism' and the post-Constantinian settlement, Duchrow's thinking contains this strong residual echo of Christendom and the assumption of Christian rule.

The economy is not only a suitable topic for Christian ethical enquiry – it is, in many ways, a test case for the adequacy or otherwise of a Christian ethical approach. Not many ethicists have engaged substantively with

---

[36] Ronald H. Preston, *Confusions in Christian Ethics: Problems for Geneva and Rome*, London: SCM Press, 1994, p. 69.
[37] Ronald H. Preston, *Religion and the Ambiguities of Capitalism*, London: SCM Press, 1991, p. 86.

economic questions, so my criticisms of Novak and Duchrow must be tempered with respect for their willingness to stand out in doing so. But it remains that neither a liberal nor a communitarian approach seems adequate to address the question which market economics poses: how to arrive at a model for distributional justice in a plural world, without either coercion or neglecting the poor. The market theory tries to address the problem of plurality, however ineptly and unjustly the market economy turns out to handle it. In the earlier part of this book, I argued that the best prospect for a revived public theology may lie in some kind of corrective synthesis between liberal and communitarian approaches to Christian ethics. The test case of the economy suggests that this must, again, be our conclusion.

Further reading

It helps, in considering the ethics of the market economy, to be clear what economics as a discipline is trying to do. Here is a dialogue between a Christian ethicist and an economist which explores the extent of overlap in the structures and principles of the two disciplines: Andrew Britton and Peter Sedgwick, *Economic Theory and Christian Belief*, Oxford, Bern, etc.: Peter Lang, 2003.

Two excellent introductions to the debate about Christianity and market economics are: John Atherton, *Christianity and the Market*, London: SPCK, 1992; Rob van Drimmelen, *Faith in a Global Economy: A Primer for Christians*, Geneva: WCC Publications, 1998.

More communitarian approaches to Christian ethics and the market include: Tim Gorringe, *Capital and the Kingdom: Theological Ethics and the Economic Order*, Maryknoll, NY: Orbis Books, and London: SPCK, 1994; Kathryn Tanner, *Economy of Grace*, Minneapolis: Fortress Press, 2005.

A more varied range of approaches are explored in this collection of essays: John Atherton and Hannah Skinner (eds), *Through the Eye of a Needle: Theological Conversations over Political Economy*, Peterborough: Epworth Press, 2007.

11

Sex and sexuality: trouble for the Churches

It is a brave person, these days, who attempts to write on the subject of sexual ethics while seeking to retain trust across a broad cross-section of members in the mainstream Churches. Not only the Anglican Communion, but many other denominations have been deeply split by opposing understandings of sexuality – usually meaning homosexuality – and even those Churches which appear to be riding above the fray contain many dissidents within their ranks. This is a topic where the heat of the arguments has obscured the light, to the extent that it might very well be included alongside the debates on abortion and nuclear deterrence in MacIntyre's list of interminable arguments pursued from incommensurable positions.

On the other hand, to dodge the issue is to evade a responsibility to the many faithful Christians who are alert to the argument but honestly unclear where they stand within it. Moreover, questions about sexuality in today's Western culture are at once so prevalent and so vexed that the ethicist may reasonably feel a duty to the whole community to try to illuminate the issue. But no one does so without a risk of making enemies these days.

At times, the disputes over homosexuality are presented in the public media as if they are entirely internal arguments within the Church – and often as if they confirm the idea that religions are essentially irrational and refuse to take on board new knowledge of any kind. Within the Churches, the same dispute is often portrayed as a conflict between authentic Christian ethical teaching and a sell-out by some Christians to the obsessions and mores of the culture around them. At the centre of the problem, therefore, lies the relationship between Christian ethics and the assumptions of Western societies, especially the secular aspects of the latter. (To characterize Western culture as purely secular is to ignore its longer history as a culture influenced very strongly by Christian assumptions.)

One good reason for looking into the dispute about sexuality is that it helps uncover the complex, and at times misleading, ways in which the terms 'conservative' and 'liberal' are used. At the same time, the increasing tendency – especially in America and in some evangelical circles in Britain – to adopt a terminology of 'left' and 'right' to identify the opposing positions arouses a strong suspicion that there are political as well as ethical and ecclesiological dimensions to the issue.[1] We cannot hope to resolve all

---

[1] See, for example, the *Church of England Newspaper* on many occasions since about 2007 for this usage of 'left' and 'right'.

the questions here, but it may help to try to tease out some of the points at issue and, perhaps, to suggest some alternative approaches which might be fruitful.

The Bible, culture and sexuality

Many have been puzzled by the way in which the question of homosexuality has been presented as fundamentally a matter of biblical authority. Texts on the subject, whether in Old or New Testament, are few and do not always seem capable of being detached from a very specific socio-historical context without considerable loss of meaning. As is well known, the issue is not mentioned at all in the Gospels and there is no intimation that Jesus himself spoke about it. On the other hand, he spoke on other matters of sexual ethics, notably divorce, in ways which appear to convey a plain meaning – but the meaning in terms of practical ethics has been adapted, without much rancour, by many Churches in order to conform better to social conventions (whether such accommodations are a good precedent or an awful warning is, of course, disputed). Meanwhile, the book of Leviticus in the Old Testament, and a number of passages in the Epistles, appear to condemn sexual relationships between members of the same sex out of hand.

This is not the place to examine each of the relevant biblical texts in detail – many others have done so in considerable depth, although their conclusions do not always agree.[2] Two main strands of argument, however, need to be considered. First, do the biblical utterances against homosexual relationships actually mean what we take them to mean? Second, even if their meaning is not obvious, does the overall ethical trajectory of the Bible suggest a clear judgement, one way or the other, on homosexuality? For, even if specific texts are ambiguous, the collective thrust of biblical teaching may still suggest an ethical conclusion.

The first point turns, to a great extent, on the question of whether sexual relationships in biblical times carried the same meanings as they do today. For example, it is clear from both Old and New Testaments that marriage was seen much more in property terms than would be common in our culture today. One can go further and argue that most sexual relationships in the Bible, and in antiquity, have overtones of power, at least as much as desire, which we find alien. Of course, the association between marriage (and, hence, sexual relationships), property and power persisted long after biblical times and remains strong in many cultures – the children of the Enlightenment are, in this respect, the odd ones out. Nevertheless, in detaching marital relationships from property rights, Enlightenment ideas have worked in step

[2] A good introduction to the opposing views within biblical scholarship is: Dan O. Via and Robert A. Gagnon, *Homosexuality and the Bible: Two Views*, Minneapolis: Fortress Press, 2003. Via explores the 'liberal' approach while Gagnon articulates the 'conservative' position.

with Christian ethics by helping to weaken the treatment of other human beings as commodities.[3]

It is well-known that Paul's epistles are concerned, not only with systematizing Christian doctrine and helping the nascent churches to grasp the nature of discipleship in the light of the resurrection, but also with understanding the significance of God's self-revelation in Christ in relation to Judaism and to Greek and Roman thought. As his condemnation of homosexuality is about distinguishing proper Christian conduct from that of pagans, the context of same-sex relationships in antiquity is clearly significant. Did homosexuality then mean what it means to us today?

From Greek culture it is clear that sexual penetration was very much about the exercise of power. To penetrate a man sexually was to reduce him to the lowly status of a woman – literally, to un-man him. Nor is this just a long-forgotten understanding from antiquity. In all-male prisons today, homosexual rape is not infrequently deployed as a means of reinforcing hierarchies among violent prisoners. There is a considerable difference between that kind of oppressive action and a loving, enduring, same-sex relationship (which is not to say that same-sex relationships are any freer from exploitation than heterosexual ones). The context of the New Testament references to same-sex relationships does suggest that it is this kind of sexual dominance and humiliation that is in Paul's sights – but that is not to say that this is the limit of his concern about homosexual relationships. Those who are disposed to find faithful same-sex relationships acceptable for Christians argue that an unambiguous biblical prohibition is not implied by the Scriptures, but for anyone who places a high value on the authority of biblical texts the presumption is that the obvious meaning is the true meaning unless absolutely conclusive evidence to the contrary can be sustained.

The biblical arguments deserve considerably more scrutiny than I can give them here, and the reader would be well advised to follow up the arguments in the books by Via and Gagnon, or Dormer and Morris. Sufficient for now that the biblical evidence has not convinced those who argue for the theological legitimacy of same-sex relationships (known in most contexts as the 'liberals') that they are wrong, nor have the opponents of same-sex relationships (the conservatives or traditionalists) been persuaded that the Bible is not clear on this point. Doing both sides the courtesy of assuming that they read their Bibles with equally prayerful attentiveness (and noting the extensive and serious biblical scholarship which supports both sides) it is clear that the argument is not capable of resolution on solely biblical grounds. This conclusion, of course, will please almost nobody – but the fact that scholarship has failed to arrive at a definitive textual reading shows that the problem is not with the texts but with how we read them. It has often been

---

[3] See Andrew Mein, 'Threat and Promise: The Old Testament on Sexuality', in Duncan Dormer and Jeremy Morris (eds), *An Acceptable Sacrifice?: Homosexuality and the Church*, London: SPCK, 2007.

said that the Bible is not so much a book which we read, as a book which reads us. In the present instance, the dispute tells us more about the preconceptions and allegiances of the protagonists than about the direct teaching of Scripture.

The St Andrew's Day Statement

But, if the question cannot be resolved by direct appeal to texts, how does it appear through the prism of Christian doctrine which, after all, is generated out of reflection on the whole Bible and reflections on the nature of God, humanity and the created order which flow out of the biblical sources? There have been a number of attempts to argue from doctrine to a position on homosexuality, and one of the most useful is the so-called St Andrew's Day Statement, not least because it appears in a collection of essays which include a critique of the Statement itself.[4]

The St Andrew's Day Statement, first published in 1995, is the work of seven theologians within the evangelical tradition, including Michael Banner and Oliver O'Donovan. They start by distancing themselves from the strident disagreements that are dividing the Church: 'That the issue should have become so highly dramatized calls for repentance on the part of all members of the Church. It suggests that the Gospel has not been directing the acts, words and thoughts of Christians on this subject.'[5] The aim of the group was explicitly to bring a fresh precision and theological clarity to the question, both for those who would agree with their conclusions, whose thinking would be sharpened, and for those who would disagree, to prompt them to be clear about where the disagreement lay.

The Statement itself begins with three fundamental creedal principles and moves on to suggest how those principles should be applied in the context of the question of homosexuality. The principles are those of orthodox Trinitarian theology – first, Jesus Christ as the one Word of God and the work of atonement which makes us God's children. 'His promise and his call are for every human being: that we should trust in him, abandon every self-justification, and rejoice in the good news of our redemption.' The second principle outlines the work of the Holy Spirit: '...guided by the Spirit of God to interpret the times, the Church proclaims the Word of God to the needs of each new age, and declares Christ's redeeming power and forgiveness in mutual encouragement and exhortation to holiness'. Third, 'The Father of Jesus Christ restores broken creation in him', as we live 'awaiting the final revelation of the children of God'.[6]

[4] Timothy Bradshaw (ed.), *The Way Forward?: Christian Voices on Homosexuality and the Church*, 2nd edn, London: SCM Press, 2003.
[5] Bradshaw, *The Way Forward?*, pp. 5–6.
[6] Bradshaw, *The Way Forward?*, pp. 6–7.

Stating basic theological truths in this way does, of course, prefigure the direction the application of those principles will take – the emphasis on the brokenness of the creation, the call to holiness and the warning against self-justification, all tend to draw back from the language of fulfilment, celebration and the wideness of God's mercy which have characterized the theological arguments of those seeking to understand some homosexual relationships as blessed. It is not self-evident that one approach is more theologically authentic than the other. Already we see clues that the corrective influence of different strands within the Christian tradition may need to be brought to bear.

Not surprisingly, the sections of the statement which focus on practical application emphasize the disjunction between the world and the Christian calling rather than the world-affirming strands of Christian theology. These sections of the statement will be persuasive to anyone who is uneasy about the shape of contemporary sexual discourse. Because, in Christ, we know 'both God and human nature as they truly are', the statement argues that ways of categorizing human identity in terms of particular characteristics, whether sexuality, ethnicity, class or nationality, are inadequate – and, in consequence, there is no special calling for people of any particular sexual orientation; all are called to follow in the way of the cross. 'The struggle against disordered desires, or the misdirection of innocent desires, is part of every Christian's life.'

Then the statement considers how theology relates to other sorts of knowledge. Of course, it says, the Church must be open to empirical evidence, but 'guided by God's Spirit' the gospel remains the touchstone for discerning truth. Here, the authors make a key point: the question is not so much that empirical knowledge and scriptural evidence may point in different directions but that the whole framework within which we understand things may, in a flawed culture, be itself deeply flawed. The assumptions of modernity are called into question: 'To "interpret the times" in the midst of . . . theological confusion, the Church must avoid being lulled by the vague idea that there is a transparent and necessary progress of thought working itself out in history, with which it has only somehow to keep abreast.'[7] As we have seen, there are some critical questions to be asked about the central assumptions of modernity: here those assumptions are taken from the outset to be misleading.

The statement concludes with the assertion that there are only two options open to Christians, all of whom are called to live chastely: marriage between a man and a woman or singleness. 'In neither vocation . . . does fulfilment require or allow the exercise of every power or the satisfaction of every desire that any individual may reasonably have.'[8] Wanting to live otherwise is not authority to do so.

---

[7] Bradshaw, *The Way Forward?*, p. 8.

[8] Bradshaw, *The Way Forward?*, p. 9.

So the St Andrew's Day Statement simultaneously seeks to relativize the significance of homosexuality as a pivotal question for Christian ethics and to reaffirm, through doctrinal arguments, that it is not a valid practice for Christians. But the main significance of the statement is its insistence that practice must follow from the application of doctrinal principles, themselves grounded in Scripture. This is immensely more profound than mere proof-texting: those who disagree with the authors' conclusions must respond with something equally attentive to the scriptural and dogmatic roots of faith.

Bradshaw's book allows the statement itself to be followed by just such a critique, written by Rowan Williams before he became Archbishop of Canterbury.[9] Williams warmly welcomes the Statement's theological method. With its authors, he deplores the treatment of homosexuality as a litmus test issue for orthodoxy and, like them, he rejects what he calls 'the casting off of "traditional" or even scriptural norms' which for some is 'part of a general programme of emancipation from the constraints of what they conceive to be orthodoxy, part of a package that might include a wide-ranging relativism, pluralism in respect of other faiths, agnosticism about various aspects of doctrine or biblical narrative, and so on.'[10] All these he rejects in favour of the theological method exemplified in the statement – start with creedal statements then move to application. (Williams was no instinctive liberal, even before becoming Archbishop of Canterbury.) Moreover, he has no difficulty accepting the statement's three foundational principles. It is in the move from principle to application that he begins to part company with the authors. First, he queries the running together of ethnicity, class, sexuality and so on as equally peripheral aspects of human identity. Whereas class-identity may change, racial identity does not – and the experience of many black Christians is often that 'the particular ways of living associated with this racial and cultural history may by the grace of Christ be shown as transparent to Christ, ways of expressing and witnessing to the richness that is in him'. It matters, in other words, that arguments resting on analogy get their analogies right. If homosexuality is analogous to ethnicity rather than class, a different set of conclusions may follow. The statement tends to treat sexual orientation more like class – more as something that can be changed – and so the analogy, despite its doctrinal seriousness, is skewed in a particular direction. Similarly, Williams notes that the statement treats the scriptural references to homosexual orientation as plainly referring to the same phenomenon that we understand by the term – but as we have seen, this is not self-evidently the case, and he goes on to suggest that the vices listed in Romans 1 (on which the statement depends heavily) do not immediately suggest the kind of orientation that we now mean when speaking of homosexuality.

---

[9] Rowan Williams, 'Knowing Myself in Christ', in Bradshaw, *The Way Forward?*, pp. 12–19.

[10] Williams, 'Knowing Myself in Christ', p. 12.

In terms of ethical conduct, as Williams says, 'if the basic point that homo-sexual desire is always the symptom of a fundamental spiritual confusion or error is accepted, what follows [the statement's points about conduct] makes good sense' – but his central point is that the statement does not clinch that basic point incontrovertibly. In short, Williams is saying to the authors, I love your method, but it does not lead inexorably to one set of conclusions, since your premises (and maybe your use of analogy) can be called into question. He concludes: 'How does the homosexually inclined person show Christ to the world? That must be the fundamental question, and theological and pastoral discussion of this theme ought to begin from there rather than from rights on the one hand or law on the other ... What we disagree about is, I hope, not the principle but how knowledge-in-Christ is mediated and made actual in the church's life.'[11]

Reframing the questions: Milbank

So whether approaching the subject from the point of view of Scripture or of doctrine, the question of homosexuality seems not to have been answered conclusively – although the arguments on either side are treated as conclusive by many. Indeed, it is the very intractability of the issue which suggests that there is more going on here than a dispute about ethics. Nor is this simply one further example of a MacIntyrean interminable argument between incom-mensurable positions – or at least, not obviously so – since all concerned are seeking to work from within the Christian tradition. True, there are some who express the liberal position in terms of the 'common sense' of the wider culture, and some conservatives who hold their position solely on the grounds that this is (as they see it) what the Church has always taught – but neither are serious endeavours to wrestle with the theology. Likewise, the old tension between pastoral and ethical imperatives is sometimes seen here, with claims that affirming homosexual people is a matter of pastoral care and that doctrine and ethics must serve that imperative. There is an interesting variant to that argument, which proposes acceptance of homosexuality as a necessity for mission, claiming that, in a world which already accepts homosexuality as unproblematic, the Church's continued difficulties with this subject are making it harder for the gospel to be heard. Neither of these arguments need detain us – we have already had a good deal to say about the difficulties of prioritizing pastoral concerns over ethics, and the view which sees the Church's ethical arguments as a barrier to mission has clearly lost sight of the fact that a constantly malleable Church is hardly worth calling people to join. But putting aside these half-thought-through positions, the continued stalemate between serious theologians does suggest that other approaches might be illuminating.

---

[11] Williams, 'Knowing Myself in Christ', pp. 18–19.

At this point, John Milbank has some useful observations to contribute. He says:

> I think we are totally wrong to approach contemporary sexual issues as primarily a moral matter, or of what should and should not be done. On the whole, disagreements about sexual morality are a farcical unreality, masking grotesque depths of hypocrisy. 'Liberals' always seek more fidelity and security than they own up to; 'conservatives', in practice, will usually put life before principle. In this realm, the sham of argument is forever overshadowed and defeated by anxiety. So the Church should forthwith cease its participation in these unedifying disputes.[12]

Easier said than done, perhaps, since few churches choose the battles which threaten to divide them. But behind the rhetorical flourishes, Milbank makes a good point about how the protagonists actually behave, and goes on to explain his reasoning.

He speaks of the 'increasing displacement of erotic affinity by a general system of market competition for sexual conquest that is entirely complicit with the pursuit of economic power and advantage', and reminds us that our culture's insistence that sexual fulfilment demands constant novelty is completely wrong, because any depth of sexual encounter requires what he calls the 'relaxed presence of the ever-different-familiar' which requires time to unfold.

Milbank, as we might suspect, is attacking the culture-shaping imperatives of capitalism within a wider conception of modernity from which he seeks to rescue the truer insights of faith. In modernity and under capitalism, he suggests, all our understandings of sexuality are distorted. It is within this wider critique of contemporary sexual assumptions that he analyses same-sex relationships. In modernity (which he identifies as 'since the Renaissance'), attitudes to sexuality have oscillated between a 'disciplinary Puritanism unknown to the Middle Ages', and the 'promotion of a dark, death-obsessed, and narcissistic eroticism'.[13] Strikingly, he goes on to claim that it is not homosexuality but heterosexuality with which the Church has the deepest problem.

How does he arrive at this bold assertion? His argument is that our culture (using that term as shorthand for Milbank's analysis of capitalism within modernity) is uninterested in profound difference since culture constantly reduces the conception of the human to mere individuals who treat each other as means not ends. Thus, the deep and mysterious difference between male and female is lost in an obsession with 'difference' in general which

---

[12] John Milbank, 'The Gospel of Affinity', in Carl E. Braaten and Robert W. Jenson (eds), *The Strange New World of the Gospel: Re-evangelizing in the Postmodern World*, Grand Rapids, MI: Eerdmans, 2002, p. 15.

[13] Milbank, 'The Gospel of Affinity', p. 16. (Note the implication that the Middle Ages are the touchstone for authentic Christian society. Cf. his 'half turn back to pre-modernity' in 'Postmodern Critical Augustinianism' – see p. 106.)

never reaches beneath the superficial. Gender, then, becomes superfluous in a capitalist structure which requires individuals who look only to themselves, thereby enhancing consumption and generating a highly 'flexible' labour force. Indeed, he asserts that capitalism seeks to commodify the 'production' of children so as to leave the adult population more free to work and to consume, and that this requirement to commodify children contributes to the culture's inability to comprehend the profound differences between women and men. Here he takes a swipe at the way we express equality of the sexes by diminishing, rather than affirming, the real differences between male and female.

So, Milbank argues, all our understandings of sexuality are disordered and the 'problem' of homosexuality is just one manifestation of the wider malaise. He is quite prepared to accept that 'homosexual practice is part of the richness of God's creation' but holds that it can, nonetheless, never fully reflect or embody the sacramental significance of 'the unity in difference of man and woman' any more than can our culture's disordered grasp of sexuality in general.[14] Indeed, he makes the claim that, in a culture of narcissistic individualism, all our sexuality is 'transcendentally homoerotic'.

Milbank's ideas do not, of course, close the question of sexuality within Christian ethics. I offer them as an example of how the question can be reframed in a way in which the 'problem' is not projected onto some caricatured 'other' but becomes a problem for everyone, mired as we are in structural sin. The power of Milbank's analysis is that it looks upon homosexuality, not as uniquely aberrant but as a facet of a more widely disordered sexual culture. Few Christians, I think, could claim with a straight face that our contemporary culture is not deeply confused around sexual matters, although not all would agree with Milbank's version of why this is so.

. . . and Hauerwas

As we considered Milbank's work alongside that of Stanley Hauerwas in Chapter 6, it is interesting to find that Hauerwas too has turned his attention to reframing the question of homosexuality within a wider narrative of Christian ethical practice. The style, as we would expect, is different – more direct and polemical, less full of striking paradox, but no less rhetorical or surprising. Typically, for Hauerwas, his most interesting essay on this subject (first delivered as a sermon) has been given an 'in your face' title: 'Why Gays (as a Group) Are Morally Superior to Christians (as a Group)'.[15]

As we saw, Hauerwas's central motif is that the Church does not *have* a social ethic, the Church *is* a social ethic; and that ethic revolves around the vision of the peaceable kingdom. Hauerwas first gave this sermon at the time

---

[14] Milbank, 'The Gospel of Affinity', p. 17.
[15] To be found in John Berkman and Michael Cartwright (eds), *The Hauerwas Reader*, Durham, NC, and London: Duke University Press, 2001, pp. 519–21.

when America was at odds over whether gay men and women should be allowed to join the armed forces. His argument is that it ought to be Christians, not gay people, who are treated with suspicion and mistrust in the context of military service. Typical of Hauerwas's barn-storming approach are his parodies of arguments used by those opposed to gays in the military: 'Would you want to shower with such people [Christians]? You never know when they might try to baptize you.'

Hauerwas's main point here is not, of course, about homosexuality but about pacifism in the Christian tradition, but it is also a ringing critique of the way in which America was tying itself in knots over what he saw as, theologically, the wrong question. Gay people are regarded as untrustworthy in the heat of battle, but: 'Could you really trust people in your unit who think the enemy's life is as valid as their own or their fellow soldier? Could you trust someone who would think it more important to die than to kill unjustly? Are these people fit for the military?' The implication for the debate about homosexuals in the Church is that we too are barking up the wrong tree. Much is made, at times, in the course of the homosexuality debate, about the need for the Church to stand out counter-culturally, and same-sex relationships are treated as a totemic issue which can crystallize that counter-cultural calling. Hauerwas makes it clear that it is possible to be counter-cultural on different fronts and that it is not obvious that the gospel treats sexual matters as of greater concern than questions of violence and war.

But, more significantly for our reflections here, Hauerwas is arguing that gay people are morally superior to most American Christians because gay people have understood that camouflaging themselves in order to be acceptable to the dominant culture is a lost cause – they can be true to their nature only by standing out publicly for their gay identity. In Hauerwas's school of Christian ethics, the scandal is that the Churches have not recognized a similar truth.

Considering sexuality on a wider canvas than same-sex relationships, it is worth considering other contributions on the subject from Hauerwas, notably his equally provocatively titled essay, 'Sex in Public: How Adventurous Christians Are Doing It'.[16]

Hauerwas uses the essay to reiterate some of his central themes, including the MacIntyrean principle that if I want to know what I ought to do, I need to start with the question, 'Who do I want to be?' Like Milbank, he argues that contemporary approaches to sex are deeply disordered – and this includes times when the Church's teaching has colluded with the romanticism or the realism of the age (as ever, Hauerwas is not specific about exactly which Church is guilty of this). In keeping with his insistence that it is not the Church's job to underwrite an ethic for everybody but to be a community

---

[16] In Berkman and Cartwright, *The Hauerwas Reader*, pp. 481–504.

embodying its own distinctive narratives and practices, Hauerwas is arguing here for a Christian sexual ethic to be derived from the Church's political understanding of marriage. In other words, what place does marriage hold in the Church's self-understanding and what does that imply for sexual ethics? This is a more substantial departure from conventional under-standings than it might appear since it means a decisive rejection of attempts to ground sexual ethics in natural law. Hauerwas's aim is not to discern a purpose for sexual relationships deduced from their intrinsic nature but to ask, first, what the Church is for and then to ask what kind of sexual ethic fits that purpose.

Whereas, in much contemporary social thought, the family is treated as 'a voluntary society justified by its ability to contribute to the personal enhance-ment of each of its members',[17] Hauerwas instead speaks of the family as an expression of the Christian's hope for the world. Here, he makes an ingenious move from a discussion about singleness as an authentic Christian vocation to a discussion of the theological significance of having children. In the early Church, singleness was a no less valid calling than marriage, and singleness gained its virtuous standing from the ability of single people to put the mission of the Church first in their lives. Because the single person gives up, not just sex but, more significantly, the promise of having heirs, singleness is a powerful expression of the Christian's belief that his or her future is now safeguarded by the community of the Church and not by the family. And this is not contradicted by the equal esteem given by Christian theology to marriage, since marriage, and specifically having children, expresses the hope, 'in spite of the considerable evidence to the contrary, that God has not abandoned this world'.[18]

Marriage, therefore, is a political statement by the Church. It is, says Hauerwas, a 'heroic' institution because Christians are called to enter into marriage, not for their personal gratification or fulfilment, but to express precisely that hope for the world. Hauerwas gently punctures the romantic illusion that a Christian marriage is necessarily a happy marriage in the con-ventional sense – for while Ephesians 5.22ff. can be used to justify happy marriages, 'there seems to be nothing in the text itself to suggest that Christ's love and unity with the Church implies that unity is without discord'.

Like Milbank, Hauerwas is arguing that only within marriage can the full theological meaning of sex be realized. And he too is clear that contemporary society's whole understanding of sexuality is deeply disordered. So for both Hauerwas and Milbank, the battle over homosexuality in the Churches is a sideline which misses the crucial point.

That said, our earlier critique of the communitarian theologies of Hauerwas and Milbank raises some important questions. Is it true to the Church's vocation to say, as Hauerwas does, that it is not the Church's job to develop

---

[17] Hauerwas, 'Sex in Public', p. 496.
[18] Hauerwas, 'Sex in Public', p. 499.

an ethic for society? Milbank implies that, unless one is already committed to the Christian narrative, the Church's sexual ethics simply don't make sense outside the theological framework. It is as if the rest of the world has the choice of going to hell or signing up to the full theological world-view on offer from an idealized Church. Might the horrors of modernity, which both of them deplore, be mitigated or even reversed by a Church which sees its mission more in terms of engagement with the society we have than creating in embryo the society we would like? Are not Christians citizens? The theological ethics of Hauerwas and Milbank excite and inspire many in the Church (myself included) and encourage greater theological rigour, deeper questioning of transient cultural assumptions and a profound cherishing of the Scriptures, the Church and its traditions. But how they translate into practical missiology seems to me less clear.

There is a further dimension which gets short shrift in the writings of these theologians, but which – especially in the realm of sexual ethics – is raised again and again in the missiological context. This is the baleful history of the Church's collusion in the subjugation of minorities and of women. If starting with theological first principles always serves to underpin the positions regarded as 'traditional' in the Church's teaching, there needs to be some acknowledgement of the ways in which those teachings have been used in the past to reinforce attitudes and practices which are usually now recognized to be contrary to the Christian vision. It is not unfair to ask what kind of community would fully embody the sexual ethics which these theologians propose. The empirical Church of history has almost always combined the 'traditional' sexual ethic with a low status for women, sacralizing their childbearing role to bind them into subordinate positions, and has policed other aspects of its sexual ethic in ways which have reinforced a human hierarchy that seems at odds with the thrust of the Gospels. It does not seem adequate to offer only the alternative scenarios of a profoundly disordered modernity or a Church which has difficulty learning new insights into the gospel. What seems to be missing is a liveable model for the empirical Church which, called to cut through the confusions of contemporary modernist attitudes, nonetheless has to overcome its own history of an equally distorted traditionalism. On the other hand, if that traditional ethic has been adequately expressed in the Church of history despite our modernist distaste for its consequences, that surely needs saying too, with no nonsense about being a community where women and men enjoy equal esteem.

The wider context of disagreement

Hauerwas's and Milbank's work suggests that there is potential for reframing the so-called debate about sexuality in terms which might cause members of the Church to re-examine what is at stake. Where a desire to reinforce traditional teaching is part of a reaction against the confusions, inconsistencies and trivialities of modernism, it helps to have a thoroughgoing analysis of what, exactly, is wrong with modern societies. Where the urgency stems from the perceived marginalization of the Christian faith, there must be reflection about whether the Church is called to be at the centre or at the margin. Most of all, reframing the problem offers hope that sincere Christians who disagree might find a vocabulary for working at their disagreements and recognize in each other a fellow disciple seeking to live faithfully. Yet all these attempts to make the debate truly theological have failed to prevent issues of sexuality – specifically homosexuality – from doing grave damage to Churches and Communions. What else has been added to the equation, besides theology, which makes the issue so toxic? In Part 1, we considered the significance of dialogue between traditions as a prerequisite for an authentic public theology. We need to be clear whether the sexuality debate proves the impossibility of dialogue across differences, or whether other factors are muddying the waters.

Global church politics and many not-so-hidden agendas have made questions of sexuality impossible to resolve calmly. Two observations may be worth rehearsing. First, the vehemence of the 'debate' may be a reflection, not of un-Christian lack of charity, but of the profound significance which the question holds for many. Second (and notwithstanding the first point), when an issue becomes a proxy for a wider set of discontents and agendas, no search for common discourses is likely to make much headway because the wrong questions are being asked.

To expand on the first point: when 'reasonable' church members abhor discord, it may obscure a failure to take religious concerns seriously enough. In a culture where religious susceptibilities are often regarded as essentially trivial private pursuits, it is hard to communicate a passionate belief that sexual behaviour is a factor in either the common good or the objective good of an individual. If I believe that your immortal soul is at risk if you pursue certain actions, should I be indifferent to your choices? If I believe that the future integrity of the Church is in jeopardy if it compromises with the disordered spirit of the age, should I remain mild-tempered and avoid rocking the boat? If I believe with equal conviction that the Church has been apostate in preferring a limited vision of God merely because that vision is familiar, should I not fight valiantly to expand the Church's grasp of God's love? Of course, when passion spills over into self-centred certainty – the belief that, despite the depredations of human finitude, I must be right and others utterly wrong – righteousness has been overshadowed by sin. But that is not to say that culturally specific assumptions of politeness are the only Christian mode of discourse.

Having said that, it is hard to believe that all the protagonists in the argument about sexual ethics are motivated by such passionate concern for God's truth, otherwise the caveat that my sight may be clouded by my own sin might have a wider moderating effect. The 'elephant in the room' is the way the issue has become a key spot where many American culture warriors have chosen to stand and fight. We have already looked at the way in which un-resolved political differences in American culture have absorbed a kind of rudimentary Christian vocabulary and how this has raised the political stakes so that the imperative to win an argument is equated with faithfulness, and losing an argument with traducing God. A trawl through the websites of some American independent Churches reveals a language of conflict and, often, hatred which is quite alien to British church life (at present, at least). As noted earlier in this chapter, the adoption of the terminology of 'left' and 'right' to denote the pro-gay and anti-gay factions gives the game away: the real dispute may be less theological than political. And the adoption of that same vocabulary in some British church circles justifies my parenthetical comment above – in an age dominated by American economic and cultural power, all manner of attitudes and vocabularies are among the things exported from the United States. Add the legacy of colonialism in Africa (a British, rather than an American legacy – although a new style of Pentecostalism is flowing rapidly from the USA to Africa forging, perhaps, a new colonial relationship), and the dispute is clearly not susceptible to resolution by theology alone.

For this reason, it is clear that there is not a precise correlation between 'liberals' and 'conservatives' on issues of sexuality, and the 'liberals' and 'communitarians' of the ethical typology in previous chapters. When anti-liberal communitarians like Hauerwas and Milbank are unconvinced by either side of the argument and even see moral virtue in the homosexual community's stance within modernity, it is clear that 'communitarian' does not always equate with 'conservative'. And the very vehemence of the dispute has driven liberals back to the Bible, doctrine and the tradition. Indeed, if the identification of the theological liberals as being on the 'left' has any accuracy, it is they, not the conservatives, who are counter-cultural in political terms. The liberal/communitarian typology is not a particularly good fit in terms of the way this dispute is taking shape.

That, perhaps, is a good point on which to end this chapter. Perhaps the debate about sexuality has more in common with MacIntyre's interminable arguments between incommensurable positions than I initially allowed since, if the global political context is a reliable guide to what is going on, the fact that the various antagonists are all Christians becomes a secondary factor. This may be a conflict between the world-view of the liberal Enlightenment and the conservative reaction against it but, if so, it is not being fought out on MacIntyrean lines. Indeed, since the political right is committed to liberal market economics, this seems to be a war between rival versions of liberalism – economic liberalism plus social authoritarianism on the one hand, and market scepticism plus social liberalism on the other.

In the case of Christian sexual ethics, despite all the good work by serious theologians striving to present the matter through a close examination of Scripture, doctrine and social analysis, the clamour continues. Here is more evidence that secularization theories, predicting the rapid eclipse of all religions under the rising tide of modernity and reason, are deeply flawed. Religion still matters – religions and Churches are still worth hijacking for political causes. But a real Christian sexual ethic doesn't start there – and perhaps only a great deal more work along the lines of the St Andrew's Day Statement will eventually clear the fog.

Further reading

For the Church of England's key document on questions of homosexuality, see: *Some Issues in Human Sexuality: A Guide to the Debate*, London: Church House Publishing, 2003.

For a development of the arguments in the St Andrew's Day Statement, and a partial response from an evangelical perspective to some of the statement's critics, see: Oliver O'Donovan, *A Conversation Waiting to Begin: The Churches and the Gay Controversy*, London: SCM Press, 2009.

For views on wider topics of sexuality, from a broadly liberal perspective, see: John Davies and Gerard Loughlin (eds), *Sex These Days: Essays on Theology, Sexuality and Society*, Sheffield: Sheffield Academic Press, 1997.

For a wide-ranging exploration of the issues, looking at sex in its biblical and social contexts, see: L. William Countryman, *Dirt, Greed and Sex: Sexual Ethics in the New Testament and their Implications for Today*, Minneapolis: Fortress Press, 1988, and London: SCM Press, 2001.

Third interval: anniversary thoughts on Darwin, science and belief

In an ethics seminar, it can be illuminating to take an anecdote from a participant's recent experience and tease it out to reveal the ethical insights it contains. Here is something that happened to me.

2009 was the two hundredth anniversary of the birth of Charles Darwin. A friend working in the field of practical theology once commented that the challenge the Church faced was to start thinking as if Marx, Freud and Darwin had really lived. In other words, the Church needed to accept that these three had changed the way we think about ourselves and our relationships. Whether Christians agree with them or not, the Church, as much as the secular world, needed to absorb their ideas and frame its view of the world accordingly. That was back in the 1980s. I had no idea at the time that so much conflict could have been stirred up in religious circles by the bicentenary of Charles Darwin.

As part of the anniversary, London's Natural History Museum set up a comprehensive exhibition on Darwin and his work and, as part of the programme accompanying the exhibition, I was invited to be on a panel debating the question 'Can science and religion coexist?' My fellow panellists were a scientist, formerly of the Royal Society, who was also an Anglican priest, and a member of the museum staff who specialized in researching weevils. The discussion was attended by well over a hundred people who had chosen to spend an evening considering the question and had paid for the privilege of doing so. One can only guess at the composition of a group of that size, but my estimate was that most were under 40 and well-educated.

The occasion had been complicated by something I had written a few weeks before, commemorating the Darwin bicentenary.[1] Arguing that Christian theology had not, historically, been at odds with scientific enquiry, I had suggested that the early response to Darwin by churchmen such as Wilberforce had been deeply mistaken, driven not so much by sound theology as by anxiety that new and surprising ways of thinking would destroy every social foundation. A line of argument which I had regarded as unexceptional – certainly in Church of England circles – had, however, become controversial as a result of the American presidential election campaign, then in full swing, and the creationist views of the Republican vice-presidential candidate, Sarah Palin. One national newspaper, responding to what I had written, attempted

---

[1] Malcolm Brown, 'Good Religion Needs Good Science', The Church of England Website, <http://www.cofe.anglican.org/darwin/malcolmbrown.html>. Accessed: 10 October 2009.

to spin it into a 'Church opposes Sarah Palin' story, but in a half-hearted way which suggested the story was unlikely to go very far. However, this was sufficient to alert a Sunday paper which ran a 'shock horror' account of how the dreadful liberal Church of England was 'apologizing' to the long-dead Charles Darwin, and wheeled out a Conservative politician to call me 'ridiculous'. I had, of course, made matters worse by deploying a rhetorical flourish which was interpreted by the Press as the Church of England's official, and belated, apology to Darwin (which it wasn't).

So I turned up at the Natural History Museum, one rainy night in November 2008, half expecting a claque of Christian creationists to be there ready to attack the scientists on the panel, and to attack me once they had heard what I had to say. I was half right. There were plenty of attacks on the scientists, but not from creationists; and, in fact, there was almost no sign of any Christian motivation among those who spoke from the floor.

I suppose that, in the context of a national museum committed to reasoned debate and not to show business, the event was predictably well-mannered. It would be easy to imagine the sort of 'debate' on the subject that could be engineered by someone who was more interested in the drama of controversy than in seeking truth – perhaps putting a prominent atheist scientist like Richard Dawkins up against an American creationist, with a nice Anglican like me in the middle to be the patsy whom no one listened to. What we got in the end was, in its way, more disturbing than that.

The scientist from the museum opened the proceedings. He spoke of the nature of scientific enquiry; what it was and what it was not. He explained the experimental method, the way a theory is tested and tested until it begins to have predictive potential and how new knowledge can falsify or confirm a theory. He spoke of what science cannot do – how science can describe something but not ascribe value to it. And he added that the scientist also requires faith – not in the religious sense, perhaps, but in the sense of trusting in what is only part-known in the expectation that deeper knowledge will follow. As a succinct exposition of the nature of science it was superbly lucid.

The scientist-priest expanded on this theme from a more historical angle, speaking of the quest for understanding and meaning throughout human history, and how religion had paved the way by making the created world significant enough to study. Religion had only relatively recently ceded ground to scientific methods which had enormously accelerated and expanded our knowledge of the world around us. Yet, he too noted, religion and science were not rival ways of explaining the world, even if they had sometimes been thought of in this way, but addressed different areas of human enquiry.

Having no formal scientific background I was, by this point, feeling a touch out of my depth, but my contribution was to go further into the 'is/ought' distinction, with empirical and moral understanding complementing one another and thus making religion and science, at least potentially, comfortable bed-fellows.

Then the contributions from the floor began.

The opening shot set the agenda for the next three-quarters of an hour. It was a question directed to the scientist from the museum: Why had he not got the courage of his convictions to say that science had debunked religion once and for all?

I hadn't expected the audience to be sympathetic to my argument that science and religion had nothing to fear from each other, but I had not anticipated that the same kind of argument from a scientist would be received with such aggression – and to the obvious approval of much of the audience. Nothing the museum scientist could say would satisfy the audience's desire to hear 'science' wipe the floor with 'religion'. In vain he asked them to reflect on what he had actually said about scientific method and its limits. The slightly cosy unanimity of the three speakers, all of whom in our different ways had answered the question, 'Can religion and science coexist?' with a pretty firm 'Yes', was clearly not what this audience had come to hear.

The discussion eventually moved to a more direct attack on religious thought. Yet the level of understanding was weak, even for a predominantly secular group. One speaker argued that religion and science were obviously and insuperably at odds, since, 'religion says that homosexuality is wrong but science has proved it's perfectly OK'. How do you start to answer such mis-conceptions except to remember that most people gain their understanding of religion – and, indeed, science – from popular media not renowned for subtlety, or even accuracy. The comment received responses from all three panellists: a priest who had worked as a scientist in the field of human sexuality, a scientist who pointed out some of the limits of anthropology in explaining, as opposed to describing, what it is to be human, and a theologian who emphasized that both religion and science involved weighing dissenting views.

As the discussion rolled on, the contributions maintained the general hostility to religion. Another natural scientist stressed that he had no problem in understanding himself as the sum total of his inherited genes and that the thought that being human was qualitatively different from being any other sort of animal was incomprehensible to him. Altruism, kindness or virtue were, to him, no more than complex programmes which helped bring about optimal outcomes for the species. Hardly poetry, I thought, but if you are happy to explain the poetic aspect of existence in those terms too, it has a certain consistency. Then came a diatribe from another speaker, rehearsing the old chestnut about religion being the source of all human conflict and misery whereas science was all about improving the human condition . . . except, of course, where science was deployed to make more and more destructive weapons, in which case (happy inspiration!) that was an example of science being corrupted by ideologies which behaved like religions. For fear of drifting into the interminable argument about whether Stalin's initial studies in the seminary had made him the atheist tyrant of later history, I stayed silent.

But it was the early skirmishes which had surprised and even shocked me. What is happening when an uncontroversial (as I thought) account of scientific method is treated as selling the pass in the battle to the death between science and religion? The event took place at a time when Richard Dawkins's *The God Delusion* was still being advertised on large posters across London's Underground and was to be seen grasped in the hand of many a fellow commuter each morning. But the contributions from the floor of the debate didn't seem like recently read insights, or even to be based on such secondary sources – they felt as if the speakers not only believed their position to be unassailable but had arrived there after serious journeys of their own. I repeat that most members of the audience who spoke did not come across as superficial, unreflective or stupid – rather the opposite.

I believe that the events of that evening were deeply significant for the practice of Christian ethics today. What was demonstrated was not just the difficulty of understanding a faith from outside, as it were, when the basic vocabulary of faith is no longer socially current; it also demonstrated how the perceived irrationalities of religion have been replaced, not with the empirical rationalism of good scientific method, but by a caricature of science which has more in common with fundamentalist religion than anything that takes place in a well-run laboratory.

We never did get as far as considering what Darwin would have made of it all.

The participant who was satisfied that being human amounted to no more than the sum of his genetic inheritance was, perhaps, voicing a thoughtful version of a more pernicious position. Characteristically, this approach has a strong reductionist element – sexual ethics, for example, is *just* a codification of behaviour that maximizes genetic advantage; kindness is *just* a learned behaviour that helps preserve the race from self-destruction – one could go on. Reductionist positions like these are a kind of closed world which cannot be falsified on the grounds of evidence since the 'arguments' for the position contain within them the rejection of other views. Rather like astrology, or some forms of religious fundamentalism, the propositions cannot be falsified because the attempt to falsify them is itself explained within the overarching theory – what MacIntyre, we recall, referred to as epistemological defences. This is precisely the opposite of the good scientific method that was offered at the Natural History Museum and which had allowed Darwin to develop his theories and his successors to test them.

Darwin's significance lies not only in the breadth and grandeur of his theory of natural selection but in the manner by which he showed that empirical methodology could reveal great truths about the nature of the created world. Of course this was a challenge to the religion of his time, although it is doubtful if, say, Augustine or Aquinas would have had any problem with his general approach. What may be less obvious is that Darwin's theories were so far-reaching that they seem to have prompted a real hubris among the kind of people who hope to find and possess a grand theory of everything.

This over-reaching in the name of science has sometimes been called scientism, and its characteristics are not dissimilar to some forms of religious commitment which the 'rational' world often graces with the term fanaticism. 'Scientism' is so far removed, not only from Darwin's work but also from Darwin's character, that it is depressing to see how his bicentenary has helped bring it to prominence. Is it reading too much into the initial religious opposition to Darwin by Wilberforce and the like to suggest that in some half-formed way they could see how Darwin's theories might be misused?

Darwin's ideas of natural selection, as a way of understanding evolutionary processes over thousands of years, make sense. Translate them into a half-understood notion of 'the survival of the fittest', imagining the processes to work on a day-to-day basis, and evolution gets mixed up with a social theory in which the weak perish – the very opposite of the Christian vision in the Magnificat (Luke 1.46–55). This 'Social Darwinism', in which the strong flourish and losers go to the wall, is also the complete converse of what Darwin himself believed about human relationships. From this social misapplication of Darwin's theories have sprung insidious forms of racism and other forms of discrimination which are more horribly potent for having the appearance of scientific 'truth' behind them. Darwin's immense achievement was to develop a big theory which went a long way to explaining aspects of the world. But to treat it as an all-embracing theory of everything is to travesty Darwin's work. The difficulty is that his theory of natural selection has been so effective within the scientific community, and so easily understood in outline by everybody, that it has been inflated into precisely that general theory of everything – which is not only erroneous but dangerous.

Christians will want to stress, instead, the human capacity for love, for altruism, and for self-sacrifice. There is nothing here which, in principle, contradicts Darwin's theory. Humanity has acquired the capacity to reflect, to imagine, and to reason inductively from what is known to what is not yet known. Some animals may have these features in a very rudimentary form, but the human capacity is very much greater. What marks us out is our awareness, through the capacity to imagine, of other people not only as bodies but as persons. It is that, above all, which has enabled the human mind and will to achieve so much. If this capacity – which we can characterize as the capacity for love – is consistent with Darwin's ideas of natural selection, it suggests that it is our capacity as a species to act in ways which appear to be against our personal interests which has, paradoxically, enabled us to survive as 'fitted' to our context and environment. So the pseudo-Darwinian reductionism which elevates selfishness into a virtue and celebrates power and dominance, is not only a misunderstanding of Darwin but may conceivably contribute to human decline by eroding those aspects of being human which have given us such a natural advantage. Even the more sophisticated versions of social Darwinism, which interpret all human behaviour in terms of the struggle for dominance and the maximization of genetic advantage through the generations, risk presenting us with an image of being human which makes us slaves to some kind of evolutionary imperative as if we are pro-grammed in ways we cannot overrule. But the point of natural selection is that it is precisely by being most fully human that we demonstrate our fitness. Being fully human means refusing to abdicate our ability to act selflessly, lovingly or even irrationally. It is vital that Darwin's theories are rescued from political and ideological agendas that are more about controlling human imagination and unpredictability than about good science.

All this will remain contentious in some circles. Some Christian move-ments still make opposition to evolutionary theories a litmus test of faithful-ness and – the other side of the coin – many believe Darwin's theories to have finally destroyed religious belief and therefore reject any accommodation of one by the other. Why should this be?

The Church of England in 1860 was already facing challenges to its former pre-eminence. Freethinking and non-conformist Christianity were challenging the power of the established Church – and then came Darwin. These were nervous times for Anglicans, and when worldly power is believed to be God-given, threats to power are perceived as attacks on God. What was true for Anglicans in 1860 is largely true for all kinds of Christians today, although (depending where you are in the world) the threat may be perceived to come from radical Islam, secularism, consumerism or atheism. The cultures within which Christians try to be faithful are widely seen to be hostile, at least in some respects, and discipleship means, at some level, standing against social trends. The problem for all Christians is discerning where the surround-ing culture is really a threat and where God's hand can still be seen at work. Because 'science' has been widely regarded as offering a total theory of everything; because some scientists have encouraged this claim; perhaps because we all know how reliant we are on scientific ideas which we barely under-stand and which make us nervous of our ignorance; and perhaps because the Churches have not been good at equipping people to see God at work in the contemporary world – for all these reasons and others, a parody of science has become a focus for certain forms of social unease. In so far as science has its hubristic side, there is a case for science to answer. In so far as 'social Darwinism' has diminished our sense of being human and being in relationships, there are real problems to address. But first it is important to recognize that the anti-evolutionary fervour in some corners of the Church may, like the conflicts over sexuality, be a kind of proxy issue for other discontents; and perhaps most of all, an indictment of the Churches' failure to tell their own story with conviction in a way which works with the grain of the world as God has revealed it to be, both in the Bible and in the work of scientists of Darwin's calibre.

At a university in Kansas some years ago, I asked a biology professor how he coped with teaching Darwin's theories to students whose Churches insisted that evolution was heresy and whose schools taught creationism. 'No problem', he replied. 'The kids know that if they want a good job they need a degree, and if they want a degree they have to work with evolution theory. Creationism is for church, as far as they're concerned. Here, they're Darwinists.' Perhaps he was over-cynical. But he was also pointing to young lives which could not be lived with integrity – the very opposite of how Christians are called to live. There is no integrity to be found either in rejecting Darwin's ideas wholesale or in elevating them into the kind of grand theory which reduces humanity to the sum of our evolutionary urges. For the sake of human integrity – and thus for the sake of good Christian living – some *rapprochement* between Darwin and Christian faith is essential. At the very least, we need to acknowledge the degree to which, for good and ill, Darwin has changed the way we think.

Further reading

For an excellent recent study of Darwin's work and its theological implications, see: Nick Spencer, *Darwin and God*, London: SPCK, 2009.

12

Waging war: and peace

From conflict within the Christian tradition we turn to the tradition's handling of conflict in the world at large. Christians worship the Prince of Peace and the liturgy constantly repeats the angels' prayer for peace upon earth. Yet war and armed conflict are a continual fact of human existence which has marked the age of Christendom no less than any other age. As Christendom wanes, the arguments within the Church about an authentic ethical approach to war, not surprisingly, intensify. At the same time, the nature of war itself continues to change. The Cold War stand-off between super-powers, which generated the nuclear arms race and irreconcilable arguments about deterrence and disarmament, has given way to a situation, paradox-ically perhaps, less stable. Wars are no longer a matter just for belligerent nation-states but are more likely to be within states, as with the numerous civil wars which have scarred Africa in recent years, between major military powers and rogue or failing states, or in that hinterland to war which is international terrorism. In none of these cases do former assumptions about the nature of warfare apply straightforwardly.

Three strands appear to be emerging within Christian ethics to accom-modate these shifts: the reworking of the just war tradition in order to address new contexts, a newly confident understanding of Christian pacifism, and a radical rereading of Scripture which underpins a practice of passive resistance. We shall look at each, and at the connections between them.

In each case, it is worth asking who is the presumed audience. An ethical reflection on war and conflict may be addressed to governments and those who decide whether and how to wage war; it may be addressed to the soldier who may, or may not, be aware of the *causus belli*; it may address the citizenry as a whole, or it may be part of the Church's exploration of its counter-cultural vocation. The implicit audience, not surprisingly, reveals the place Christian ethics is taken to have in the public realm, indicating who is assumed to be listening when the Church speaks. This, inevitably, reflects the place Christians ascribe to themselves in history, whether accurately or otherwise.

Just war revisited

If you are part of a minority group, separate in some ways from mainstream culture and misunderstood or even persecuted, your experience of war and violence is likely to come in two forms: either as a victim of others' aggression or by being enlisted into someone else's conflict. The earliest Church, negotiating its relationship to the surrounding cultures on the basis of its new insights from the life, teaching, death and resurrection of Jesus, was more concerned with how to cope with coercion than with the responsibilities of power. It is a moot point whether the relative marginalization of Christianity within contemporary Western cultures has restored the Church to a position analogous to the early Church or whether the legacy of its once-powerful status makes such identification impossible. What is certain is that, since the rise of Christianity to a more favoured place within the Roman empire, many new moral questions, associated not with marginalization but with power and authority, had to be faced. The crucial theological figure in the transition into a Church which sought to play a full part in the world was Augustine. As Charles Reed puts it:

> St Augustine's genius and probably his greatest gift to Christian political theology was his ability to reconcile a non-Christian theory of civil society with the promise of the New Testament. By urging the early Church to distinguish between the Church in the earthly and the heavenly city, he encouraged it to engage with and challenge all that is corruptible and imperfect in a fallen world.[1]

Grounded in Augustine's theology, and developed by Aquinas, the theory of the just war emerged, not as a theology of war, but as a set of largely pragmatic guidelines (Max Stackhouse calls them 'moral maps').[2] Perceived to be consistent with Christian beliefs, their aim was to constrain the destructive impact of war, both on the material world and on the souls of human beings − since, on this side of the eschaton, it could not be eliminated. The fundamental principle is that the believer is also a citizen committed to the common good and driven to engage with politics in order to secure a just peace. There is a basic democratic assumption here: understandings of just war are not directed simply to leaders and military decision-makers (although such people may be Christians, in which case the Church has a duty to inform their thinking) but to citizens whose consent is understood to legitimate actions by their leaders. In the thought of Augustine or Aquinas, as Stackhouse puts it, 'God is not only concerned about the pure heart or the holy church, but the course of human history and the redemption of the world.'[3]

As is well known, there are two strands to the just war tradition, concerning the justification for war (*ius ad bello*) and the conduct of war (*ius in bello*). In the case of the first, the presumption of peace entails that going to war must be a last resort. How to discern the last resort is, of course, deeply

---

[1] Charles Reed, *Just War?* London: SPCK, 2004, p. 35.
[2] Max Stackhouse, 'Theologies of War: Comparative Perspectives', in Jon L. Berquist (ed.), *Strike Terror No More: Theology, Ethics and the New War*, St Louis, MO: Chalice Press, 2002, p. 209.
[3] Stackhouse, 'Theologies of War'.

problematical, but the principle upholds the idea that war is never a desirable option but, at best, the least bad possibility. Just war thinking has been around for most of the history of the Christian faith, and Robin Gill refers to it as 'one of the more abiding theological heirlooms in the modern world'.[4]

Not only must war be a last resort, it must also be waged in a just cause. Recognizing all the difficulties of agreeing what is just, the principle establishes that some form of public scrutiny, some wider agreement about justice than mere assertion by an interested party, is necessary if a war is to be supportable.

Further, war may only be declared by a legitimate authority. Because of the destructive and chaotic implications of armed conflict, it must remain the preserve of some properly constituted political order. Although the most familiar form of legitimate authority is the nation-state, the notion of legitimacy need not inevitably be so restricted. As Stackhouse points out, the legitimacy of authority is both a legal and a moral concept. Not surprisingly, this distinction is not easy to discern or to agree upon – democratic legitimation, for instance, is far from a universal model.

Finally, going to war loses any moral justification if there is no realistic hope of success. A doomed last stand is to be equated with suicide as a denial of God's providence and puts too much at risk for too small a hope of gain. There is something in this principle which usefully serves to avoid the glorification of war. Success must mean that more good than harm is likely to emerge from the conflict – achieving limited ends while making other conditions worse is to lose sight of the ultimate objective of peace and the common good.

Having met all the conditions of *ius ad bello*, the question then arises of how a war is to be conducted within a moral framework – *ius in bello*. The desire for victory does not, of itself, justify any and every action. First, the legitimate authority must announce the conditions under which the action is to be taken. The point here is that it preserves the possibility of negotiation and reinforces the idea that going to war is a final option, since the enemy is allowed to contemplate the consequences of taking on an adversary in battle.

In the conduct of the war, it is crucial to do everything possible to distinguish between combatants and non-combatants. The difficulty of keeping this distinction clear-cut was always recognized, but to ignore the separation between soldiers and civilians is dehumanizing to the one waging war. Moreover, the theory of *ius in bello* requires that only proportionate force is applied – the lust for victory and the desire to win overwhelmingly must not lead to force and destruction beyond what is necessary to achieve the

---

[4] Robin Gill, *Changing Worlds: Can the Church Respond?* Edinburgh and New York: T&T Clark, 2002, p. 19.

declared aims. To do otherwise is to contradict the earlier provision that the effects of war must not be to create a situation worse than what went before.

An associated requirement is that the war shall cease when its declared aims have been achieved. The fact of war is not an excuse or a cover for initiating new objectives. But, most of all, the war must be conducted in such a way that it can lead towards reconciliation and the establishment of a just peace. The cycle of violence which breeds further violence is only too easy to enter. The point of trying to constrain the conduct of war within the ethical framework of justice is to uphold peace as the ultimate war aim.

That, in brief, is the outline of the just war theory. It is not a doctrine, nor is it derived in any straightforward way from doctrine. Indeed, it is not very obviously a theological theory at all. True, it holds as paramount the desire for peace and the humanity of the enemy – and while these principles can be derived from Christian theology, they might be shared by many others on other grounds. Just war theory is rather a good example of the idea that Christians can authentically stand alongside people of other traditions who arrive at the same position from different arguments. This is not quite the same as arguing that just war theory derives directly from natural law – a claim which Stanley Hauerwas makes.[5] Hauerwas wants to identify just war theory with natural law in order to contrast it with other positions which he regards as more distinctively Christian (which we shall consider later). But if Nigel Biggar is right that Christian authenticity in ethics is more important than distinctiveness, what matters is that there are sound Christian understandings underpinning just war theories. Hauerwas wants to suggest that, by arguing from natural law, just war theorists are somehow using sub-Christian concepts. Biggar's approach to authenticity, I think, happily bypasses that concern.

Hauerwas, however, hits the nail on the head when he notes that just war theory – what he calls the Augustinian solution – regards the history of the world and God's history as 'hopelessly mixed together on this side of the eschaton'.[6] That, as will have become apparent by now, is one of the main theological motifs of this book – although one which Hauerwas repudiates. We shall look further at how Hauerwas deals with that question when we consider the tradition of Christian pacifism, but some other questions must first be asked of just war theory.

Is it the case that, by appealing to just war theory when the nature of conflict has changed so radically from Augustine's or Aquinas's times, we are failing to allow ethics to give sufficient attention to new knowledge? As we saw earlier, there is a delicate line to be trodden between properly engaging

---

[5] Stanley Hauerwas, 'Should War be Eliminated? A Thought Experiment', in John Berkman and Michael Cartwright (eds), *The Hauerwas Reader*, Durham, NC, and London: Duke University Press, 2001, pp. 392–425.

[6] Hauerwas, 'Should War be Eliminated?' p. 424.

with new understandings and following slavishly the received wisdom of the moment. Given the difficulties already alluded to in applying just war theory to present realities (the question of discerning legitimate authority being just one), and recognizing that just war theory is intended not as a doctrinal statement but as a pragmatic framework to contain excessive violence and retain a promise of peace, do present conditions allow the theory to fulfil its objectives?

Charles Reed, in his detailed analyses of the Gulf War of 1990–1 and the invasion of Iraq in 2001–3 argues that classic just war theory fits contemporary conditions better than may be supposed.[7] Nevertheless, conceiving just war theory only in terms of conflict between states is too narrow. Speaking of the United Nations Charter which outlaws inter-state wars except in conditions of self-defence or perceived threat, he writes:

> It is clear that the UN founding fathers had inter-state conflict in mind when they sought to prohibit the use of force. Inter-state war has proved, however, to be the exception rather than the norm. Civil wars, ethnic conflict, cross-border guerrilla incursions and limited inter-state fighting have been more common than fully blown inter-state war. The end of the Cold War, and with it the emergence of the USA as the sole remaining superpower, has led to a more flexible interpretation of the Charter. The discernible trend is for states to use force to promote democracy, restore order in failed states, protect their citizens overseas and as a means to combat terrorism.[8]

Yet Reed argues that the principles of the just war can sometimes fit these new contexts rather well. Just war theory is ultimately about the promotion of peace, and he interprets this in terms of community in its widest sense. It is this focus on peace which, for Reed, allows the just war tradition to bridge idealism and pragmatism; 'realism' and 'pacifism'. The shifting nature of armed conflict in the late twentieth and early twenty-first centuries is far from the first such adaptation which the tradition has had to make, yet it has proved surprisingly resilient. Reed argues that the just war tradition must not be viewed as a set of law-like propositions but, precisely, as a tradition which continually attempts to hold together the Christian commitment to peace as God's norm with the irrepressible tendency of fallen humanity to wage war. (He comes close here to echoing MacIntyre's understanding that a tradition is an ongoing conversation about what it means to inhabit the tradition.) Most of all, he commends the just war tradition as a common currency between the Church and world leaders which acts as a bulwark against the temptation to divorce practices of government from considerations of ethics.

Reed's book, *Just War?*, is commended to readers who seek a detailed analysis of the political processes which led up to the Gulf War and the

---

[7] Reed, *Just War?*
[8] Reed, *Just War?* p. 46.

invasion of Iraq, and the politics which governed those conflicts. He also maps clearly the initiatives, statements and stances taken by the Churches in relation to both those conflicts. Suffice to say that he is persuaded that the Gulf War of 1990–1 stood up well to a just war analysis. Iraq's invasion of Kuwait was an act of aggression which needed to be resisted and which broke international law. Many options other than military intervention – notably sanctions of different kinds – were tried, often doggedly, and backed up with strenuous diplomatic efforts to secure a withdrawal from Kuwait. Military intervention sought to restore the status quo and ceased short of regime change in Iraq, however desirable that end might have been. Throughout, UN backing was painstakingly secured. In terms of *ius in bello*, the use of 'smart technology' to minimize civilian casualties may have been less than fully successful – but the objective was nonetheless pursued. Over-claiming for technological precision somewhat damaged the case, but just war theory has always recognized the difficulty of maintaining the distinction between combatants and non-combatants: the point is to seek to discriminate as far as is possible. Reed concedes, however, that the use of cluster bombs was a morally problematic decision which remains hard to justify within just war thinking. He concludes that the First Gulf War came close to meeting the criteria of a just war, although many of the Churches' responses did not acknowledge this – the reason, in his view, being that the Churches remained torn between realist and pacifist positions which they had not been able to reconcile in their own lives.

Turning to the invasion of Iraq, Reed (writing rather nearer to the events themselves) pins much of his analysis on the question of how much of a threat Saddam Hussein actually posed to other countries. As he says:

> Even if it is accepted that the trinity of rogue regimes, terrorism and weapons of mass destruction legitimates a doctrine of preventative action, this would not necessarily make the Second Gulf War a just war. Such a judgement depends on whether the conditions for preventative action were met.[9]

He notes that, despite the quickly achieved victory, the task of restoring order to Iraq has been deeply problematic. While the principle of proportionality may have influenced the conduct of the war itself, not least through increasingly sophisticated technology, the confusion over the war aims and the lack of a clear plan for promoting a post-war peace have seriously damaged any claims that this war was just. As more details have emerged, since Reed was writing, about the misleading intelligence data on which the decision to go to war was founded, the justice of the action begins to slip away still further.

Reed's reflections on these two military actions of recent times go a long way to establish the continuing usefulness of the just war tradition. He

---

[9] Reed, *Just War?* p. 135.

concludes that the work of rethinking the tradition to take full account of the present global order has only just begun and that the Churches have an important role in developing the tradition for new circumstances. He has little to say about the so-called 'War against terror', but it is clear that the growth of international terrorism and measures to combat it are not at all easy to incorporate into the just war tradition. This is, perhaps, a good reason to resist the designation of counter-terrorism measures as 'war' and to restore a vocabulary which retains them firmly within the field of policing action, however challenging. But the key point I want to draw out is that Reed offers a robust account of the Christian realist position, emphasizing that the way of thinking epitomized in the just war tradition is not necessarily hostile to the traditions of Christian pacifism but seeks to pursue pacifist objectives within a context of a fallen world. In this respect, just war thinking fits neatly alongside a theological emphasis on the Interim which we have explored in earlier chapters. As we shall see, it is possible to start much closer to the Christian pacifist position than Reed does, yet still find that the just war tradition is of value.

Christian pacifism

It is not surprising that Hauerwas is one of the most eloquent spokespersons for a tradition of Christian pacifism today, and it is worth looking at his arguments in some detail since he belies (not least in his own combative approach to argument) the image of the pacifist as an other-worldly idealist, unable to see the nastiness present in human affairs. We have already noted the central concept of the peaceable kingdom in Hauerwas's theology and the debt he acknowledges to John Howard Yoder and the Mennonite tradition – Mennonites, along with Quakers, being a Church known primarily for a pacifist stance.

For Hauerwas, the moral right or duty of self-defence is highly questionable. It provides, he argues, an implicit moral contradiction in that, while professing to abhor war in general, we wish to retain the possibility of war in defence of causes, including our own nation and culture, of which we approve. In other words, the idea of self-defence is deeply subjective.[10] In contrast, Hauerwas stresses the necessity of abjuring war altogether, and here he explicitly comes into conflict with the notion that we inhabit a theological interim marked by a kingdom which is, in the classic vocabulary, inaugurated but not yet here in its fullness. Instead, he emphasizes the view that the kingdom has already been made present fully in Jesus Christ. He asserts that the 'tender mercy' of Jesus 'makes it possible to stand against the world's tragic assumption that war can be the means to justice'.[11]

[10] Hauerwas, 'Should War be Eliminated?' p. 418.
[11] Hauerwas, 'Should War be Eliminated?' p. 419.

And here too, Hauerwas contradicts some of the perspectives already introduced in this book. For he explicitly rejects the idea that Christian ethics had to evolve to accommodate the Church's unfolding experience that the world as it is was not likely to end soon – or at least, he rejects that as an explanation of how Christian ethics began to look for ways to control and minimize suffering and harm, since those evils could not be finally defeated but must somehow be endured. Instead, he places himself firmly within the strand of Christian thinking which stresses the Church's calling to live within the dispensation of the kingdom as if it were fully realized now (in Milbank's terms, solely on the other side of the Cross) and thus to eschew compromises which imply that the realization of the kingdom in Christ is somehow incomplete or yet to unfold. As he says, 'the eschatology of the New Testament rests not in the conviction that the kingdom has not fully come, but that it has'.[12]

In the end, this comes down to the degree of normative authority which one gives to the New Testament. In other words, do the texts of the New Testament leave room for a continuing revelation of God's purposes to the Church, or must the Church for all time be committed to the eschatological vision of the writers of those texts? Hauerwas clearly inclines to this second position, and his stance is attractive and perhaps persuasive. Yet it remains that adopting the eschatological vision of the New Testament more than two millennia after it was first conceived does raise questions which the practices and beliefs of the earliest Church seem ill-equipped to answer. Foremost among such questions is, as we saw earlier, the question of the Christian's proper stance towards a long-term future. Elsewhere in his *oeuvre*, especially in his writings on children and families, Hauerwas puts great store by the Church's belief and trust in a future. How does he square this with the rejection of war as illegitimate in all circumstances, since war may be joined with the express purpose of safeguarding a future which embodies peace and justice? It comes down to his understanding of history.

For Hauerwas, just war theories make the mistake of imagining that God's understanding of history, and human understandings, can be seen as flowing together rather than as radically divergent. War, he asserts, is not part of how God would have his kingdom present in the world. War, rather, is 'the desire to be rid of God, to claim for ourselves the power to determine our meaning and destiny'.[13] Instead, the Church is the manifestation of God's invitation to join a community which has learned to love one's enemy. This involves, for Hauerwas, the supreme trust that God will enable his people to have a history without that history entailing war. The Church exists to 'free our imaginations from the capacity of war'.[14]

---

12 Hauerwas, 'Should War be Eliminated?' p. 420.
13 Hauerwas, 'Should War be Eliminated?' p. 421.
14 Hauerwas, 'Should War be Eliminated?' p. 423.

One feels at times that Hauerwas's rhetoric loses sight of the tragic dimension in human history which just war thinking seeks to embody. His description of war as humanity's expression of fear and hatred of the other is recognizable in many circumstances <u>but leaves no room for the regretful acceptance of war as the last resort to defend justice and peace itself</u>. The problem may not be my sense of fear and hatred but someone else's fear and hatred of me – and it may be beyond my power to subdue irrational fear and hatred in another without some resort to force. But Hauerwas argues that such regretful and tragic resorts are themselves manifestations of unfaithfulness – a refusal to commit ourselves (and, presumably, our neighbour also) into God's hands rather than taking on God's prerogatives for ourselves. Although Hauerwas rejects the accusation that pacifism is parasitic upon those who do not shy away from conflict in the name of peace and justice, it is tempting to repeat that accusation since he leaves no room in his descriptions of war for the kind of conflict that has sometimes preserved the Church from atheistic totalitarianisms. In the end, the question of whether any form of Christian Church, or Christian virtue, would have survived two millennia, had the actual, empirical, Church not been prepared to endorse defensive military action, is the kind of 'counterfactual conditional' which is impossible to solve. For Hauerwas, the answer from the perspective of faith is obvious – but the consequence is to call into question the faithfulness of those who have, in human history, answered the question differently.

Yet it would still be wrong to characterize Hauerwas's pacifism as politically inert. 'Christians', he says,

> cannot avoid . . . attempting one step at a time to make the world less war-determined. We do that exactly by entering into the complex world of deterrence and disarmament strategy believing that a community nurtured on the habits of peace might be able to see new opportunities not otherwise present. For what creates new opportunities is being a kind of people who have been freed from the assumption that war is our fate.[15]

This seems to be an invitation to engage in politics, but not on politics' terms. Quite what it entails in terms of a Christian practice or a programme for the Church is unclear. As ever, Hauerwas's readers are left to do a good deal of work to draw his ideas and rhetoric into a course of action that covers all the bases he sets out. Yet it is difficult, whatever one's hesitations and misgivings, to deny that Hauerwas paints such an attractive picture that it *ought* to be realizable. In place of the resigned acceptance of compromise and the dampening presumption that sin will continue to persist (even if that is borne out by our constant experience), the pacifist vision reminds us of the radical difference which believing in God makes to our evaluation of the world and its affairs. Hauerwas is determined not to compromise with natural law, since natural law suggests that Christians do not have a monopoly of God's truth,

---

[15] Hauerwas, 'Should War be Eliminated?' p. 424.

and thus he will not entertain just war ideas based on pragmatism which do not emphasize the distinctiveness of the gospel. Others embrace natural law precisely because they refuse to claim that Christians have nothing to learn about God from others. It is also worth recalling that Hauerwas is, quintessentially, a theologian for an American context, and the perspective on war which prevails in the United States is not identical with that which informs 'old Europe', whose history of mutual destruction (and also of the proximity of totalitarianism) is rather different. Nonetheless, I am not yet ready to jettison the insights which the pacifist tradition offers and which Hauerwas epitomizes. In a Church which is still adapting to the end of Christendom, but also carries its enduring legacy, renegotiating its relationship to political power is an ongoing project. That must mean looking again at what a Christian ethic, situated much more than an arm's length away from power, might look like.

Pacifism and the just war: two traditions or one?

As we noted earlier, Charles Reed describes the theory of the just war as an attempt to pursue pacific objectives in a fallen world. However, by choosing to portray Christian pacifism through the work of Stanley Hauerwas, I have deliberately sought to emphasize the gap between pacifism and the just war tradition. As a matter of observation, the just war tradition is usually called upon by Christians who are emphatically not pacifist, while Christians who adopt pacifist positions are likely to regard just war theory as a 'sell-out'. This polarization broadly corresponds to the political right and left within church life. Theologically, the just war tradition rests upon an understanding of the interim which Hauerwas rejects (as does Milbank), but Hauerwas's rejection of the theological interim, like his rejection of natural theology, is part of the rhetoric on which his wider project is based – it need not be intrinsic to every form of Christian pacifism. Perhaps, rather than having two, mutually irreconcilable, ethical traditions here, what we have are two ways of looking at war and conflict from within one, Christian, tradition.

This is possible because, as I have emphasized, the just war tradition is not itself an ethic directly derived from doctrine but a pragmatic programme, designed to be intelligible both within and beyond the household of faith. Follow its principles backwards, and their derivation from a Christian understanding of humanity, the world and God can be made explicit, but it is not overt. This need not be a failing since, of all ethical issues, avoiding war and conflict most involves seeking understandings with people of traditions, histories and beliefs other than one's own. It remains that the process of 'showing the theological working' has often been assumed rather than practised, so that just war theories are often taken to be self-evidently Christian tenets.

Reed starts from a position in sympathy with just war theory and regards it as compatible with pacifist principles. But it is also possible to start from

Christian pacifism and still recognize and respect just war theory. An example of this approach is pursued by Gerald Schlabach in a book co-edited by Hauerwas and Samuel Wells.[16] Schlabach's governing motif is the concept of the Eucharist as the place where the Christian rejection of violence is made manifest. 'The Eucharist', he says,

> is an offer of life … as Christians now celebrate the Eucharist around the globe, it makes more real than ever what was already clear when the God of Israel offered new life to Gentile nations through Jesus Christ: this is a gospel that breaks the confines of even the most sacred nationalism.[17]

But Schlabach is not oblivious to the ways in which this vision can be, and has been, subverted. He reminds us that, in Pinochet's Chile, Christian supporters of the regime emerged from sharing the Eucharist with others who opposed violence and torture, immediately set upon them and turned them over to the police. The Eucharist is not a panacea, as the history of the Church through the ages bears out. But Schlabach focuses more on the implicit tension which is apparent when Christians who find it impossible to forgo violence come to God's table:

> even those who cannot quite imagine how they will cease their own disputes, extricate themselves from systems of greed, and undo their complicity in killing (cf. James 4), find themselves quietly disquieted when they fail to show others anything less than the generous non-violent love that God has shown them.[18]

So, for Schlabach, the Eucharist is the reminder that, despite the incorrigible fallenness of the human condition, violence and war have no part in the kingdom of God. Schlabach is much more open to a theology of the interim than is Hauerwas. He refers to this period of the 'already and not yet' by the term 'eschatological tension', and he notes how Christians who are more attuned to the 'not yet' element of the tension are likely to understand reluctantly that witness in a contingent world may involve the cautious use of force. Those, however, more attracted to the 'already' side of the tension will seek rather to live in ways which signpost the future possibilities offered by God. Yet this is not merely a matter of personal disposition and temperament, for the Eucharist is itself a manifestation of the 'already and not yet' in that the mundane meal of bread and wine is a sign, but not the fulfilled totality, of all the gifts of God to the world. So for the participant in the Eucharist, the tension becomes so much more unbearable – and this, says Schlabach, is as it should be, since the Christian should neither be divorced from the world as it is, in all its anguish, nor reconciled to the world in ways which obscure the radical promise of God's kingdom.

---

[16] Gerald W. Schlabach, 'Breaking Bread: Peace and War', in Stanley Hauerwas and Samuel Wells (eds), *The Blackwell Companion to Christian Ethics*, Oxford: Blackwell, 2004, pp. 360–74.
[17] Schlabach, 'Breaking Bread', p. 367.
[18] Schlabach, 'Breaking Bread', p. 367.

From this theological position, Schlabach considers the just war tradition to begin with commitments shared with pacifists. Violence is never the norm for Christians: always it is the exception which must be justified:

> Even if war is justifiable ... Christians can only approve it cautiously, reluctantly, with regret and without any spirit of revenge. In this way, a *presumption against violence* continues to work its way not only through Christian pacifism but through the just-war tradition.[19]

The gap between Christian pacifism and the just war tradition need not be seen as unbridgeable; and, again, it is a theology of the interim that helps the bridge to be built.

Non-violent resistance

Not quite synonymous with Hauerwas's pacifism, yet no less separate from the just war tradition, Walter Wink's radical reframing of the gospel ethic as politicized non-violence offers a third perspective between those of aggression and pacifism.[20] He maintains that Jesus' teaching, notably in the Sermon on the Mount, has been perverted into a position of passive non-resistance which Wink sees as profoundly different from active non-violence.

Wink's case rests upon a rereading of Matthew 5.38–41. Whereas Jesus' command to 'turn the other cheek' has usually been interpreted as surrendering to violence, Wink notes that, in the culture of the gospel period, a gesture with the left hand was shameful since the left hand was used only for unclean tasks. Thus, being struck on the right cheek, presumably means a right-handed backhander from one's assailant, and this is the kind of blow intended, not to injure so much as to humiliate. Turning the other (left) cheek then places the assailant in a morally compromised position, since he would have to break the cleanliness laws by striking with a left backhander. Wink interprets the turning of the other cheek as a refusal to be humiliated – as a statement of fundamental human equality, whatever the social or economic disparity between the protagonists. 'This is not submission, as the churches have insisted. It is defiance.'[21]

As a second example, Wink offers Jesus' proposal that 'if anyone wants to sue you and take your coat, give your cloak as well' (Matthew 5.40). The context for this saying, he suggests, is that of extortionate interest rates imposed on the local people by the Roman empire, which could result in one being sued even for the clothes one stood up in. The translation I have quoted above is from the New Revised Standard Version, but Wink draws on a different translation to suggest that Jesus is saying, 'when they sue you for

---

[19] Schlabach, 'Breaking Bread', p. 363 (author's italics).
[20] See: Walter Wink, 'We Must Find a Better Way', in Jon L. Berquist (ed.), *Strike Terror No More: Theology, Ethics and the New War*, St Louis, MO: Chalice Press, 2002, pp. 329–36.
[21] Wink, 'We Must Find a Better Way', p. 331.

your outer garment, give them your undergarment too'.[22] Thus, he says, the oppressor is humiliated because it was shameful to look upon the nakedness of another.

Wink's final example comes from the following verse: 'if anyone forces you to go one mile, go also the second mile'. This, Wink maintains, refers to the law which permitted a Roman soldier to force a person to carry his heavy military pack – but only for one mile. If the imposed-upon civilian insists on carrying it for a second mile, he puts the soldier in the position of having broken military law. Again, the tables are turned and the oppressed score moral victories over their oppressors.

I am not a historian of first-century Palestine and cannot vouch for the accuracy of Wink's historical contextualization. But natural scepticism, rather than an entrenched textual conservatism, does raise some questions. From an experience of playground scraps at primary school, I cannot quite see how a quick 'one–two' – backhand and forehand, both with the right – is an impossible response to the proffered left cheek. We children had learned that tactic from the movies, but it probably dated back many centuries and crossed many cultures. Some have argued that, in the first century, a forehand slap had a different meaning from a backhander and, again, this may be true. But arguing on these lines either distances the text more and more from our own world and experience or requires us to assume a degree of subtlety in Jesus' words which verges on the obscure. In the second example it matters a great deal for Wink's credibility whether the text is best translated as 'undergarment' or 'cloak'. Then again, an expert in Roman military law would be able to tell us whether the limit of one mile was applicable only to an unwilling pack-bearer and whether the question of distance arose at all if there was no coercion involved. When one puts so much emphasis on little-known aspects of a distant culture, these details count for much.

Nevertheless, one may agree that Christian discipleship requires some kind of active defiance without recourse to Wink's contextual reconstructions. There should be no illusion that the oppressor, thus humiliated, will slink surreptitiously away – on the contrary, active defiance is likely to lead to an even harder time (another lesson from the school playground). Wink's point is to distance Jesus from the charge of passivity and to stress that pacifism, properly understood, is not inert. He wants to make this move because, on other scriptural grounds, he sees Jesus' resistance to oppression and injustice as the 'bigger story', and so the limp passivity implied in most interpretations of Matthew 5 must be wrong. Wink interprets the texts as a statement of the equality of all humankind under God, regardless of the injustices and humiliations heaped upon oppressed peoples. The turned cheek and proffered undergarment say, in effect, 'you can oppress me but you cannot reduce me to something less than human, for it will be you who will be dehumanized'.

---

[22] Wink notes that this is his own translation of the text.

Wink goes on to apply this understanding to the post-9/11 context of America. The 'War against Terror' could, he argues, have been avoided by dealing with some of the manifest injustices perpetrated in the Middle East and elsewhere. So Wink believes that the sanctions against Iraq should have been lifted. This contrasts with Reed, who understands the sanctions as crucial steps in ensuring that military action was indeed a last resort. The sanctions, for Wink, eroded the moral stance of the West and made us into oppressors. He stops short of claiming that the terrorist attacks on America and Britain were any moral equivalent of the active resistance which he attributes to Jesus' teaching, although by pointing to the West as oppressor, he is forced to distinguish resistance from destructive violence. Terrorism, he says, has terror as its only rationale and cannot be dignified as resistance. But as is well known, my resistance can be your terrorism – it depends who is defining the terms, since vocabulary itself is a source of political power.

Wink is arguing, both in the biblical and the contemporary conflicts, for the principle of non-retaliation. The 'War against Terror' violates this principle in his eyes, even if the moral non-equivalence of the USA and Osama bin Laden is not established comprehensively in his short essay. And he is concerned to rescue pacifism from what he sees as un-Christlike passivity in the face of injustice. How one develops practices of resistance in the multitude of different social and political situations of conflict around the globe is left as further work for the reader.

A question of perspective

Comparing the three approaches considered above, it becomes clear that each assumes a location from which the moral question of conflict is being addressed, each reflecting different understandings of where the Church is most authentically to be found. In other words, different ecclesiologies inform different ethical approaches to the question of war.

As we noted earlier, just war theory appears to address most directly the decision-makers, politicians and military commanders who amass the evidence which may justify war, take the decision to prosecute war and control the strategies and mechanics of war. To the extent that such leaders may still, in some countries and cultures, be Christians, or may be strongly influenced by a Christian inheritance, this assumption about whom the just war theory is addressing may be justified. But it is worth noting that the decision to go to war is not one for politicians and military leaders alone. As the American service personnel who went AWOL rather than serve in Iraq suggest, members of the armed forces are not simply 'cannon fodder' with no moral responsibility for their actions. The Nuremberg trials established that 'only obeying orders' is a morally inadequate stance when the justice of the conflict is patently lacking. The difficulty is that the evidence by which the conditions of just war theory may, or may not, be met are seldom fully articulated to the public at large or even to the mass of military personnel. Nor, once a

Importance ?

conflict has begun, are the rules of engagement (the *ius in bello*) always consistent since the fortunes of war are changing all the time. It remains that just war has a continuing *salience*, not only for nations and authorities grounded in a Christian inheritance but for every member of a democracy whose participation in, or endorsement for, conflict may be required.

The pacifist tradition, in contrast, locates the Church at some distance from the immediacy of political and military decision-making. The pacifist must, to be consistent, refuse all positions in which going to war would be required by the role, and a national leader who eschewed all war on principle is unlikely to survive long in post. The travails of nuclear disarmament, and diplomacy in general, suggest that pacific outcomes can be achieved only through pragmatic, realist, negotiation. The role of the pacifist may, however, be to offer a lived example which stands as a constant reminder that pragmatism and realism descend into cynicism if the possibility of a better way is not kept in view. This locates the pacifist tradition outside the realms of political power but decidedly not as apolitical.

It is unsurprising that, given its grounding in a contextualized reading of the Gospels, Wink's approach to non-violent resistance seems to fit most effectively into a political and social context analogous to that of Jesus' day. Political oppression by a very proximate occupying force provides a setting where small acts of defiant resistance can be envisaged as practical opportunities. It is harder to translate such action into the context of global armed conflict. The world, however, is not short of examples of face-to-face oppression, comparable with occupied Judaea, and in such places Wink's approach may speak volubly to the situation.

Further reading

There have been a number of reappraisals of the just war tradition in the light of the changing dimensions of international conflict in the late twentieth and early twenty-first centuries. Among the best are: Oliver O'Donovan, *The Just War Revisited*, Cambridge: Cambridge University Press, 2003, and a collection of essays: Charles Reed and David Ryall (eds), *The Price of Peace: Just War in the Twenty First Century*, Cambridge: Cambridge University Press, 2007.

13

Human rights and God

We have given a good deal of consideration to the possibility that Christians and others may be able to find ethical common ground in various places. We have also seen how the quest for universal approaches to ethics – a characteristic of the Enlightenment and of liberal thought – sits ambiguously alongside Christian theology which is grounded in a particular story and yet which shares a missionary desire to communicate itself to all peoples. Again, we have seen how tricky it can be to understand conceptions of the good which are forged simultaneously in the narratives of our faith community and in the assumptions and 'common sense' of the cultures we inhabit. One example of an ethical issue in which all these issues are 'in play' is the question of human rights. In the prevailing culture of the twenty-first-century West, the concept of human rights is widely accepted as a rallying point for everybody. Who dares publicly to oppose the idea of basic standards of treatment for fellow human beings? Yet the ways in which human rights are incorporated into law, especially (in the British context) in relation to European law, are politically contentious.

Some communitarian strands in theology are inclined to portray the idea of human rights as deeply flawed by its Enlightenment origins. This line of argument cannot be conducted solely from the safe haven of academic life, since human rights address matters of life and death for innumerable people around the world. To drive a wedge between Christian theology and the politics of human rights risks aligning the Churches with the perpetrators of genocide and human abuse. So this is an instance where trends within Christian ethics matter deeply in terms of practical politics and public discipleship. Are Christians therefore bound into Enlightenment universalism by a practical commitment to human rights, despite the difficulty of squaring this project with the particularities of the Christian narrative? Or does Christian counter-culturalism extend to agnosticism about (or even opposition to) laws and structures erected against the bloodiest totalitarians of history? Or can the question be expressed differently so that Christians are enabled to negotiate this apparent trap?

Inevitably, there is an undercurrent of scepticism in the Christian Churches on the question of human rights, since the concept has its roots in a historical context which linked talk of rights to rejection of the Church's moral authority and, often, to outright atheism. This association with the works of the atheist Tom Paine (*Rights of Man*, 1791) and with the French Revolution, means that the concept of human rights is sometimes perceived not only to lack authentic Christian roots but to be the offspring of militant atheism. The atheistic overtones might, perhaps, be mitigated by the fact that Paine's work is associated not only with the French Revolution but with the American War of Independence, and that although the concept of human rights figures prominently in the Virginia Declaration of 1776, the United States has emerged as one of the most religious environments in the developed world today. Perhaps, in practice, human rights and belief in God can sit together reasonably comfortably. But where Christian theology seeks to avoid becoming subsumed into Western, individualistic, culture, the fact that a vocabulary of human rights and a thriving Church can coexist in America is not the point: the question is whether the concept of human rights can be authenticated from Christian principles.

The ways in which different historical analyses impact upon the matter of human rights is interesting. The idea of rights emerges quite strongly at the time of Magna Carta (1215). No disjunction between Magna Carta and the idea of Christian England has ever seriously been put forward (although, to be fair, neither has the connection been consistently stressed). Similarly, the political impetus to establish a global agreement on human rights which followed the genocides and totalitarian atrocities of the Second World War was very widely supported, not least by Christians, and associates the idea of human rights with a historical moment of which the West, and the Churches, can generally be proud. Nevertheless, whether caused by the fading of Christendom, the waning memories of totalitarianism, or the widespread feeling that the post-war consensus is incapable of resuscitation, human rights looks set to become another issue which divides Christians along roughly liberal versus communitarian lines.

Human rights, liberals and communitarians

Much turns upon whether a concept of human rights can be built upon authentically theological premises. In this, the US Declaration of Independence (1776) is significant since it begins: 'We hold these truths to be self-evident, that all men are created equal; that they are endowed by their Creator with certain unalienable rights ...' Here, the attribution of human rights to the Creator is grounded, not in Scripture or any aspect of the unique Christian narratives, but in the idea that the proposition is 'self-evident'. In a helpful discussion of human rights, Nicholas Wolterstorff calls this 'a piece of epistemological bluster'.[1] Nevertheless, others have taken this preamble to imply that human rights are a completely deracinated concept, starting from a conception of the human which imagines the person to be independent of community, tradition or narrative. It is, partly, this assumption that talk of

---

[1] Nicholas Wolterstorff, *Justice: Rights and Wrongs*, Princeton and Oxford: Princeton University Press, 2008, p. 319.

human rights is irrecoverably grounded in the person-from-nowhere of the liberal imagination, which has done much to turn communitarian thinkers away from an endorsement of human rights. MacIntyre, memorably, claims in *After Virtue* that 'there are no such rights, and belief in them is one with belief in witches and unicorns'.[2] His reason is precisely that there are no truths independent of external or contextual evidence, so the argument that human rights are self-evident is fatally flawed. Ideas like human rights, claims MacIntyre, purport to give us an objective and impersonal measure of moral behaviour, but they do not do so because they fail to see that to talk of persons in a way which detaches them from particular communities and traditions is meaningless. Only in community do we become persons, so the idea of rights attaching to persons extrapolated from particular contexts is meaningless.

Attracted as I am to MacIntyre's work, this passage has always bothered me. I agree with MacIntyre's arguments about the vacuity of the context-less person-from-nowhere as any basis for ethical thought, and with the emphasis on community, narrative and tradition. But to move from these commitments to a summary dismissal of human rights seems to uncouple the exploration of ethics from the pursuit of the good in practical terms for innumerable people. Is MacIntyre – usually so humane in his observations – here forgetting that the ethicist has a responsibility, not just to the academy, but to the life of the world? Is his line on human rights proof that the communitarian ethicists are uninterested in solving questions of bloody and barbaric conflict between different traditions – the very conflicts that a discourse of human rights was designed to prevent? But, equally, does my unease here suggest that I am happier to contradict my ethical beliefs the moment they pose a serious challenge to the conventional wisdom of the age?

It may be worth, at this point, noting that the decoupling of human rights from the specifics of tradition and community is not just a theoretical problem but a puzzle in terms of practical politics and law-making. To be an effective check against totalitarian state power, human rights need some authority beyond that of the individual nation-state. Hence, we see the grounding of human rights in the UN Declaration on Human Rights and the European Convention on Human Rights. But one consequence is that judgements in the European Court of Human Rights (for example) are made without regard to the specific tradition of law within each member state – and the traditions of law in, say, Britain, are very different from those in France. Incorporating the judgements of the Court into domestic law has created complications and anomalies, but the transnational status of human rights legislation inevitably means that it trumps local or national

---

[2] Alasdair MacIntyre, *After Virtue: A Study in Moral Theory*, 2nd edn, London: Duckworth, 1985, p. 69.

legal frameworks. The idea of universal human rights, possessed by individuals regardless of their social context, by definition ignores the nature of the social fabric within which they exercise personhood, and the notions of tradition and community suffer as a result. But if the diverse politics of different nations are allowed to trump the idea of human rights, the defence against the kind of nationalism that dehumanizes the foreigner or the 'other' all but disappears.

For Hauerwas, as we would expect, abuses of human rights are wrong, not because they offend against a universal principle but because they are incompatible with the Christian understandings of the world. Thus, apartheid is wrong, not as a breach of human rights, but because it precludes the sharing of the Eucharist between black and white Christians. Christians do not adopt moral positions because they are committed to universal ideals but because they believe in God and are committed to discipleship. All of which may be fine in the case of apartheid, which took place in an avowedly Christian country, but would leave the Church mouthing pieties incomprehensible to those living in the context of (say) the elimination of dissidents in Mao's China. Christians are not concerned only with the good for people within their own purview – abuses in China remain no less evil to Christian eyes. One lesson of the Second World War which, at the time, was compelling to many Christians, was that in the face of the utter denial of God entailed by totalitarianism, Christian ethics must connect with practical politics to resist and prevent these things from happening again. Looking back to our earlier consideration of economic issues, this is precisely the point which Duchrow sought to extrapolate from the experience of the Confessing Church and the experience of the Churches under apartheid to apply to the ethics of the Church in a market economy.

Problems with human rights in practice

One consequence of the weakness of liberal ideals is that attempts to impose or enforce human rights have proved deeply problematic. Liberals who assume that their conceptions of the good are, in fact, universal, have had to realize that theirs is a historically and geographically particular ideology. Indeed, the concept of human rights causes some strain to the liberal ideal of tolerance. Two contemporary examples might be attitudes towards Islam's treatment of women and international relations with China.

All aspects of the relationship between the West and Islam (and, therefore, between Christianity and Islam) have been brought under intense scrutiny since 9/11. It therefore becomes difficult to discern how far the problems of understanding and coexistence are exacerbated by unacknowledged fear and political reactions to threat, and how much they are aspects of the wider problem of plurality. It remains that, in the eyes of many Western liberals, Islam's treatment of women fails to honour their autonomy and equal status with men. One point of very obvious public tension here is the traditional

Islamic dress for women which, to Western eyes, appears to reinforce women's subjugation. In France, where secular liberalism is deep-rooted in domestic politics, the Islamic headscarf has been outlawed in certain public places such as schools. At once, the tension between liberalism's virtue of tolerance and its commitment to human rights (or to a particular interpretation of human rights) becomes obvious.

My point here is not to resolve the vexed issue of Islamic dress codes in Western societies, but to illustrate how liberalism has either to maintain its honouring of difference and plurality by tolerating different practices at the expense of its avowed commitment to universal rights, or sacrifice tolerance in order to impose its view of rights. Here, 'universal' rights become uncomfortably close to 'rights as perceived by those with the power to enforce them'. Nor is it much help to appeal to the women of Islam in the hope that, when they express their oppressed plight, the universal nature of women's rights will be established. Muslim women are far from being of one mind about Islamic dress codes. Some argue that traditional dress liberates them from being treated as sexual objects and confers a freedom which their Western sisters do not enjoy. On this issue, liberals are forced to face the fact that their own beliefs cannot be both universal and relative at the same time.

The case of China shows how difficult it can be to apply common understandings of human rights even when market economics are becoming a near-universal currency for international relations. The brutal crushing of dissident groups in Tiananmen Square in 1989 brought human rights abuses in China sharply into Western consciousness. However, Tiananmen Square also coincided with a new phase in China's relationship to the rest of the developed world as rapid industrialization on a massive scale began to make China a major economic force in the global economy. The rest of the world recognized that China mattered in two very important ways: first as a source of cheap manufactured goods, able to undercut the West thanks to much cheaper labour; and second as a very significant source of global warming which could not be ignored or alienated if mitigating climate change was to be feasible.

As Western governments pursued negotiations with China on these matters, the question of China's human rights record, especially in the light of the 'unfinished business' of Tiananmen Square, became something of an embarrassment. Nations like Britain and the USA, committed publicly to upholding human rights in their global diplomacy, now found themselves embroiled in negotiations with a nation that was not only too big an economic and military power to ignore but which appeared to have neither the will nor, perhaps, the vocabulary, to discuss the rights of its own people on shared terms with the West. The perception that Western nations are benefiting economically from trade with a country where human rights are not honoured has led to calls for economic engagement with China to be conditional on incorporating China into some shared understanding of human rights. But this is where considerations of realpolitik enter the equation; China's economic (and probably military) significance means that effective sanctions aimed at improving its human rights record could disadvantage the West most. The result has been a general downplaying of the issue. If human rights abuses can be tolerated so long as the perpetrating state is sufficiently powerful, the whole post-war ambition to secure human rights is seriously undermined.

So liberal relativism and tolerance do not sit comfortably with commitment to universal human rights, and the facts of global connectedness and international power relations make it difficult to enforce human rights except in nations which are too weak to resist interventions, thus provoking the charge that rights are little more than a smokescreen for a new imperialism.

This is not to suggest that the idea of human rights is worthless in practical terms. On many occasions since the Second World War, notably in Bosnia, where it has not been possible to prevent atrocities such as 'ethnic cleansing', the extent of consensus about human rights across the international community has at least enabled some perpetrators to be tried for their actions. It remains that, for all the reasons suggested already, there are difficulties surrounding the discourse of human rights which seem to be intrinsic, as well as the communitarian critique which is wary of ideas which purport to be grounded on some tradition-transcendent principle.

Human rights and Christian ethics

How then might Christian ethics respond? Despite the problems of applying human rights principles in practice, the concept represents an ambition which is congruent with the Christian vision – a world in which people are treated with respect on the grounds of their humanity alone and not for any earned status they may have. Because the discourse of human rights aspires to be universal, it must always seek to be intelligible across otherwise distinct communities – an approach to human rights grounded solely in any one religious or other tradition just won't do. The quarrel of some communitarian Christian ethicists with the language of human rights is the same as their critique of the liberal tradition itself: that, seeking to transcend tradition, it covertly rests upon one particular tradition – that of liberal secularism – and this makes it hard to see why such a discourse should be compelling for Christians.

Nevertheless, the political imperative of preventing or mitigating bloody ethnic or religious conflict suggests that the concept of human rights might be a very attractive candidate for the approach outlined by Nigel Biggar which we looked at earlier. That is, seeking to identify an authentically Christian ethic of human rights which can then be in dialogue with other traditions about what in those traditions might lead to commensurate conclusions. If Christian ethics is to attempt this move, it has first to be established that the discourse of universal human rights is compatible with a belief in God as the ultimate source of our humanity.

Here, I want to consider two approaches. The first, by Nicholas Wolterstorff, seeks to establish theological grounds for a discourse of human rights. The second, by Rowan Williams, goes further in proffering a theological approach which holds the potential for eliciting much wider agreement from other traditions.

A theistic grounding for human rights

Wolterstorff is quite clear that a secular grounding for universal human rights does not work. To summarize a detailed argument, secular accounts of the worth of a human being always come back, sooner or later, to questions of capacity or dignity. The consequence of this is that persons who lack dignity or capacity – those with Alzheimer's disease, infants, those in comas, and so on – do not inevitably fall within the category of beings which possess rights. Careful formulation of the principles of human rights can get around this problem for some such cases, but not for others. Wolterstorff asks, 'Is it possible, without reference to God, to identify something about each and every human being that gives him or her a dignity adequate for grounding human rights?'[3] Looking in detail at a number of arguments from Kant, Dworkin and others, he concludes that none are sufficiently robust to meet the challenge without leaving some, whom we instinctively recognize as human, insufficiently endowed with dignity to possess human rights. It seems, then, that the attempt to secure human rights without appeal to God has failed – but can an approach to human rights built upon God do any better? In other words, does theology allow us to speak of human rights for all regardless of faith? Wolterstorff is drawing here explicitly on Christian theology, although he suggests that other faiths – Judaism and perhaps Islam – might be able to come to similar conclusions from the resources of their traditions.

In search of theistic groundings for a discourse of human rights, Wolterstorff turns to the concept of the Image of God – the *Imago Dei*. Does the idea that human beings are created in the image of God secure for them intrinsic rights? The problem here is that the idea of the likeness of God appears to imply that humans have certain capacities in which they resemble God. That just takes us back to the problems associated with secular accounts of rights. Might we, instead, argue from the *Imago Dei* to an understanding of human nature which takes us beyond questions of capacity? Wolterstorff suggests that the concept of human nature is promising since one does not regard the person with Alzheimer's as lacking human nature. One says, instead, that, while such a person lacks rationality, capacity to do many things, and

---

[3] Wolterstorff, *Justice: Rights and Wrongs*, p. 324.

so on, there is something wrong with them that, one day, might be avoidable or curable. Their human nature has not been taken away from them. As Wolterstorff says, 'fundamental to medical science – cosmetic medical science excepted – is this idea of human nature'.[4]

But Wolterstorff's argument goes further than this, turning not so much on the nature of humans as created by God, as on the nature of God in relation to humans. There are, as he shows, many ways of construing human worth, but a foundation for human rights requires

> some worth-imparting relation of human beings to God that does not in any way involve a reference to human capacities. I will argue that being loved by God is such a relation: being loved by God gives a human great worth.[5]

This is what Wolterstorff calls 'bestowed worth'. He illustrates the concept with examples from human relationships and explains that, while one can be loved in many ways which do not confer worth, worth is bestowed by the kind of love understood as attachment (an example from human relationships: being befriended by royalty). 'I conclude,' says Wolterstorff, 'that if God loves, in the mode of attachment, each and every human being equally and per-manently, then natural human rights inhere in the worth bestowed on human beings by that love.'[6]

Wolterstorff's achievement here is not that he has constructed a foundation for a universal system of human rights on which all people can agree, but rather that he has shown that, for those who believe in God, universal human rights can be seen to follow from their understanding of God's love. This, he says, is not so much a new insight as the recovery of an old one which was implicitly recognized in the Hebrew and Christian Scriptures, the Church Fathers and through to the Middle Ages. 'The general recognition of such rights remained an exceedingly slow and halting process, however, until, quite surprisingly, it burst forth after the horrors of World War II in the UN Declaration.'[7]

Rights, and the right

Not all Christian ethicists have been convinced by Wolterstorff's arguments. Oliver O'Donovan, for example, suggests that the language of rights is far more problematical, and goes on to analyse three sorts of problem with it.[8] The first problem is political: individual human rights conceived independ-ently of the social order within which people relate to each other will tend to be destructive of the social order. O'Donovan suggests that the impact of

---

[4] Wolterstorff, *Justice: Rights and Wrongs*, p. 350.
[5] Wolterstorff, *Justice: Rights and Wrongs*, p. 352.
[6] Wolterstorff, *Justice: Rights and Wrongs*, p. 360.
[7] Wolterstorff, *Justice: Rights and Wrongs*, p. 361.
[8] Oliver O'Donovan, 'The Language of Rights and Conceptual History', *Journal of Religious Ethics* 37.2 (2009), pp. 193–207.

judgements in the European Court of Human Rights on the legal systems of member states is a case in point. The second is conceptual, and here O'Donovan seeks to distinguish carefully between the idea of 'rights' in the plural and 'the right' in the singular. Should justice be conceived in terms of rights which are inherent in persons, or as the right order of society? In other words, are rights the foundation from which we build conceptions of justice, or is the notion of 'right' the foundation and 'rights' derived from it? This is much more than a linguistic quibble – when rights appear to conflict with ideas of justice, it is essential to understand which is the foundational concept if we are to know whether 'justice' must be seen as relative compared to inalienable and universal human rights, or vice versa. Third, O'Donovan identifies a historical problem: he maintains that the language of rights (in the plural) is not found in the ancient world at all. Rather, he says, it began to emerge in the twelfth century, and saw further development in the four-teenth, sixteenth and eighteenth centuries. As the concept is not an ancient one, Wolterstorff is mistaken in seeing the origin of a discourse on human rights somewhere in a scriptural world-view.

O'Donovan turns to a practical example to examine what he sees as the limitations of grounding morals on concepts of individual human rights. In 1984, cyanide fumes were released from the Union Carbide plant at Bhopal in India, causing some 15,000 deaths and many times as many injuries. If we rely only on a language of rights, we need to consider the event in terms of some 560,000 infringements of rights (at the minimum). Is it not both intuitively true, and more useful, to speak of a single wrong? In other words, the language of right and wrong (singular) makes more sense than the language of rights in the plural. O'Donovan sees the language of rights as a despairing attempt to put something, however minimal, in place to counter the moral fragmentation of a plural world; and 'The question of despair and confidence is, for the theologian, the most important question to be raised by this whole theme.'[9] For the Christian, then, some reconstitution of the notion of the right – the right structure for a society which reflects the right ordering of human relationships and humanity's relationship with God – is the way ahead; not a reliance on a discourse of human rights.

For O'Donovan, Wolterstorff leaves too many questions unanswered to be able to overcome these problems. Wolterstorff grounds his account of human rights on an assertion of human worth, but the question arises of whether he establishes that human worth is part of

> a general account of human nature. Is it merely a contingent truth that God's worth-conferring love is conferred on *each* member of the human race, or is the love of God to 'one and all' connected, after all, with the fact that 'one and all' are members *of the human race?*[10]

---

[9] O'Donovan, 'The Language of Rights and Conceptual History', p. 204.
[10] O'Donovan, 'The Language of Rights and Conceptual History', p. 206 (O'Donovan's emphases).

In other words, does God bestow worth on me because I am human or because I am me?

These are important arguments because of the dilemma outlined at the start of this chapter. Christians generally wish to support the objectives of human rights in terms of protecting people from the arbitrary and often oppressive power of the state, acting as a bulwark against the tendency to dehumanize people who are different or provoke fear or resentment, and so on. If Christians can only support these objectives by adopting concepts and rules which do not sit authentically within the narratives of Scripture and tradition, are they selling their birthright? So there appear to be three choices: buy into a language of human rights and make distinctive Christian narratives subordinate; reject the language of human rights and remain indifferent to the likely abuses and atrocities which may follow; or find a way to ground universal human rights in the particular narratives of Christian theology. I think that Wolterstorff succeeds in showing that there are good theological grounds for Christians to share the objectives enshrined in a discourse of human rights. The second option is therefore inadmissible for Christians. However, O'Donovan wants to avoid the plural concept of rights and return to a singular understanding of 'the right'. Whether a Christian account of the right can be constructed which can be equally accessible to other faiths and traditions is, however, another question. We face, once again, the tension between the need for ethics to be authentically Christian and yet to make common cause beyond the household of faith. Is there another way to conceive the idea of human rights which can build this bridge? Here we turn, once again, to the work of Rowan Williams.

The body as the foundation for human rights

Rowan Williams developed his ideas about religious faith and human rights in a lecture at the London School of Economics in May 2008. As yet, the lecture is only available online, although I suspect that it will not be long before it starts appearing in collections and anthologies. The lecture as delivered is important, not only in the context of human rights but as a way of conceiving theology in public debate. It well repays a few clicks on the mouse to find it on the Archbishop of Canterbury's website.[11]

Williams starts with a thoughtful discussion of MacIntyre's dismissal of human rights, with which he broadly agrees. Not that either MacIntyre or Williams are against the things which human rights legislation seeks to preserve, but rather, as opponents of oppression and abuse, they both fear that human rights need a much more solid foundation than can be found in Enlightenment liberalism. As Williams notes, the way we actually talk about

---

[11] Rowan Williams, *Religious Faith and Human Rights*, lecture delivered at the London School of Economics, 1 May 2008. <http://www.archbishopofcanterbury.org/2087>. Accessed 29 September 2009.

human rights tends to lack precision in a way which suggests that the concept itself may be inadequately defined:

> If we speak without qualification of the right to life, the right to a fair trial, the right to raise a family and the right to a paid holiday under the same rubric, it is very hard to see how this language can plausibly be understood as dealing with moral foundations.

Williams acknowledges that the language of human rights is worth salvaging because, as things stand, it is the best defence we have against the state simply doing what it wants. To provide the necessary robustness, Williams turns, paradoxically as he acknowledges, to what he calls 'Christianity's confused and uneasy relationship with the institution of slavery'. In the Scriptures and in the life of the early Church, he contends, despite the fact that slavery was still regarded as an unchallengeable social institution, slaves and slave owners are nevertheless embraced together within the Church. Because all Christians belong to 'one divine Master' it is impossible for a slave to be nothing more than the property of another person. It was this perception which built into Christian thinking the insight that, since the human body could not be owned by other people, there were significant limits to what anyone could do to the body of another. The language of ownership is inappropriate when speaking of the human body. As Williams says,

> I may talk about 'my body' in a phrase that parallels 'my house' or 'my car', but it should be obvious that there is a radical difference. I can't change it for another, I can't acquire more than one of it, I cannot survive the loss of it.

And, Williams goes on, the significance of the body is that it is the means of communication whereby we take our place in social relationships. 'The recognition of a body as a human body is, in this framework, the foundation of recognising the rights of another.' So, encountering another person, we perceive that here is another like me with whom communication is possible. This is a person who, because they are embodied, has feelings, expresses him or herself to others, and so on. It is not rationality that endows persons with personhood but the fact that they are embodied. Recognizing the embodiment of another confers on them the right not to have that body treated as a commodity. 'Grasping that the body cannot be an item of property is one of the things that is established by the Christian doctrine of communion in Christ and shared obedience to Christ.' This, he argues, is a theological insight that has helped move Christians in the direction of universal doctrines of right. However, Williams bases this universalism, not on shared rationality as in the liberal Enlightenment tradition, but on the fact of the body.

One consequence of this is that rights are not dependent on the ability to reciprocate with duties. Indeed, human rights founded on embodiment are not dependent on anything other than being a person with a body. Rights, on this count, do not depend on notions of human dignity and cannot be taken away from those who are deemed by others to lack dignity or capacity – the physically or mentally disadvantaged, the demented, the dying or the embryo. Immediately it will be seen that Williams is offering an account of the foundations of human rights which has consequences across many ethical questions. In the light of this account of human rights, one can revisit the questions of the beginning and end of life and consider the implications. As Williams notes, there are consequences here, too, for matters of torture and capital punishment, however slow the Church may have been to work out these consequences in practical ethics.

But the focus on the body leads still further into a discourse of human rights. Because we are free to 'make bad or inadequate sense of our bodily lives', restrictions on the way we use and treat our bodies should, except for the necessary protection of the vulnerable, be outside the power of the state to determine:

> If the state legislates against sexual violence and abuse, as it must, it is because of the recognition that this is an area in which the liberty to make sense of or with one's body is most often put at risk by predatory behaviour on the part of others.

Moreover, when we base the idea of rights on the fact of embodiment, context becomes important. It no longer seems absurd to lump together the right to a fair trial and the right to a paid holiday as if they were rights of different orders since, depending on context, each might be just as important an aspect of 'possessing adequate bodily/communicative liberty'.

Part of Williams's argument here is also about the nature of public theology. He is offering Christian theology as a response to the 'bereavement' felt by the Enlightenment's attempt to transcend tradition and as a rich source of understanding which can engage with the concerns of the world on terms which are intelligible beyond the company of the faithful. He is offering the Christian inheritance as a more robust foundation for something the world craves – a viable discourse of human rights – than secular understandings which seem too flimsy to bear their own ambitions. The fact of embodiment is, after all, something that all can recognize. It offers grounds for an approach to universal ethics which, much better than the ground of shared rationality, is able to express the instinctive desire to protect the person from the power of the state. At this point it would be worth going back to Chapter 1 and asking what difference Williams's focus on the body would make to my account of the weaknesses of Enlightenment liberalism and the liberal/communitarian tension. His argument here brings together the centrality of tradition (the Christian tradition) with liberalism's yearning for an ethic which communicates across the diversity of traditions. For while the concept of the body is comprehensible to all, 'the inviolability of the body is ultimately grounded in the prior relation of each embodied subject to God'.

Here, then, in the tension between secular accounts of human rights and the desire of the Church to champion those things which human rights are designed to defend, there are insights into the whole venture of Christian ethics today. The need for accounts of ethics to be grounded in the Christian story can sit alongside the Christian's calling to be a disciple in the world and not to walk away from the demands of citizenship. In Williams's consideration of human rights, we see how an ethic of the body not only builds on the struggles of the early Church to make sense of its vocation but starts to resolve the tension between a Hauerwasian emphasis on the Church's calling and the liberal insistence on communicability. Williams's lecture deserves a very wide readership.

Further reading

The edition of the *Journal of Religious Ethics* (37.2, May 2009) from which the essay by Oliver O'Donovan, quoted above, is taken, is given over almost entirely to a series of articles discussing Nicholas Wolterstorff's *Justice: Rights and Wrongs*, and is recommended for anyone wishing to dig deeper into Wolterstorff's important book.

For more of O'Donovan's political theology, written from within the evangelical traditions, see: Oliver O'Donovan and Joan Lockwood O'Donovan, *Bonds of Imperfection: Christian Politics, Past and Present*, Grand Rapids, MI and Cambridge: Eerdmans, 2004.

For a different approach to the problems of arriving at concepts of justice which are both theological and address the problem of plurality, see: Raymond Plant, *Politics, Theology and History*, Cambridge: Cambridge University Press, 2001.

For a rather more accessible, yet very thorough, consideration of theology and the concept of justice, see: Nicholas Sagovsky, *Christian Tradition and the Practice of Justice*, London: SPCK, 2008.

14

The next turn on the road for Christian ethics?

I suggested at the outset that Christian ethics is one of the fastest moving disciplines in the theological curriculum. If that is true, then the structure of this book may date no less quickly than aspects of its content, since the tensions and arguments about how we do ethics will evolve as fast as the problematics they seek to address. Nevertheless, the underlying tension between liberal and communitarian approaches – even if not always under those names – seems likely to endure since, although liberals are on the retreat in the Church today, they have certainly not stopped thinking, and although communitarian positions are becoming more confident and sophisticated, the nature of the Church as a community which shapes lives (and hence ethics) is still hotly contested. The Church's vocation to be a missionary community in the midst of a culture dominated by the legacies of classic liberalism means that translating ideas between traditions and cultures remains vitally important.

But while the liberal/communitarian tension seems likely to endure, what are the new questions which are now emerging? Three developments seem to point towards the next turning on the journey of Christian ethics today: the growing sense that theological liberalism need not always be subservient to classic Enlightenment liberalism; the turn in communitarian Christian ethics to a deeper rootedness in worship as the source of Christian identity; and the understanding that Christian ethics in the public domain is a mode of mission.

A new theological liberalism

I noted earlier that, while most liberal theologians retain a strong concern for the significance of community (and especially for the Church), communitarians such as Hauerwas and Milbank, Banner and O'Donovan rarely have anything sympathetic to say about liberalism in any form. Similarly, MacIntyre is arguing deliberately against liberalism and thus sets it up on particular terms in order to demolish it. But as Jean Porter has observed, MacIntyre may commend the world of mediaeval Catholic Thomism as superior to that of liberal modernity, but he cannot enter that world without taking with him, as it were, the very modernity from which he wishes to escape:

he [MacIntyre] remains ineluctably an inhabitant of his original tradition as well. That is, he continues to be a late-twentieth century, native-English speaking, liberal philosopher whose work is defined by the distinctively modern problematics of conceptual incommensurability and irreducible moral pluralism.[1]

It may be, therefore, that the communitarians cannot escape from liberalism any more than most liberal theologians wish to escape from the rich lives of communities. While few communitarian theologians are prepared to see much virtue in liberal ideas (Nigel Biggar is an obvious exception) it may be that the ability of liberalism and communitarianism to act as correctives to one another will gain wider recognition.

How might theological liberals modify their position in the light of the communitarian critique without merely abandoning everything that makes them liberal? It is significant that most liberals, when asked to explain what liberalism stands for, will reach, not for the principle of autonomy, the subordination of the theological to the secular or the primacy of human reason, but will speak of qualities such as tolerance, humility, and the import-ance of doubt and contingency as expressions of human limitation. (This does not, of course, mean that liberals always act with tolerance or humility, or that liberalism as a mode of thought always points in these directions – only that most liberals seem to be motivated by a desire to embody these qualities.) There is only a small gap between words like these and the notion of virtue, despite the fact that virtue ethics is normally conceived in com-munitarian terms. Is it possible, then, to speak of the liberal virtues in a way which avoids the denigration of tradition and community implicit in so much liberalism?

I introduced liberalism as emanating from a specific historical context – the gradual globalization of commerce which required some mode of discuss-ing value, independent of culturally specific traditions. It is precisely that historical perspective which leads to the 'project' to transcend traditions of all kinds through a focus on the universality of human reason. Liberalism's tendency to marginalize tradition has naturally proved an uncomfortable bedfellow for religion. Hence the sniping at liberals by Hauerwas and others for, as they see it, constantly making Christian wisdom subservient to a bogus rationalism.

But what if the history of liberalism could be told differently? What if, instead of the story about transcending tradition, liberals emphasized instead the way liberalism emerged in a predominantly Christian society precisely because it offered an expression of certain key Christian insights which chimed with the way the world was coming to be understood?

---

[1] Jean Porter, 'Openness and Constraint: Moral Reflection as Tradition-Guided Inquiry in Alasdair MacIntyre's Recent Works', *Journal of Religion* 73.4 (1993), p. 526.

First, liberalism emerged as the natural sciences were beginning to suggest that the beauty and grandeur of God's creation, as exposed in Scripture, could be discovered in new and important ways through human enquiry and the experimental method. Of course this led to hubristic claims about reason usurping faith (which, as we have seen, persist strongly), but that was neither a necessary reaction nor an especially common one until fairly recent times. For a very large number of Christians since the Enlightenment, reason has been celebrated within the tradition: a God-given faculty through which people are enabled to praise God with greater awe. If reason and faith are compatible and mutually enhancing, it does not seem self-evident that liberalism's commitment to reasonableness is theologically misplaced. When the tradition-constituted nature of reason is accepted, the formative significance of faith and the Christian community become central.

Second, we have already noted how attention to the theological times we inhabit – the theological interim – means that contingency and finitude become ethically significant since they are characteristic of the persistence of sin on 'this side of the cross'. Moreover, since corrective insights from both sides of the cross are necessary for theological reflection in the interim, we are made constantly aware of the dangers of premature closure and unwarranted certainty. So the 'liberal virtue' of humility emerges as an authentic hallmark of orthodox theology – the antithesis of the implicitly idolatrous belief that God has so favoured his preferred people that they are not subject to sin and do not err in their assertions of truth. To be sure, humility in this sense can be overdone (although the 'wishy-washy liberal' is more a lampoon by liberalism's enemies than a reality – most liberals have hard edges when pressed). But the point is, not that Christians can never be certain of anything in this world, but that discernment becomes a cardinal virtue for Christian living, always with the risk that God's truth will be mis-discerned by fallible humanity and the fallible empirical Church.

Third, we have already noted Ian Markham's six theological arguments for tolerance. They begin to make the case that tolerance is indeed a godly virtue grounded authentically in the traditions of Scripture and the Church. Notoriously, of course, liberals can act with considerable intolerance towards those who do not accept liberal ideology as a given. But tolerance is never an absolute virtue – it must be combined with discernment so that the limits to what can be tolerated are understood. That is why we looked at the ways in which Shanks and Selby discern proper partners in dialogue. The fact that tolerance can be overdone does not make it any less a virtue – and, on Markham's account, a Christian virtue.

The emphasis on discernment is, perhaps, the link between these 'liberal virtues' and the communitarian insight that reason and perception emerge from formation within a tradition and within a community marked by rich practices of its own. How to discern a way between conflicting accounts of what faith requires; how to discern the limits to tolerance – it all has to be learned since it cannot be arrived at intuitively. And the learning takes place within communities such as the Church. Not many theological liberals, I think, would quibble with that understanding.

None of this is to deny that liberalism – within theology and on a wider canvas – has often been frighteningly hubristic, seeing its own positions as the only possible ways to understand the world, and those who do not share them as either primitive or deviant. Nor is it denying the destructiveness of claims that liberalism is a universal panacea, gradually eroding the irrationality at the centre of religious belief. The fruits of such claims are being felt in the baleful disintegration of civil and political life in the twenty-first-century West. But it is a fallacy – though a frequently committed one – to think that failure in practice always invalidates the principles supporting the practices that fail. The best creeds, beliefs and systems can overreach themselves – as even a cursory reading of church history suggests. If it will reject the claim to have transcended the particularities of mere tradition, liberalism can be understood as one tradition among others – as one strand of tradition within the tapestry of traditions that constitute Christian theology and Christian ethics. It is a tradition which seeks to embody particular virtues – humility, contingency, tolerance – and which grounds these virtues in the revelation of God in Christ through Scripture and the Church. Like most movements in Christian thought, liberalism emerged as a response to new problems thrown up by an evolving world, necessitating corrective yet authentic insights to compensate for old emphases and old neglects which no longer served the Church in its missionary calling. For precisely those reasons, liberalism has required correctives from the communitarian branches of theology and ethics – but that is not to deny its distinctive insights.

Three things should keep liberal insights in play. First, the Church's calling to make its message intelligible to the surrounding culture necessitates a degree of 'literacy' in the thought-patterns of that culture. Second, the sheer extent of human knowledge and expertise which (*contra* Milbank, in my view) means that a deductive ethic drawn solely from a pre-modern Christian tradition cannot, as it did in mediaeval times, dominate and govern all knowledge and enquiry. Third, the fact that Christians continue to be formed, in part, by communities other than the Church, and continue to perceive goodness, justice and many virtues operating with no apparent religious foundations. These perceptions of goodness and so on may be no more than shadows or fragments of Christian virtues, but few Christians are inclined to lose the potential of fragmentary wisdom or to be indifferent to their own contribution to goodness in their wider citizenship.

These are arguments for not throwing out the liberal baby with the bathwater of liberal inadequacy. If John Atherton is right that, in the twentieth century, an Age of Atonement gave way to an Age of Incarnation, and that a new Age of Atonement has now emerged, then the possibility remains open for a further swing of the theological pendulum.

Christian ethics and liturgy

Meanwhile, the communitarian strand in Christian ethics is enjoying a period of great creativity, coupled with a degree of dominance in the academy. Although there are many implicitly conservative aspects to communitarian theologies, there is simultaneously a very strong radicalism which constantly presents apparently familiar dilemmas in terms of newly formulated questions. Partly because they set themselves so sternly against liberalism in all its perceived inadequacy, the more radical communitarians like Hauerwas and Milbank occupy an interesting space within current ecclesial politics. Where the only ecclesial home for those dissatisfied with liberal theology is often assumed to be one or other mode of reactionary conservatism, Hauerwas and Milbank demonstrate a more rigorously theological, and infinitely more challenging, stance for non-liberal believers. Some Christians, of course, are theologically (and politically) conservative by choice or inclination, just as some remain incorrigible liberals. But for Christians who seek something more counter-cultural, and more rooted in the tradition, than liberal theology is perceived to be, who retain a radicalism and are disinclined to impose the political categories of right and left onto church life, some communitarian theologies are attractive.

The latest move within communitarian theology is typified by Stanley Hauerwas's and Samuel Wells's recent work.[2] We have already noted Hauerwas's eclectic ecclesial identity. Wells is an English Anglican, who has worked as a priest in hard-pressed parishes, and a distinguished scholar, now based with Hauerwas at Duke University in the United States. The combination of Wells's rootedness and Hauerwas's confrontationalism is powerful.

In their introductory chapters to the *Blackwell Companion to Christian Ethics*, Hauerwas and Wells take us deeper into the nature of the community which is the Church, out of which come understandings of living well, of justice, goodness, obligation and so on. The nature of the Church, they argue, is discovered pre-eminently in the Eucharist, and it is through the prism of worship that they, and their fellow contributors, explore Christian ethics as the activity of the Church in the world. This is, perhaps, the most detailed development yet of Hauerwas's slogan that the Church does not *have* a social ethic: the Church *is* a social ethic. For the characteristic activity of the Church is worship – this is where the Church is uniquely and most profoundly itself. And the Eucharist, with its multi-layered enactment of the central drama of Christ's death and resurrection, wherein lies the whole doctrine of salvation and atonement, is the Christian act of worship unlike any other.

---

[2] Stanley Hauerwas and Samuel Wells (eds), *The Blackwell Companion to Christian Ethics*, Malden, MA, and Oxford: Blackwell, 2004.

Typically for Hauerwas, however, the focus on the Eucharist is presented as a kind of anti-ethics. As ever, he insists on demonizing modernity and, in fact, every turn in philosophy and theology since Kant. Ethics, for Hauerwas and Wells, is only a pseudo-subject, created out of a bogus separation of public life from the practices of worship. Ethics only becomes a necessary component of Christian life when the divorce between worship and daily life has been completed by liberal modernity's fracturing of the integrated life of faith. Christian ethics, then, is what happens when the Church becomes neglectful of the richness of its own traditions and accepts unquestioningly the secular assumption that living well can be separated from the practices of community.

As we might expect, there is much in Hauerwas's and Wells's analysis that rings true to some aspects of our condition. They argue that many Christians

> have a thriving life of personal devotion, an active life within a worshipping community, and an engaged life fulfilling a range of professional and public roles in the workplace, neighbourhood and family, but comparatively seldom do lay Christians have an equally developed way of bringing these three parts of their lives together.[3]

Many, even most, church members can relate to this. The diagnosis of why this situation exists, with its constant denunciation of the Churches' sell-out to Kantian modernity, is more contentious. Of course it has taken the communitarians to make central the role of worship in determining how we should live. But this is, perhaps, not such a radical insight when one remembers that something very similar is found at the heart of the work of an unreconstructed liberal like Ronald Preston.[4] Hauerwas and Wells express their case as a series of polar opposites. It is, they say, assumed (by whom is not clear – liberals, presumably) that 'ethics is about the real, worship is about the unreal', whereas the editors hold that worship is the greater reality and that 'life *is* a rehearsal' for the kingdom of God which is foretasted in the Eucharist.[5] Worship, they argue, is subjective, whereas ethics is objective – worship being about beauty whereas ethics is about the good. Worship is about the internal, ethics about the external, and worship about words, ethics about action.[6] All these false dichotomies are challenged by the editors.

---

[3] Hauerwas and Wells, *The Blackwell Companion to Christian Ethics*, p. 4.
[4] See R. John Elford and Ian S. Markham (eds), *The Middle Way: Theology, Politics and Economics in the Later Thought of R. H. Preston*, London: SCM Press, 2000. In Elford's introduction and in Preston's own 'After Word', it is clear that Preston's liturgical work as a canon of Manchester Cathedral was wholly integral to his academic approach to ethics. It also explains that, because of the responsibilities of these roles, Preston only began to publish substantially in retirement and his fundamental theological position often has to be inferred from his books rather than being set out systematically.
[5] Hauerwas and Wells, *The Blackwell Companion to Christian Ethics*, p. 4.
[6] Hauerwas and Wells, *The Blackwell Companion to Christian Ethics*, p. 6.

Whether the implied hard separation of worship and ethics is actually the way many theologians, or Christian ethicists, think, is another matter – no direct evidence is offered.

We have already noted one example from among the contributors to Hauerwas's and Wells's *Companion* when we considered Gerald W. Schlabach's treatment of war. Schlabach, with his careful analysis of the just war tradition, avoids the stark dichotomies which seem to inform the editors' framework of thought. He is not alone among the contributors and it would seem that seeing the Eucharist as the practice which defines the Christian understanding of the good, of justice and so on, can be a widely accessible insight.

Another example comes in Robert Song's essay on hunger and food.[7] Starting from the fact that starvation is rife in a world where many have more than enough, Song asserts that, while hunger and starvation may appear to be ultimate realities to be met with resignation, 'the Eucharist proclaims that hunger and poverty, disease and death, are not the last word about the human situation.'[8] He suggests that Christians may need reminding that, in the Eucharist, it is not their own hospitality that is being celebrated (which would imply divine sanction for acts of charity) but God's hospitality which invites us to participate. The relationship between the believer and the poor of the world is thus reorientated from one of charity, which cements an unequal relationship, to one in which all perceive themselves to belong within a single social network. The Eucharist celebrates Christ's power to reunify the broken body, and this has implications for how Christians relate to hungry and starving people.

Song goes on to suggest some practical ethical outcomes. He wonders aloud about reinforcing the theme of one body by receiving communion in the round rather than trooping one by one to the altar for what can become interpreted as a private blessing. He reminds us of the old practice of fasting before communion and develops this both as a small act of solidarity with the hungry and also as a check on the temptation to be enslaved to particular patterns of eating. He looks at the Fair Trade movement and notes that, despite its weaknesses and the risk of tokenism, it is a way of emphasizing the human relationship between purchasers and growers.

Here, Song points us to a significant difference between a Hauerwasian ethic and the kind of Christian ethics which seeks small steps towards the kingdom of God through political outcomes: 'from the point of view of eucharistic witness, the first criterion of discernment is not its effectiveness in reforming the world but its aptness as a symbol of the world renewed in

---

[7] Robert Song, 'Sharing Communion: Hunger, Food and Genetically Modified Foods', in Hauerwas and Wells, *The Blackwell Companion to Christian Ethics*, pp. 388–400.
[8] Song, 'Sharing Communion', p. 390.

Christ'.[9] While acknowledging the considerable power of such symbols, and understanding them to lie at the heart of Christian formation (which, in turn, is the root of Christian ethics), it seems not unreasonable to ask whether such symbols lead with sufficient reliability towards concrete political programmes for change. Communitarian strands in Christian ethics, despite their proper emphasis on the doctrine that this world is not God's last word, can at times imply that Christians can abdicate from the kind of citizenship which furthers the good in the world. To be sure, the focus on the formation of Christian consciences – not least through intelligent reflection on practices like the Eucharist – is a welcome reminder that right actions and right motivations go together, and this is well expressed in Song's essay. But the criticism already noted – that Hauerwasians are content to belittle the achievements of modernity while enjoying the freedoms it offers, including freedom from want – still lingers.

Alan Suggate, reviewing Hauerwas's and Wells's *Companion*, rejects the hard line drawn between Christian practices and modernity. Whereas the book's editors define scarcity as a consequence of sin which contradicts their central assertion that 'God gives his people everything they need to follow him',[10] Suggate finds this simplistic. 'In our finite world much potentiality is locked away awaiting human ingenuity.'[11] He invokes the theological principle of the interim to argue for the need to discern truth within complexity and not simply to dismiss 'modernity' as if the global economy (for instance) exemplified the whole of science and technology.

> Above all, modernity is actually inhabited by people, who are assuredly not ideology on legs. They are often worried, by consumerism and violence and so on, and are struggling to see more constructive ways forward. In this book few such people appear . . . Can we not both inhabit our distinctive tradition and struggle with others, whatever their ultimate beliefs, for our common humanity? Does not the classical Christian tradition itself warrant this?[12]

From my preceding chapters, the reader will have discerned that my sympathies lie with Suggate's critique of Hauerwas and Wells. But (as Suggate concedes) the contributors to the *Companion* do not all adopt the confrontational dichotomies that the editors see as their main framework, although all make the Eucharist, and surrounding practices like baptism, the key to their understanding of ethics. So I am drawn to the idea that worship – and specifically the Eucharist – is a much more suggestive ethical environment than I have, so far, allowed. As we have identified already, contemporary

---

[9] Song, 'Sharing Communion', p. 395.

[10] Hauerwas and Wells, *The Blackwell Companion to Christian Ethics*, p. 13.

[11] Alan Suggate, review of *The Blackwell Companion to Christian Ethics*, ed. S. Hauerwas and S. Wells, *Crucible* (April–June 2005), p. 48.

[12] Suggate, review, p. 49.

Christians are members of many overlapping communities, each of which contributes to the formation of their ethical outlook. In many respects, the secular cultures have a head start – it is fatally easy to regard faith as optional, and faithful observance as a kind of hobby for those who like that sort of thing. If Christian ethics is about connecting what we believe about God with what we do as citizens, then the power of the Christian story to mould character and to make the Church not only an attractive but a necessary source of community attitudes, must be enhanced as strongly as possible. Hauerwas and Wells are right that too few resources exist for most Christians in the West to integrate the different worlds they inhabit. The symbolic richness of worship as a practice which articulates Christian belief and moulds Christian action makes it the source of precisely that necessary integration. And if it runs the risk of introspection and abdication from citizenship, the necessary corrective may lie in a revitalized sense of Christian ethics as mission.

Christian ethics: mission in the world

Part 1 of this book asked whether it is possible to do Christian ethics in the public forum today and concluded that, under certain conditions, public theology is still viable. But it is beyond question that theological language can no longer take a role in public discourse without a great deal of explanation and interpretation. Even if a degree of religious literacy was common in public life in the first half of the twentieth century, when the religious affiliations of people in power might be expected to be more than superficial, that time has long gone. A recent report, commissioned by a Church of England bishop to look at the role of the Church in delivering welfare programmes, pointed to 'immense religious illiteracy' among government ministers and senior civil servants.[13] Although religion has a much higher public prominence than for many years (mainly because of the political implications of religiously inspired civil unrest), the depth of public understanding of religion, in government, in the media and among the so-called commentariat, is often shallow. Most significantly for the Churches, the assumption that the Christian faith is part of the warp and weft of the social fabric is challenged by a prevalent assumption that the default position of the British is a secular – even atheistic – rationalism and that all religions are essentially similar phenomena, characterized by belief in a fantasy god beyond scientific proof, and therefore a mark of regressive irrationality. In such a context, the task of Christian ethics in the public domain has clearly changed from the days when bishops could speak with the authority of their office to influence public policy and expect to be listened to.

---

[13] Francis Davis, Elizabeth Paulhus and Andrew Bradstock, *Moral, But No Compass: Government, Church and the Future of Welfare*, Chelmsford: Matthew James, 2008, p. 49.

As in so many things, the scene is significantly different in America. In the era of George W. Bush, and especially since the election of Barack Obama to the White House, some have taken 'faith-based' politics to an extreme rarely encountered before, in which mere facts have no place if they contradict gut 'beliefs', tending to confirm the view that 'religion' equates to a massive detachment from reality, objective truth and socially responsible behaviour. One might imagine that American right-wing evangelicals had, by 2009, taken counter-culturalism to a point where it had willingly detached itself from reason, except that the policies espoused by the neo-conservative right are recognizably part of an economic project which enthusiastically espouses rational self-interest.

If we reject this strident counter-cultural warfare, Christian ethics in public debate today must spell out its distinctive and authentic world-view in ways which make the Churches' stance on citizenship and public issues intelligible, even to those who reject them. The Churches' mission imperative calls on Christians to explain to the world, not just the stances they take – not even the reasons why Christian ethics can lead people to counter-cultural conclusions – but why a Christian understanding of being human and part of the created order can generate an ethic that is attractive, persuasive and life-enhancing.

Therein lies the chief difficulty. The popular view of Christianity, fuelled by most of the media, is moulded by second-hand impressions of American extremism coupled with vague memories of bumbling pantomime vicars. Moral interventions from members of the Churches are reported through a prism of media values which seem to have only two stories about the Christian faith in Britain. One pits irrational religion against the common-sense rationality of secular wisdom; the other is the charge of moral vacuity whenever the Church fails to reflect the social authoritarianism which, it is supposed, is the authentic Christian message. How to break through the deadlock?

One approach is that of Nigel Biggar, which we have examined already. Biggar has written for the British press on issues such as assisted suicide, utilizing arguments which are by no means exclusive to Christians or to any religious tradition, but seeking a vision of the common good which can be apprehended by a wide-ranging constituency. On this principle, so long as the writer knows how the arguments have been arrived at theologically, there is no need to rehearse the development of ideas from within the tradition, only to expound the conclusions.

Another is represented by a recent Church of England report on the Human Genome Project.[14] Here, chapters about genetic science, the patenting of the genome, the medical and therapeutic implications and so on, are interspersed with a number of chapters by theologians exploring the biblical

---

[14] Mark Bratton (ed.), *God, Ethics and the Human Genome*, London: Church House Publishing, 2009.

tradition, the significance of doctrinal perspectives and the relationship of Christian ethics to secular philosophy. Although no attempt is made to ensure that all the contributors toe the same line, or to reach final conclusions or recommendations, there is a common theme running through the report which affirms the necessity of bringing critical faculties of all kinds to bear on a matter of massive human significance. Reason and the sciences are indispensable in leading to informed moral positions, but the role of theology (in the widest sense of the Church's rich tradition of reflecting on the world through its own narratives) is acknowledged as crucial in offering a framework wherein the 'fact/value', 'is/ought', connection can be forged. This is, explicitly, a development in the Anglican social tradition, moving away from attempts to set out an official church 'position' and avoiding the trap of generating arguments on the grounds of secular wisdom with theology as an afterthought. It seeks to offer material that is intelligible beyond the household of faith, but also to present sufficient substantial theological material to make the case that the Christian tradition brings unique and worthwhile resources to the question.

If neither of these examples seems to be the definitive response to the difficulties faced by Christian ethics as mission in public today, it is probably because, after Christendom, there is no one definitive answer but only constant attempts to bring Christian perspectives into a beneficial dialogue with the surrounding, ever changing, culture. But a first step to effective engagement is to understand the nature of the problem. Many in the Churches are unaware how deep the ignorance of their faith actually is among the figures with the greatest influence on culture. And becoming a member of the Church has taken on a distinctly odd-ball character, so no wonder that, having decided to stand out among their secular friends, many now seem to want their religion to be as odd-ball as possible. In such a setting, Christian ethics can seem like a catalogue of extreme positions, adopted over against a supercilious culture and motivated (so it seems) more by a desire for controversy than for reasons rooted deeply in a centuries-old tradition.

The task for the Christian ethicist therefore becomes inseparable from that of the missioner. Both are charged with making the Christian story known in such a way that it shapes the perceptions of the whole world and our place in it. As part of the story, the questions about what is right, what is just, what is true and what one ought to do, become more than just puzzles and dilemmas but aspects of who I am. And the question, 'Who am I?' only makes sense in the context of the kind of people I live among as my friends and neighbours.

I said at the beginning that Christian ethics is related in interesting ways to other areas of the theological curriculum such as doctrine and pastoral theology. Hauerwas and Wells have added liturgy and worship as a further connection which informs the ethicist. Drawing on their work, it is important to remember that the Eucharist ends with the command to go out into the world. Christians do not cease being citizens, nor do they cease drawing

245

some of their perception of ethics from communities, stories and practices that lie beyond the Church. Making sense of lives lived in this way has been the theme of this book, and a clear sense that the public role of Christian ethics is embedded within the mission of the Church may be the most important perception on which to end.

Bibliography

Aquinas, Thomas, *Summa Theologica*, vol. XXVIII, London: Blackfriars with Eyre & Spottiswoode, and New York: McGraw Hill, 1966.

Archbishop of Canterbury's Commission on Urban Priority Areas, *Faith in the City: A Call for Action by Church and Nation*, London: Church House Publishing, 1985.

Atherton, John, *Christianity and the Market*, London: SPCK, 1992.

Atherton, John, *Social Christianity: A Reader*, London: SPCK, 1994.

Atherton, John, *Public Theology for Changing Times*, London: SPCK, 2000.

Atherton, John, *Marginalization*, London: SCM Press, 2003.

Atherton, John, and Hannah Skinner (eds), *Through the Eye of a Needle: Theological Conversations over Political Economy*, Peterborough: Epworth Press, 2007.

Augustine, *City of God*, Penguin Classics, trans. Henry Bettenson, ed. David Knowles, Harmondsworth: Penguin, 1972.

Badham, Paul, *Is There a Christian Case for Assisted Dying?*, London: SPCK, 2009.

Banner, Michael, 'Nothing to Declare', *Church Times*, 16 June 1995.

Banner, Michael, *Christian Ethics and Contemporary Moral Problems*, Cambridge: Cambridge University Press, 1999.

Berkman, John, and Michael Cartwright (eds), *The Hauerwas Reader*, Durham, NC, and London: Duke University Press, 2001.

Berquist, Jon L. (ed.), *Strike Terror No More: Theology, Ethics and the New War*, St Louis, MO: Chalice Press, 2002.

Biggar, Nigel, *Aiming to Kill: The Ethics of Suicide and Euthanasia*, London: Darton, Longman and Todd, 2004.

Biggar, Nigel, '"God" in Public Reason', *Studies in Christian Ethics* 19.1 (2006), pp. 9–19.

Biggar, Nigel, 'A Methodological Interlude: A Case for Rapprochement Between Moral Theology and Moral Philosophy', in Mark Bratton (ed.), *God, Ethics and the Human Genome*, London: Church House Publishing, 2009.

Biggar, Nigel, and Donald Hay, 'The Bible, Christian Ethics and the Provision of Social Security', *Studies in Christian Ethics* 7.2 (1994), pp. 43–64.

Blond, Philip, 'Rise of the Red Tories', *Prospect* (February 2009).

Board for Social Responsibility, *Something to Celebrate: Valuing Families in Church and Society*, London: Church House Publishing, 1995.

Bonhoeffer, Dietrich, *Letters and Papers from Prison*, ed. Eberhard Bethge, London: SCM Press, 1971.

Boyle, Nicholas, *Who Are We Now?: Christian Humanism and the Global Economy from Hegel to Heaney*, Notre Dame, IN: University of Notre Dame Press, 1998.

Braaten, Carl E., and Robert W. Jenson (eds), *The Strange New World of the Gospel: Re-evangelizing in the Postmodern World*, Grand Rapids, MI: Eerdmans, 2002.

Bradshaw, Timothy (ed.), *The Way Forward?: Christian Voices on Homosexuality and the Church*, 2nd edn, London: SCM Press, 2003.

Bratton, Mark (ed.), *God, Ethics and the Human Genome*, London: Church House Publishing, 2009.

Britton, Andrew, and Peter Sedgwick, *Economic Theory and Christian Belief*, Oxford, Bern etc.: Peter Lang, 2003.

Brown, Malcolm, *After the Market: Economics, Moral Agreement and the Churches' Mission*, Oxford, Bern etc.: Peter Lang, 2004.

Brown, Malcolm, *Faith in Suburbia: Completing the Contextual Trilogy*, Contact Monograph 15, Edinburgh: Contact Pastoral Trust, 2005.

Brown, Malcolm, 'Good Religion Needs Good Science', The Church of England Website, <http://www.cofe.anglican.org/darwin/malcolmbrown.html>. Accessed 5 October 2009.

Brown, Malcolm, and Peter Sedgwick (eds), *Putting Theology to Work*, London and Manchester: CCBI and William Temple Foundation, 1998.

Bruce, Steve, *Politics and Religion*, Cambridge: Polity Press, 2003.

Burridge, Richard A., *Imitating Jesus: An Inclusive Approach to New Testament Ethics*, Grand Rapids, MI, and Cambridge: Eerdmans, 2007.

Church of England, The, *Some Issues in Human Sexuality: A Guide to the Debate*, London: Church House Publishing, 2003.

Clark, Henry, *The Church Under Thatcher*, London: SPCK, 1993.

Clark, Stephen R. L., *Biology and Christian Ethics*, Cambridge: Cambridge University Press, 2000.

Coleman, Terry, *The Railway Navvies*, Harmondsworth: Penguin Books, 1968.

Countryman, L. William, *Dirt, Greed and Sex: Sexual Ethics in the New Testament and their Implications for Today*, Minneapolis: Fortress Press, 1988; London: SCM Press, 2001.

Davie, Grace, *Europe the Exceptional Case: Parameters of Faith in the Modern World*, London: Darton, Longman and Todd, 2002.

Davies, John, and Gerard Loughlin (eds), *Sex These Days: Essays on Theology, Sexuality and Society*, Sheffield: Sheffield Academic Press, 1997.

Davis, Francis, Elizabeth Paulhus and Andrew Bradstock, *Moral, But No Compass: Government, Church and the Future of Welfare*, Chelmsford: Matthew James, 2008.

Dawkins, Richard, *The Selfish Gene*, Oxford: Oxford University Press, 1976.

Dawkins, Richard, *The God Delusion*, London: Bantam Books, 2006.

Deane-Drummond, Celia, *A Handbook in Theology and Ecology*, London: SCM Press, 1996.

Dormer, Duncan, and Jeremy Morris (eds), *An Acceptable Sacrifice?: Homosexuality and the Church*, London: SPCK, 2007.

Drimmelen, Rob van, *Faith in a Global Economy: A Primer for Christians*, Geneva: WCC Publications, 1998.

Duchrow, Ulrich, *Global Economy: A Confessional Issue for the Churches*, Geneva: WCC Publications, 1987.

Duchrow, Ulrich, 'The Witness of the Church in Contrast to the Ideologies of the Market Economy', in *Poverty and Polarisation: A Call to Commitment*, Manchester: William Temple Foundation, 1988.

Duchrow, Ulrich, 'Let's Democratize the West as Well', in Christa Springe and Ulrich Duchrow (eds), *Beyond the Death of Socialism*, Manchester: William Temple Foundation, 1991.

Duchrow, Ulrich, 'Christianity in the Context of Globalized Capitalistic Markets', *Concilium* 97.2 (1997).

Elford, R. John, and Ian S. Markham (eds), *The Middle Way: Theology, Politics and Economics in the Later Thought of R. H. Preston*, London: SCM Press, 2000.

Etzioni, Amitai, *The Spirit of Community*, London: Fontana, 1993.

Evans, Christopher H. (ed.), *The Social Gospel Today*, Louisville, KY: Westminster John Knox Press, 2001.

Evans, G. R., *The Mediaeval Theologians*, Oxford: Blackwell, 2001.

Fergusson, David, *Community, Liberalism and Christian Ethics*, Cambridge: Cambridge University Press, 1998.

Flanagan, Kieran, 'Sublime Policing: Sociology and Milbank's City of God', *New Blackfriars* 861 (1992), pp. 333–41.

Forrester, Duncan, *Christian Justice and Public Policy*, Cambridge: Cambridge University Press, 1997.

Gill, Robin (ed.), *The Cambridge Companion to Christian Ethics*, Cambridge: Cambridge University Press, 2001.

Gill, Robin, *Changing Worlds: Can the Church Respond?* Edinburgh and New York: T&T Clark, 2002.

Gill, Robin, *A Textbook of Christian Ethics*, Edinburgh: T&T Clark, 1st edn 1985, 3rd edn 2006.

Gorringe, Tim, *Capital and the Kingdom: Theological Ethics and the Economic Order*, Maryknoll, NY: Orbis Books, and London: SPCK, 1994.

Gorringe, Tim, *Crime*, London: SPCK, 2004.

Graham, Elaine L., and Esther D. Reed, *The Future of Christian Social Ethics: Essays on the Work of Ronald H. Preston, 1913–2001*, New York and London: T&T Clark, 2004.

Griffiths, Brian, *Morality and the Market Place: Christian Alternatives to Capitalism and Socialism*, London: Hodder & Stoughton, 1982.

Hare, John, 'Neither Male nor Female: The Case of Intersexuality', in Duncan Dormer and Jeremy Morris (eds), *An Acceptable Sacrifice?: Homosexuality and the Church*, London: SPCK, 2007, pp. 98–111.

Harvey, Anthony (ed.), *Theology in the City*, London: SPCK, 1989.

Hauerwas, Stanley, *A Community of Character: Towards a Constructive Christian Social Ethic*, Notre Dame, IN, and London: University of Notre Dame Press, 1981.

Hauerwas, Stanley, *The Peaceable Kingdom: A Primer in Christian Ethics*, Notre Dame, IN: University of Notre Dame Press, 1983, and London: SCM Press, 1984.

Hauerwas, Stanley, *Christian Existence Today*, Durham, NC: Labyrinth Press, 1988.

Hauerwas, Stanley, 'Should War be Eliminated? A Thought Experiment', in John Berkman and Michael Cartwright (eds), *The Hauerwas Reader*, Durham, NC, and London: Duke University Press, 2001, pp. 392–425.

Hauerwas, Stanley, 'Sex in Public: How Adventurous Christians Are Doing It', in John Berkman and Michael Cartwright (eds), *The Hauerwas Reader*, Durham, NC, and London: Duke University Press, 2001, pp. 481–504.

Hauerwas, Stanley, 'Why Gays (as a Group) are Morally Superior to Christians (as a Group)', in John Berkman and Michael Cartwright (eds), *The Hauerwas Reader*, Durham, NC, and London: Duke University Press, 2001, pp. 519–21.

Hauerwas, Stanley, *With the Grain of the Universe: The Church's Witness and Natural Theology*, Grand Rapids, MI: Brazos Press, and London: SCM Press, 2002.

Hauerwas, Stanley, and L. Gregory Jones (eds), *Why Narrative? Readings in Narrative Theology*, Eugene, OR: Wipf & Stock, 1997.

Hauerwas, Stanley, and Charles Pinches, *Christians Among the Virtues: Theological Conversations with Ancient and Modern Ethics*, Notre Dame, IN: University of Notre Dame Press, 1997.

Hauerwas, Stanley, and Samuel Wells (eds), *The Blackwell Companion to Christian Ethics*, Malden, MA, and Oxford: Blackwell, 2004.

Hay, Donald A., and Alan Kreider (eds), *Christianity and the Culture of Economics*, Cardiff: University of Wales Press, 2001.

Hayek, F. A., *Law, Legislation and Liberty*, vol. 2: *The Mirage of Social Justice*, London and Henley: Routledge & Kegan Paul, 1976.

Higginson, Richard, *Transforming Leadership: A Christian Approach to Management*, London: SPCK, 1996.

Hirsch, Fred, *Social Limits to Growth*, London: Routledge & Kegan Paul, 1977.

Hitchens, Christopher, *God is not Great*, New York: Twelve Books, 2007.

Holland, J., and P. Henriot, *Social Analysis: Linking Faith and Justice*, Maryknoll, NY: Orbis, 1983.

Jenson, Robert, 'The Hauerwas Project', *Modern Theology* 8.3 (1992), pp. 285–95.

Jones, Christopher, and Peter Sedgwick (eds), *The Future of Criminal Justice: Resettlement, Chaplaincy and Community*, London: SPCK, 2002.

Kairos Europa, *The European Kairos Document*, Salisbury: Sarum College Press, 1998.

Kairos Theologians, The, *The Kairos Document: A Theological Comment on the Political Crisis in South Africa*, 2nd rev. edn, London: CIIR/BCC, 1986.

Kerr, Fergus, 'Simplicity Itself: Milbank's Thesis', *New Blackfriars* 861 (1992), pp. 306–11.

Kraybill, Donald B., 'Amish Economics: The Interface of Religious Values and Economic Interests', in Donald A. Hay and Alan Kreider (eds), *Christianity and the Culture of Economics*, Cardiff: University of Wales Press, 2001, pp. 76–90.

Lash, Nicholas, 'Not Exactly Politics or Power?', *Modern Theology* 8.4 (1992), pp. 353–64.

Lazareth, William, *Citizens in Society: Luther, the Bible and Social Ethics*, Minneapolis: Fortress Press, 2001.

Lindbeck, George A., *The Church in a Postliberal Age*, London: SCM Press, 2002.

Loughlin, Gerard, 'Christianity and the End of the Story, or the Return of the Master-Narrative', *Modern Theology* 8.4 (1992), pp. 365–84.

McCoy, Alban, *An Intelligent Person's Guide to Christian Ethics*, London and New York: Continuum, 2004.

MacCulloch, Diarmaid, *Thomas Cranmer*, New Haven and London: Yale University Press, 1996.

MacIntyre, Alasdair, *After Virtue: A Study in Moral Theory*, 2nd edn, London: Duckworth, 1985.

MacIntyre, Alasdair, *Whose Justice? Which Rationality?* London: Duckworth, 1988.

MacIntyre, Alasdair, 'I'm Not a Communitarian, But . . .', *The Responsive Community* 1.3 (1991).

MacIntyre, Alasdair, 'A Partial Response to my Critics', in J. Horton and S. Mendus (eds), *After MacIntyre*, Cambridge: Polity Press, 1994.

MacIntyre, Alasdair, 'Epistemological Crises, Narrative and the Philosophy of Science', in Stanley Hauerwas and L. Gregory Jones (eds), *Why Narrative?: Readings in Narrative Theology*, Eugene, OR: Wipf & Stock, 1997, pp. 138–57.

MacIntyre, Alasdair, *Dependent Rational Animals: Why Human Beings Need the Virtues*, London: Duckworth, 1999.

Markham, Ian S., *Plurality and Christian Ethics*, Cambridge: Cambridge University Press, 1994.

Markham, Ian S., 'Ronald Preston and the Contemporary Ethical Scene', in R. John Elford and Ian S. Markham (eds), *The Middle Way: Theology, Politics and Economics in the Later Thought of R. H. Preston*, London: SCM Press, 2000.

Mathews, Charles, *A Theology of Public Life*, Cambridge: Cambridge University Press, 2007.

Mein, Andrew, 'Threat and Promise: The Old Testament on Sexuality', in Duncan Dormer and Jeremy Morris (eds), *An Acceptable Sacrifice?: Homosexuality and the Church*, London: SPCK, 2007.

Messer, Neil (ed.), *Theological Issues in Bioethics: An Introduction with Readings*, London: Darton, Longman and Todd, 2002.

Messer, Neil, *Christian Ethics*, SCM Study Guides, London: SCM Press, 2006.

Milbank, John, *Theology and Social Theory: Beyond Secular Reason*, Oxford: Blackwell, 1990.

Milbank, John, 'Postmodern Critical Augustinianism', *Modern Theology* 7.3 (April 1991), pp. 225–37.

Milbank, John, 'Enclaves, or Where is the Church?', *New Blackfriars* 861 (1992), pp. 341–52.

Milbank, John, *The Word Made Strange: Theology, Language, Culture*, Malden, MA, and Oxford: Blackwell, 1997.

Milbank, John, 'The Gospel of Affinity', in Carl E. Braaten and Robert W. Jenson (eds), *The Strange New World of the Gospel: Re-evangelizing in the Postmodern World*, Grand Rapids, MI: Eerdmans, 2002, pp. 1–20.

Milbank, John, Catherine Pickstock and Graham Ward (eds), *Radical Orthodoxy: A New Theology*, London and New York: Routledge, 1999.

Moe-Lobeda, Cynthia, *Healing a Broken World: Globalization and God*, Minneapolis: Fortress Press, 2002.

Mulhall, Stephen, and Adam Swift, *Liberals and Communitarians*, 2nd edn, Oxford: Blackwell, 1996.

Murphy, Mark C., *Alasdair MacIntyre*, Cambridge: Cambridge University Press, 2003.

Nation, Mark Thiessen, and Samuel Wells (eds), *Faithfulness and Fortitude: In Conversation with the Theological Ethics of Stanley Hauerwas*, Edinburgh, T&T Clark, 2000.

Niebuhr, Reinhold, *Moral Man and Immoral Society: A Study in Ethics and Politics*, New York: Charles Scribner's Sons, 1932.

Northcott, Michael, *The Environment and Christian Ethics*, Cambridge: Cambridge University Press, 1996.

Northcott, Michael, *A Moral Climate: The Ethics of Global Warming*, London: Darton, Longman and Todd, 2007.

Novak, Michael, *The Spirit of Democratic Capitalism*, Lanham, MD: Madison Books, 1982; London: Institute of Economic Affairs Health and Welfare Unit, 1991.

Nozick, Robert, *Anarchy, State and Utopia*, Oxford: Blackwell, 1974.

O'Donovan, Oliver, *Begotten or Made?*, Oxford: Clarendon Press, 1984.

O'Donovan, Oliver, *Resurrection and Moral Order: An Outline for Evangelical Ethics*, Leicester: Inter-Varsity Press, and Grand Rapids, MI: Eerdmans, 1986, 2nd edn 1994.

O'Donovan, Oliver, *The Just War Revisited*, Cambridge: Cambridge University Press, 2003.

O'Donovan, Oliver, *A Conversation Waiting to Begin: The Churches and the Gay Controversy*, London: SCM Press, 2009.

O'Donovan, Oliver, 'The Language of Rights and Conceptual History', *Journal of Religious Ethics* 37.2 (2009), pp. 193–207.

O'Donovan, Oliver, and Joan Lockwood O'Donovan, *Bonds of Imperfection: Christian Politics, Past and Present*, Grand Rapids, MI, and Cambridge: Eerdmans, 2004.

Oldham, J. H. (ed.), *The Churches Survey Their Task: The Report of the Oxford Ecumenical Conference on Church, Community and State*, London: George Allen & Unwin, and Chicago: Willett, Clark & Co., 1937.

Pattison, Stephen, *The Faith of the Managers: When Management Becomes Religion*, London and Washington, DC: Cassell, 1997.

Pinches, Charles R., *A Gathering of Memories: Family, Nation and Church in a Forgetful World*, Grand Rapids, MI: Brazos Press, 2006.

Plant, Raymond, 'Community: Concept, Conception and Ideology', *Politics and Society* 8.1 (1978).

Plant, Raymond, *Social Justice, Labour and the New Right*, Fabian Pamphlet 556, London: Fabian Society, 1993.

Plant, Raymond, *Politics, Theology and History*, Cambridge: Cambridge University Press, 2001.

Plant, Raymond, and others, 'Conservative Capitalism: Theological and Moral Challenges', in Anthony Harvey (ed.), *Theology in the City*, London: SPCK, 1989, pp. 68–97.

Porter, Jean, 'Openness and Constraint: Moral Reflection as Tradition-Guided Inquiry in Alasdair MacIntyre's Recent Works', *Journal of Religion* 73.4 (1993), pp. 514–36.

Preston, Ronald H., *Church and Society in the Late Twentieth Century: The Economic and Political Task*, London: SCM Press, 1983.

Preston, Ronald H., *Religion and the Ambiguities of Capitalism*, London: SCM Press, 1991.

Preston, Ronald H., *Confusions in Christian Ethics: Problems for Geneva and Rome*, London: SCM Press, 1994.

Preston, Ronald H., 'A Comment on Method', in Malcolm Brown and Peter Sedgwick (eds), *Putting Theology to Work*, London and Manchester: CCBI and William Temple Foundation, 1998, pp. 36–7.

Rawls, John, *A Theory of Justice*, Oxford and New York: Oxford University Press, 1972.

Reed, Charles, *Just War?* London: SPCK, 2004.

Reed, Charles, and David Ryall (eds), *The Price of Peace: Just War in the Twenty First Century*, Cambridge: Cambridge University Press, 2007.

Roberts, Richard H., *Religion, Theology and the Human Sciences*, Cambridge: Cambridge University Press, 2002.

Rowland, Christopher, and Mark Corner, *Liberating Exegesis: The Challenge of Liberation Theology to Biblical Studies*, London: SPCK, 1990.

Sagovsky, Nicholas, *Christian Tradition and the Practice of Justice*, London: SPCK, 2008.

Schlabach, Gerald W., 'Breaking Bread: Peace and War', in Stanley Hauerwas and Samuel Wells (eds), *The Blackwell Companion to Christian Ethics*, Oxford: Blackwell, 2004, pp. 360–74.

Sedgwick, Peter (ed.), *God in the City*, London: Mowbray, 1995.

Sedgwick, Peter, 'Refusing to Despair over Families', *Church Times*, 30 July 1995.

Selby, Peter, *Grace and Mortgage: The Language of Faith and the Debt of the World*, London: Darton, Longman and Todd, 1997.

Shanks, Andrew, *Civil Society, Civil Religion*, Oxford: Blackwell, 1995.

Snyder, T. Richard, *The Protestant Ethic and the Spirit of Punishment*, Grand Rapids, MI, and Cambridge: Eerdmans, 2001.

Song, Robert, *Human Genetics: Fabricating the Future*, London: Darton, Longman and Todd, 2002.

Song, Robert, 'Sharing Communion: Hunger, Food and Genetically Modified Foods', in Hauerwas, Stanley, and Samuel Wells (eds), *The Blackwell Companion to Christian Ethics*, Oxford: Blackwell, 2004, pp. 388–400.

Spencer, Nick, *Darwin and God*, London: SPCK, 2009.

Springe, Christa, and Ulrich Duchrow, *Beyond the Death of Socialism*, Manchester: William Temple Foundation, 1991.

Stackhouse, Max, 'The Fifth Social Gospel and the Global Mission of the Church', in Christopher H. Evans (ed.), *The Social Gospel Today*, Louisville, KY: Westminster John Knox Press, 2001.

Stackhouse, Max, 'Theologies of War: Comparative Perspectives', in Jon L. Berquist (ed.), *Strike Terror No More: Theology, Ethics and the New War*, St Louis, MO: Chalice Press, 2002, pp. 200–11.

Storrar, William F., and Andrew R. Morton (eds), *Public Theology for the 21st Century*, London and New York: T&T Clark, 2004.

Stout, Jeffrey, *Ethics After Babel: The Languages of Morals and Their Discontents*, Cambridge: James Clarke, 1988.

Stout, Jeffrey, 'Homeward Bound: MacIntyre on Liberal Society and the History of Ethics', *Journal of Religion* 69.2 (1989).

Suggate, Alan M., *William Temple and Christian Social Ethics Today*, Edinburgh: T&T Clark, 1987.

Suggate, Alan M., 'Whither Anglican Social Ethics?, *Crucible* (April–June 2001), pp. 106–22.

Suggate, Alan M., Review of *The Blackwell Companion to Christian Ethics*, ed. S. Hauerwas and S. Wells, *Crucible* (April–June 2005).

Tanner, Kathryn, *Economy of Grace*, Minneapolis: Fortress Press, 2005.

Taylor, Charles, *Philosophical Arguments*, Cambridge, MA, and London: Harvard University Press, 1995, pp. 181–2.

Temple, William, *Christianity and Social Order*, Harmondsworth: Penguin, 1942.

Thiemann, Ronald, *Religion in Public Life: A Dilemma for Democracy*, Washington, DC: Georgetown University Press, 1996.

Via, Dan O., and Robert A. Gagnon, *Homosexuality and the Bible: Two Views*, Minneapolis: Fortress Press, 2003.

Waldron, Jeremy, *God, Locke, and Equality: Christian Foundations of John Locke's Political Thought*, Cambridge, New York, etc.: Cambridge University Press, 2002.

Ward, Graham, 'John Milbank's *Divina Commedia*', *New Blackfriars* 861 (1992), pp. 311–19.

Watts, Fraser, 'Christian Theology', in Fraser Watts and Liz Gulliford (eds), *Forgiveness in Context*, London and New York: T&T Clark, 2004, pp. 55–7.

Watts, Fraser, and Liz Gulliford (eds), *Forgiveness in Context*, London and New York: T&T Clark, 2004.

Webb, Stephen H., 'A Voice Cursing in the Wilderness', *Reviews in Religion and Theology* 10.1 (February 2003).

Wells, Samuel, *Transforming Fate into Destiny: The Theological Ethics of Stanley Hauerwas*, Carlisle: Paternoster Press, 1998.

Williams, H. A., *Tensions: Necessary Conflicts in Life and Love*, London: Mitchell Beazley, 1976.

Williams, Rowan, 'Saving Time: Thoughts on Practice, Patience and Vision', *New Blackfriars* 861 (1992), pp. 319–26.

Williams, Rowan, 'Knowing Myself in Christ', in Timothy Bradshaw (ed.), *The Way Forward?: Christian Voices on Homosexuality and the Church*, 2nd edn, London: SCM Press, 2003, pp. 12–19.

Williams, Rowan, 'Abortion: Fundamental Convictions about Humanity Need to be Kept in Focus', *The Observer*, 21 October 2007; <http://www.archbishopofcanterbury.org/1237>. Accessed 5 October 2009.

Williams, Rowan, *Religious Faith and Human Rights*, lecture delivered at the London School of Economics, 1 May 2008; <http://www.archbishopofcanterbury.org/2087>.

Wink, Walter, 'We Must Find a Better Way', in Jon L. Berquist (ed.), *Strike Terror No More: Theology, Ethics and the New War*, St Louis, MO: Chalice Press, 2002, pp. 329–36.

Wogaman, J. Philip, *Christian Perspectives on Politics*, Minneapolis: Fortress Press, and London: SCM Press, 1988.

Wogaman, J. Philip, *Christian Ethics: A Historical Introduction*, Louisville, KY: Westminster John Knox Press, 1993 and London: SPCK, 1994.

Wogaman, J. Philip, and Douglas M. Strong (eds), *Readings in Christian Ethics: A Historical Sourcebook*, Louisville, KY: Westminster John Knox Press, 1996.

Wolterstorff, Nicholas, *Justice: Rights and Wrongs*, Princeton and Oxford: Princeton University Press, 2008.

Index